Managing
the Commons

Managing

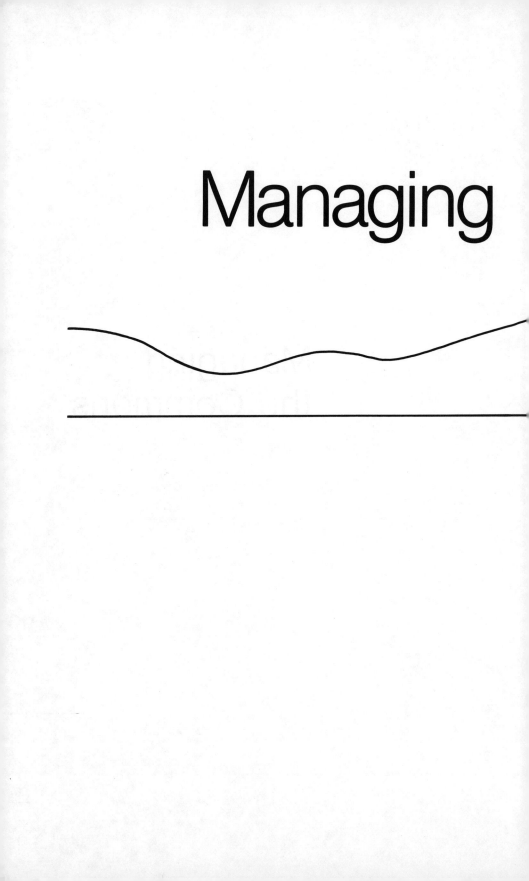

the Commons

Edited by

Garrett Hardin
UNIVERSITY OF CALIFORNIA, SANTA BARBARA

and

John Baden
UTAH STATE UNIVERSITY

W. H. FREEMAN AND COMPANY
San Francisco

Library of Congress Cataloging in Publication Data

Main entry under title:

Managing the commons.

    1. Environmental policy—Addresses, essays, lectures.
I. Hardin, Garrett James, 1915–   II. Baden, John.
HC79.E5M347   301.31   76-40055
ISBN 0-7167-0476-5

Printed in the United States of America

9 8 7 6 5 4 3 2 1

Contents

Part III: Grappling with the Commons

Preface:
The Evolution
of Cultural Norms

"All men by nature desire to know." So basic did Aristotle regard this insight that he began his *Metaphysics* with this assertion. But when does man know for sure? Individually, in private, a man may be satisfied with many degrees of "hardness" of knowledge, ranging from the mystical on up (or down?) to the sort of thing a consulting engineer must restrict himself to when he testifies in court. The world of scholarship is a court of public opinion, and so the discussion that takes place in it leans toward the "hard" end. Anticipating criticism, scholars seek rational explanations of the way the world works.

No matter how we may view ourselves, in trying to control the behavior of others we necessarily assume that others are susceptible to specifiable rewards and punishments. Part of the repertoire of behavioral reinforcements is strictly biological and not at all peculiar to human beings. But another part—and not a small one—is cultural. If I consent to serve as the chairman of the United Fund Christmas drive it is at least in part because I anticipate subtle (and sometimes not so subtle) rewards from my community. In contrast, when I stop at a red signal light at a time when no cross traffic is in sight, I do so because I anticipate the possibility of a traffic ticket. There are the two sorts of sanctions our actions are subject to—informal and formal (legal). Sanctions conserve culture.

Put slightly differently, culture rewards individuals. An obsolete culture, by definition, rewards behavior that is contrary to the larger goals of society, including survival. Sanctions that tend to destroy the society that imposes them may, in the strictest sense, be said to be tragic. Although it is obvious that destructive sanctions cannot survive in the long run because their matrix perishes, the existence of destructive sanctions at any particular moment must be regarded as a consequence of an evolutionary process. The policy problem is how to rid society rapidly of its obsolete sanctions. This is no mean problem, because any social institution that has long been in existence has accumulated an interconnected network of restrictive by-laws, legal generalizations, and semantic rationalizations. Morever, just plain habit makes us reluctant to change.

Unfortunately for those who live in the present time, the rate of change is accelerating, as Alvin Toffler has emphasized in *Future Shock*. The closing in of the world around us, as a result of population expansion, makes prompt change more necessary than ever. Actions that were adaptive yesterday are only marginally so today; tomorrow they will be maladaptive. To change the state of the system—its codified laws, and so on—we must change the accepted cultural norms that support the system. As the American experience of Prohibition taught us, without a change in cultural norms legal changes are perilous.

The present volume deals with some of the cultural changes now required for survival. What cultural norms should replace our present ones is a matter of opinion, but it is clear that independence of individual action will have to be significantly circumscribed. For a century or two, the European variant of *Homo sapiens* has assumed that the individual is the best judge of his own welfare, and that the aggregate of individual actions produces the optimal collective welfare. This belief furnishes the supposedly objective justification for asserting individual rights in the use of such nonindividually owned resources—"common pool" resources, or commons—as air and water. One has only to listen to the impassioned defense of such "rights" in a town meeting situation to recognize the religious overtones of the word "right." Like the word "sanctity," the word "right" is introduced into the discussion to put an end to the infinite regress of rational inquiry. Inquiry must, of course, be stopped at some point. Unfortunately, there is no objective criterion for determining where that point is. Uttering the word "right" does not solve the problem (unless the hearer naively supposes that it does).

No matter what may have been true in earlier cultures, American culture is committed to the belief that it is the role of education to encourage inquiry. This means that the "full stop" of "right" cannot pass unchallenged. Aldo Leopold in his celebrated essay "The Land Ethic" challenged a powerful "right" of his day in a way that left an enduring imprint on the modern mind:

> When god-like Odysseus returned from the wars in Troy he hanged all on one rope a dozen slave-girls of his household whom he suspected of misbehavior during his absence.
>
> This hanging involved no question of propriety. The girls were property. The disposal of property was then, as now, a matter of expediency, not of right and wrong. . . .

There is as yet no ethic dealing with man's relation to land and to the animals and plants which grow upon it. Land, like Odysseus' slave-girls, is still property. The land-relation is still strictly economic, entailing privileges but not obligations.

The privileges-but-not-obligations character of private property is found in certain sorts of public property as well. The danger of this coupling has sporadically been pointed out by wise men. Aristotle, for example, remarked: "What is common to the greatest number gets the least amount of care. Men pay most attention to what is their own: they care less for what is common." (*Politics,* Book II, Chap. 3.) And in the following chapter he said: "When everyone has his own sphere of interest . . . the amount of interest will increase, because each man will feel that he is applying himself to what is his own."

With regard to the investigations summarized in the present volume, some readers may regard a citation of Aristotle as little more than an act of antiquarian piety. There is no reason to think that Aristotle's assertions had much historical effect on the subsequent development of political science, political economy, or environmental studies. Why do we say this? Two considerations are relevant.

First, there is the wise observation of the philosopher A. N. Whitehead that "We give credit not to the first man to have an idea, but to the first one who takes it seriously." To take an idea seriously means to worry it as a bulldog might a bone; we try it out in a multitude of contexts seeking to discover its manifold implications. Aristotle merely mentioned the idea of common property; only in the last decade has the idea been worried sufficiently, and some of its more important implications emphasized.

Secondly, many of the theoretical consequences that were always implicit in the idea of common property were not of much practical importance for many centuries after Aristotle's death. In the most vigorously developing countries the most active agents of change were willfully blind to the perils of common property because truth threatened personal interest, narrowly defined. During the years when North America was being settled, the scarce, hence economically valuable, factors were capital and labor, particularly the former. But land and the resources within it were cheap. Good air and water were so readily available that it often seemed ridiculous even to question their value. We are told that the law does not concern itself with trifles. Neither do "practical" men; but what they call a trifle is often merely something perceived as an impediment to egoistic action. Extreme forms of individualism became the norm in rapidly expanding parts of the world like North America. The right to independence of action became deeply embedded in law.

The sudden efflorescence of environmentalism in the 1960s challenged the norm of extreme individual freedom. Things that a few lonely seers had been saying for a century or more became common knowledge. The basic ecological principle that "We can never do merely one thing" was quoted in magazines catering to businessmen. The public's attention was called to the fact that mismanagement of the environment can produce ultimate ruin even though day-to-day secular changes are difficult to observe, being dwarfed by normal fluctuations. When the time scale for environmental ruin is measured in generations it is not easy for mortal man to recognize future threats or past degradations. In 1941 Henry Miller, in *The Colossus of Maroussi,* opined that modern Greece "is what you expect the earth to look like, given a fair chance." To an ecologically educated historian nothing could be further from the truth. Greece, as well as most of the Mediterranean basin, is a dilapidated skeleton of its former glory; most of its destruction was caused by men who embraced a politico-economic system that was rich in rights and poor in responsibilities. Contrary to Miller's opinion, Greece was *never* given a fair chance. Neither was most of the rest of the world, and the end of its despoliation by men enchained by obsolete cultural norms is, unfortunately, still not in sight.

Memory decays; subconscious denial blinds; private interest corrupts; and long-standing institutions seek (so to speak) their own survival. In culture, as in biological ecosystems, we can never do merely one thing. Even when we perceive the errors of the past and the dangers of the future it is not obvious how we should, or can, alter human institutions to improve human welfare. In this crowded world of ours *unmanaged* commons are no longer tolerable: but how shall we manage them? What core norms of society need to be altered, and how? How can we best avoid the "tragedy of the commons" without provoking other evils? It is not reasonable to expect definitive answers to all these questions at once, but we cannot afford to delay looking for the answers. The contributors to this volume have opened up the discussion; let us hope that it will be continued vigorously in a myriad of intellectual centers, for we do not have much time to save the world from galloping destruction. It is (as the ancient Chinese were fond of saying) later than you think.

John Baden
Garrett Hardin

Managing
the Commons

PART I

Discovering
the Commons

1

What Marx Missed

Garrett Hardin

It is a little more than a century since Karl Marx coined one of the most influential mottoes in history: *From each according to his ability, to each according to his needs.* Before we weigh the wisdom of this ideal, let us examine the text in which it occurs. It is part of Marx's *Critique of the Gotha Program,* a polemic against a proposal made by some of his fellow communists in the town of Gotha, now part of the German Democratic Republic. Wrestling with the problem of distributional justice, Marx wrote:

> But one man is superior to another physically or mentally and so supplies more labor in the same time, or can labor for a longer time; and labor, to serve as a measure, must be defined by its duration or intensity, otherwise it ceases to be a standard of measurement. This *equal* right is an unequal right for unequal labor. It recognizes no class differences, because everyone is only a worker like everyone else; but it tacitly recognizes unequal individual endowment and thus productive capacity as natural privileges. *It is, therefore, a right of inequality, in its content, like every right.* Right by its very nature can consist only in the application of an equal standard; but unequal individuals (and they would not be different individuals if they were not unequal) are measurable only by an equal standard in so far as they are brought under an equal point of view, are taken from one *definite* side only, for instance, in the present case, are regarded *only as workers* and nothing more is seen in them, everything else being ignored. Further, one worker is married, another not; one has more children than another, and so on and so forth. Thus, with an equal performance of labor, and hence an equal share in the social consumption fund, one will in fact receive more than another, one will be richer than another, and so on. To avoid all these defects, right instead of being equal would have to be unequal.
>
> But these defects are inevitable in the first phase of communist society as it is when it has just emerged after prolonged birth pangs from capitalist society. Right can never be higher than the economic structure of society and its cultural development conditioned thereby.

> In a higher phase of communist society, after the enslaving subordina-
> tion of the individual to the division of labor, and therewith also the anti-
> thesis between mental and physical labor, has vanished; after labor has
> become not only a means of life but life's prime want; after the productive
> forces have also increased with the all-round development of the indi-
> vidual, and all the springs of cooperative wealth flow more abundantly—
> only then can the narrow horizon of bourgeois right be crossed in its
> entirety and society inscribe on its banner: From each according to his
> ability, to each according to his needs![1]

Marx is seldom crystal clear, and the above passage is no exception.
But it is evident (in the next to last paragraph) that he is being politically
realistic in accepting a definition of right that produces inequities for the
present—in order that, at some indefinite future time, true justice may
prevail, each individual being supplied according to his needs, irrespec-
tive of his contributions to society (provided, presumably, he does not
shirk his duties). The Marxist philosophy can be bluntly summarized,
Need creates right.

That acceptance of this doctrine has grown greatly since Marx's time
should be obvious to all. Scarcely a year passes without the creation of a
new right, for example, the right of the hungry to an adequate diet, the
right of the homeless to housing, the right of the aged to medical care,
and the right of the deprived, whether deprived by their social history or
by their heredity, to compensatory treatment.[2] The asserted rights are
implicitly absolute, without qualifying responsibilities; sometimes the
implicit is even made explicit.

For this historical development Marx bears a large measure of responsibility. This is not to say that the sentiment of the Gotha critique was
entirely original. As John Donne wrote:

> No man is an island, entire of itself; every man is a piece of the conti-
> nent, a part of the main; if a clod be washed away by the sea, Europe is
> the less, as well as if . . . a manor of thy friends or of thine own were;
> any man's death diminishes me, because I am involved in mankind; and
> therefore never send to know for whom the bell tolls; it tolls for thee.[3]

Despite the multitude and distinction of his predecessors, Marx has
been of supreme importance historically in spreading the doctrine of
need creates right. As has been said of musical composition, it isn't the
tune that matters so much as what you do with it. Marx did more with
this tune than anyone else. Many religions have proclaimed the brotherhood of man, but it was Marx who energized the idea with political
power. Other differences between Marxism and earlier religions are worth
noting.

In the classic religions, the call for sharing with "brothers" is largely
a Sunday thing.[4] Realistic religious leaders have seldom expected their

followers to make sharing a universal rule right away. To a certain extent, neither did Marx; the words he used toward the end of the passage quoted above show that his view was a millennial one. But among Marxists, the millennium is not something one passively waits for. Marxists try to hasten the time of its appearance. Their millennium is not a utopia but a difficult to achieve yet essentially practical arrangement—the only practical arrangement, when all is said and done. "To each according to his needs" in their view defines not an inspiring ideal high above practical achievability, but a truly possible and stable world. All it calls for is just a bit more virtue.

In matters of philanthropy many classic religions focus on the needs of the giver; Marxism shifts the focus to the receiver. Mohammedans give in order to earn their way into heaven. Marxists, by contrast, hold that the receiver has a right to receive. In the Marxist view, elites have an *obligation* to give up their advantages; in earlier religions, giving is a voluntary matter (otherwise no spiritual credit can be gained from the act).

As a by-product of this difference, the voluntary charity of traditional religions is not expected to put an end to poverty. Indeed, in those religions in which heaven is bought by alms, an end to poverty would put an end to the possibility of the individual's attaining heaven. For that reason members of such sects regard a permanent cure for poverty as unacceptable and do not seek it. Marxists obviously take the opposite position. So do most people nowadays, whatever their political persuasion. A century ago Thoreau could truly say, "There are a thousand hacking at the branches of evil to one who is striking at the root." This is not as true now as it was in Thoreau's day, but whether we are more successful in eradicating evil is questionable. We have trouble recognizing a major root when we see it.

Human beings are social animals, sensitive to the needs of others, and fearful of their envy.[5] We may even have a conscience. All of these factors predispose us to follow the path of Marx (and other religious leaders), but before we yield completely to our impulses we need to put time into the picture. It is not enough to note that the first result of sharing according to the Marxist principle is a pleasant one. We must remember that time has no stop. Our amiable efforts may immediately be met with smiles and thanks, but always we need to ask this question, *And then what?* As act becomes policy, as event gives way to a cycle of events, what are the consequences? Good intentions are not enough; the mechanism of our policy must produce good results in this time-tied world where consequences become causes.

Surely the greatest defect of utopian writers is their inability to ask, *And then what?* Marx, for all of his contempt of utopian thinking in others, fell into the same trap: he never asked what would be the ultimate consequences of organizing the world according to the rule, "to each according to his needs." Ironically, such an analysis had been carried out some time earlier by the Englishman William Forster Lloyd. Karl Marx was a high school student in Prussia when Lloyd's *Two Lectures on Population* were published in England in 1833. Young Marx could hardly have been expected to hear of them. Not until 1849 did Marx move to England, after he was expelled from the continent following the unsuccessful revolution of 1848. The standard biographies of Marx contain no mention of Lloyd, so presumably Marx never became aware of the argument of the *Two Lectures.*

It is always tempting to play the contra-factual game of history, asking "What if . . . ." such and such an event had not happened. What if Marx had not been ignorant of Lloyd's *Two Lectures?* History would probably have been no different. Lloyd is, at times, almost as difficult to understand as Marx. The difficulty of his exposition may prevent hurried scholars from discovering the profundity of his argument. Few modern treatises on population even mention him.[6] In a very thorough and scholarly United Nations document, *Historical Outline of World Population Growth,* the only mention of Lloyd is a single footnote. Speaking of the Marxist belief that with proper distribution of wealth preventive checks to population growth will arise automatically, the anonymous authors state:

> Lloyd early questioned this thesis on the ground that since the gain from restricting family size is largely diffused to others, the individual *under capitalism* [italics added] has little incentive to restrict family size.[7]

The U.N. commentators could hardly have been more mistaken. As the readers of the next two chapters will discover, Lloyd's point was precisely the opposite: it is not capitalism but the system of the commons that fails to furnish the adequate incentive. The commentators cite page 22 of Lloyd's publication; they need only have read the preceding page carefully to discover the proper referent of Lloyd's predications.

Not until 135 years after its original publication was Lloyd's argument given an adequate airing in public. It was found that the logical structure of the commons affects not only population but other critical problems of our time. The present volume is an earnest attempt to describe many of these problems and to propose ways of dealing with them. Before plunging into the present let us go back nearly a century and a half to read a shortened version of William Forster Lloyd's *Two Lectures.*

Notes

1. A convenient reprinting of this statement, first made in 1875, can be found in Robert C. Tucker, ed., *The Marx-Engels Reader* (New York: Norton, 1972). The passage quoted here is from pp. 387–388.
2. John Rawls, *A Theory of Justice* (Cambridge, Mass.: Harvard University Press, 1971). This, the most prestigious treatment of "fairness" in our time, is one long footnote to Marx.
3. From *Devotions,* XVII, first published in 1624. A statement may be beautiful without being either true or a true guide to the best action. Consider for instance Donne's assertion that propinquity is of no importance in moral matters. Should I try as hard to help a little girl with a splinter in her finger in China, 12,000 miles away, as I do to help my neighbor's child in the same need? It would be an interesting exercise to work out the practical consequences of the dogmatic assertion that distance has no bearing on ethical choice. But if this assertion is rejected, how do we reckon the quantitative effect of distance on choice?
4. It has also been a tribal thing to an extent seldom dreamed of by those who now speak for the universal brotherhood of man, i.e., of all members of the species *Homo sapiens.* Until very recent times the idea of universal brotherhood was hardly conceivable, even by the most religious of men. "Brothers" were defined in contrast to the sea of "others" outside, others to whom quite different rules of conduct applied. See Benjamin Nelson, *The Idea of Usury,* 2nd ed. (Chicago: University of Chicago Press, 1969). The subtitle of this work illuminates history: "From Tribal Brotherhood to Universal Otherhood." A key question for our time, both theoretically and practically, is this: will the rules perfected by Tribal Brotherhoods permit survival in a world of Universal Otherhood? Or, to put the matter differently: is Universal Brotherhood even possible?
5. See Helmut Schoeck, *Envy* (New York: Harcourt Brace Jovanovich, 1969). This work throws a great light on the role and many disguises of envy, a topic that is largely taboo in our society, particularly among intellectuals. Most so-called primitive peoples know far better than we the immense power of envy, and they frankly acknowledge it.
6. One of the few books in which Lloyd's work is discussed is James Alfred Field, *Essays on Population* (Chicago: University of Chicago Press, 1931).
7. *The Determinants and Consequences of Population Trends.* Population Studies, No. 17 (New York: United Nations, 1953), p. 32.

2

On the Checks to Population

William Forster Lloyd
(1833)

Suppose the case of two persons agreeing to labor jointly, and that the result of their labor is to be common property. Then, were either of them, at any time, to increase his exertions beyond their previous amount, only half of the resulting benefit would fall to his share; were he to relax them, he would bear only half the loss. If, therefore, we may estimate the motives for exertion by the magnitude of the personal consequences expected by each individual, these motives would in this case have only half the force, which they would have, were each laboring separately for his own individual benefit. Similarly, in the case of three partners, they would have only one third of the force—in the case of four, only one fourth—and in a multitude, no force whatever. For beyond a certain point of minuteness, the interest would be so small as to elude perception, and would obtain no hold whatever on the human mind.

In this, I have not assumed that the produce of the labor is to be equally divided, but merely, that all are equally interested in it, so long as it is unknown how it will be divided; and, therefore, that each person will view the future consequences, expected to result from an increase or

---

Little is known of the author of this classic statement. His name is not even listed in the fifteenth edition of the *Encyclopaedia Britannica*. According to the *Dictionary of National Biography*, Lloyd (1794–1852) graduated with a B.A. from Oxford in 1815, with a "first" in mathematics and a "second" in classics. "Although in holy orders he held no preferment, but lived on his property in Buckinghamshire." At various times he taught Greek, mathematics, and political economy. The work from which the present condensation has been made (with minor alterations in spelling) was originally published under the title *Two Lectures on the Checks to Population, delivered before The University of Oxford, in Michaelmas Term 1832*. The original volume is now quite rare. Fortunately the work has been republished as part of a collection of Lloyd's works entitled *Lectures on Population, Value, Poor-Laws and Rent* (reprinted by Augustus M. Kelley, New York, 1968).

relaxation of his own exertions, in the same light as he would any other benefit or injury extending indifferently to the whole community.

Again, suppose two persons to have a common purse, to which each may freely resort. The ordinary source of motives for economy is a foresight of the diminution in the means of future enjoyment depending on each act of present expenditure. If a man takes a guinea out of his own purse, the remainder, which he can spend afterwards, is diminished by a guinea. But not so, if he takes it from a fund, to which he and another have an equal right of access. The loss falling upon both, he spends a guinea with as little consideration as he would use in spending half a guinea, were the fund divided. Each determines his expenditure as if the whole of the joint stock were his own. Consequently, in a multitude of partners, where the diminution effected by each separate act of expenditure is insensible, the motive for economy entirely vanishes.

It may here be asked, what has this to do with the preventive check [to population]? It merely serves to illustrate those parts of a cause and of its consequences, which enter into human motives, and to show how the future is struck out of the reckoning, when the constitution of society is such as to diffuse the effects of individual acts throughout the community at large, instead of appropriating them to the individuals, by whom they are respectively committed. Where the present and the future are not opposed, of course there can be no question. I am here, therefore, referring only to cases, such as those which I have been considering, in which the endurance of a present pain or inconvenience will be the cause of a future benefit, or the gratification of a present desire will lead to eventual evil. Prudence is a selfish virtue; and where the consequences are to fall on the public, the prudent man determines his conduct, by the comparison, of the present pleasure with his share of the future ill, and the present sacrifice with his share of the future benefit. This share, in the multitude of a large society, becomes evanescent; and hence, in the absence of any countervailing weight, the conduct of each person is determined by the consideration of the present alone. The present good is chosen; the present evil is refused. This is what happens with the brute creation, and thus the obligation to prudence being placed upon the society collectively, instead of being distributed to the individual members, the effect is, that, though the reasoning faculty is in full force, and each man can clearly foresee the consequences of his actions, yet the conduct is the same as if that faculty had no existence.

Now, the objection, drawn from the theory of population, against such systems of equality, is this. Marriage is a present good. The difficulties attending the maintenance of a family are future. But in a community of goods, where the children are maintained at public tables, or where each family takes according to its necessities out of the common stock, these difficulties are removed from the individual. They spread themselves, and overflow the whole surface of society, and press equally on every part. All may determine their conduct by the consideration of the present only. All are at liberty to follow the bent of their inclinations in an early marriage. But, as we have already seen, it is impossible to provide an adequate supply of food for all who can be born. Hence, supposing the form of the society to remain, the shares of subsistence are continually diminishing, until all are reduced to extreme distress, and until, ultimately, the further increase of population is repressed by the undisguised check of misery and want.

We may observe, that, supposing the proceedings of all in respect of marriage to be alike, the aggregate amount of the several shares of pressure accruing to one person by reason of the acts of all, will be equal to the primary amount of the pressure distributed to the whole society in consequence of the act of one. Each, therefore, will feel ill effects, corresponding precisely, in character and quantity, with the consequences of his own conduct. Yet they will not be the identical effects flowing from that conduct; but, being a portion of the accumulated effects resulting from the whole conduct of the society in general, would, therefore, still be felt, though the conduct of the individual should be changed. Thus it is that the universal distress fails to suggest to individuals any motive for moral restraint.

From what has been said, I draw one general inference, viz., that the simple fact of a country being overpopulous, by which I mean its population pressing too closely against the means of subsistence, is not, of itself, sufficient evidence that the fault lies in the people themselves, or a proof of the absence of a prudential disposition. The fault may rest, not with them as individuals, but with the constitution of the society, of which they form part.

I do not profess to be here considering generally the merits of systems of equality, and, therefore, I shall not stop to inquire, whether any, and what substitute, for the motive of private interest, can be suggested, to stimulate exertion, to prevent waste, and to check the undue increase of population. My object, in now referring to them, has merely been to illustrate the principle of objection to them, derived from the theory of population—a principle, which to some may perhaps appear so plain and self-evident, as not to have required the notice I have bestowed on it, but which, while it exists in a considerable degree of force in the present condition of the laboring classes in this country, seems nevertheless, as to its bearing on those classes, in a great measure to have escaped observation. . . .

It will serve to illustrate the subject, if we compare the relation subsisting between the cases of two countries, in one of which the constitution of society is such as to throw the burden of a family entirely on the parents, and in the other such that the children maintain themselves at a very early age, with that subsisting between the parallel cases of inclosed grounds and commons; the parallel consisting in what regards the degree of density, in which the countries are peopled, and the commons are stocked, respectively. Why are the cattle on a common so puny and stunted? Why is the common itself so bare-worn, and cropped so differently from the adjoining inclosures? No inequality, in respect of natural or acquired fertility, will account for the phenomenon. The difference depends on the difference of the way in which an increase of stock in the two cases affects the circumstances of the author of the increase. If a person puts more cattle into his own field, the amount of the subsistence which they consume is all deducted from that which was at the command, of his original stock; and if, before, there was no more than a sufficiency of pasture, he reaps no benefits from the additional cattle, what is gained in one way being lost in another. But if he puts more cattle on a common, the food which they consume forms a deduction which is shared between all the cattle, as well that of others as his own, in proportion to their number, and only a small part of it is taken from his own cattle. In an inclosed pasture, there is a point of saturation, if I may so call it, (by which, I mean a barrier depending on considerations of interest), beyond which no prudent man will add to his stock. In a common, also, there is in like manner a point of saturation. But the position of the point in the two cases is obviously different. Were a number of adjoining pastures, already fully stocked, to be at once thrown open, and converted into one vast common, the position of the point of saturation would immediately be changed. The stock would be increased, and would be made to press much more forcibly against the means of subsistence.

Now, the field for the employment of labor is in fact a common, the pasture of which is free to all, to the born and to the unborn, to the present tenants of the earth and to all who are waiting for admission. In the common for cattle, the young animal begins an independent participation in the produce, by the possession of a set of teeth and the ability to graze. In the common for man, the child begins a similar participation, by the possession of a pair of hands competent to labor. The tickets for admission being so readily procurable, it cannot happen otherwise, than that the commons, in both cases, must be constantly stocked to the extreme point of saturation.

It appears then, that, neither in the actual condition of the laboring classes, nor under a system of equality with a community of labor and of goods, when the increase in the resources of the society is so slow as to require prudence in reference to marriage, is the obligation to such prudence sufficiently divided and appropriated. In neither case, if the individuals are prudent, do they alone reap the benefit, nor, if they are imprudent, do they alone feel the evil consequences. The helplessness of the first few years of life operates indeed, to a certain degree, as a weight in favor of individual prudence. But this is not enough. It ought to be an adequate weight. Nobody would maintain, that, were the helplessness to continue only for nine or ten days, or for nine or ten weeks, or for nine or ten months, it would offer a sufficient incentive to abstinence. Why then should there be any peculiar virtue in nine or ten years? If the pressure of a family during that period is disregarded, the public is not saved from the subsequent inconvenience. It does not follow, that, because the children are able to maintain themselves, as it is called, or, in other words, to purchase by their labor their daily bread, nobody else is the worse for their being brought into the world. Were this a just inference, it would be equally just could they work for their living from the moment of birth, as under the abstract hypothesis. . . .

Mr. Malthus, in treating of the effects which would result to society from the prevalence of moral restraint, infers, that "if it were generally adopted, by lowering the supply of labor in the market, it would, in the natural course of things, soon raise its price." And we may readily allow, that, abstinence from marriage, if generally and almost universally prevalent, would have this effect. But, if the principles laid down [here] be correct, it is idle to imagine, that, among laborers who have only the sale of their labor on which to depend for their maintenance, such abstinence can ever generally prevail; and this for the simple reason, that, against it, there are the natural passions which prompt to marriage, and the substantial benefits derivable from marriage; while, in favor of it, to oppose these, there is no adequate individual benefit to be derived from abstinence.

For, for the sake of argument, suppose it to prevail, and, by consequence, that the money wages of labor will command a considerable quantity of food. All laborers, therefore, without distinction, have apparently a greater power of maintaining with decency a large family. If all continue to abstain, they will retain this power. But here I ask, what is there to hinder individuals, who do not enter into the common feeling, from taking advantage of the general forbearance? What rule of prudence would they violate by doing so? Would they lower their rank in life? Would they be unable to transmit to their children the same advantages which they had themselves possessed? They might indeed have for a few years to deny themselves a few luxuries of dress or furniture, or otherwise, possibly, to submit to harder work and harder fare in order to retain them. But these inconveniences could not be sufficient, in the judgment even of the most prudent person, to counterbalance the real advantages of a wife and family, and to induce the preference of a life of celibacy.

Neither would they furnish any material grounds for delay; since, among laborers, the natural age for marriage coinciding nearly with the time when their income is the greatest, and when, being in the vigor of their health and strength, they are best able to endure privations, and, if necessary, to increase their exertions, no future opportunity would appear more favorable than the present. The wages of labor being by the hypothesis high, about the maintenance of his family the laborer would have nothing to fear. His individual act could produce no sensible effect on the market of labor, and he might therefore justly expect his children to have the same advantages which he had himself possessed.

Dr. Chalmers follows in the track of Mr. Malthus, and assumes, that by the operation of the moral preventive check, we may hope to see wages kept permanently high. And this effect he proposes to produce, through the means "both of common and Christian education." It is also to be the immediate fruit, "not of any external or authoritative compulsion, but of the spontaneous and collective will of the working classes of society."

Let us examine this question by reference to a case, which, though not exactly similar, is yet sufficiently so for the present purpose. Were unanimity essential to the enactment of every law, and, not only to its enactment, but also to its continuance, there would evidently be great difficulties in the way of government. Could we entertain the hope of removing these difficulties by means of education? And in like manner I would ask, will education produce unanimity among the working classes of society? And, if it will not, how can effect be given to their collective will, without authoritative compulsion to coerce a dissentient minority? How can we expect that some will abstain from marriage, when others may step in to take advantage of their abstinence?

The fact is, that the wages of the lowest description of labor, in every old country where competition has been tolerably free, have always bordered on the minimum necessary for maintenance. It was an observation of Swift, a hundred years ago, that there were few countries in which one third of the people were not extremely stinted even in the necessaries of life; and, were the point doubtful, similar remarks, applicable to almost every period of history, might be gleaned from other writers. We may also expect them to remain at least equally applicable in [the] future, unless some improvement shall take place in the structure of society, which shall furnish hopes of an advancement in station, leaving less to chance, and, at the same time, producing a degree of isolation, by which the consequences, whether good or evil, flowing from the actions of individuals, may be more fully appropriated to the authors of them.

Such an improvement, however, could not operate through the medium of high wages. Even in past times, when competition was much restricted, and, owing to the difficulty of communication, the field for the employment of labor did not consist of one vast common as at present, but rather of many little commons distinct from each other, and when, by consequence, a fountain of imprudence in one part, could not so readily overflow, and spread misery equally amongst all, still, in every part, there were enough at the bottom of the scale to keep down the wages of common labor. Much more must this be the case, when, by the change of circumstances, all barriers have been broken down, and the communication is free throughout England, Scotland, and Ireland. . . .

It is probable, that the obligation to moral restraint was better distributed in England a hundred years ago than it is at present. "It is seldom," says Swift, writing in 1737, and comparing the condition of Ireland with that of England, "It is seldom known in England, that the laborer, the lower mechanic, the servant or the cottager, thinks of marrying, until he hath saved up a stock of money sufficient to carry on his business; nor takes a wife without a suitable portion; and as seldom fails of making an yearly addition to that stock with the view of providing for his children. But in this kingdom, the case is directly contrary, where many thousand couples are yearly married, whose united fortunes, bating the rags on their backs, would not be sufficient to purchase a pint of buttermilk for their wedding supper, nor have any prospect of supporting their *honorable state,* but by service, or labor, or thievery." . . .

The common reasons for the establishment of private property in land are deduced from the necessity, of offering to individuals sufficient motives for cultivating the ground, and of preventing the wasteful destruction of the immature products of the earth. But to these there is another added, by the theory of population, from which we infer, that, since the earth can never maintain all who can offer themselves for maintenance, it is better that its produce should be divided into shares of a definite magnitude, sufficient each for the comfortable maintenance of a family, whence the number of families to be maintained would be determined from the number of such shares, than that all, who can possibly enter, should be first admitted, and then the magnitude of each share be determined from the number of admissions. . . .

Wealth is productive of many other beneficial consequences besides such as are intended and desired by those who seek it. For the sake of those consequences, inequality of conditions is necessary, on account of its effect in creating new and powerful stimulants to exertion, which the natural utility of wealth, considered merely in reference to the primary gratifications resulting from its use, would be utterly insufficient to produce. After the necessary wants have been supplied, the next powerful motive to exertion is the spirit of emulation, and the desire of rising in the world. Men are attracted upwards by the example of others who are richer than themselves. At the top of the scale this attraction is wanting.

At that point, therefore, it is necessary that there should be a title to wealth without the labor of producing it. A state of perfect equality, by its effect in lowering the standard of desire, and almost reducing it to the satisfaction of the natural necessities, would bring back society to ignorance and barbarism. Still, the same principle of population, which furnishes a reason for the institution of property, prescribes a limit to its concentration. To a plank in the sea, which cannot support all, all have not an equal right; the lucky individuals, who can first obtain possession, being justified in appropriating it to themselves, to the exclusion of the remainder. Where property is much concentrated, and where, by consequence, the class of mere laborers is great, the principle of population would warrant the application of the same argument, to justify the appropriation of the field of employment, and a monopoly of labor. But, since such a monopoly is not easily maintainable, we are led to look for an equivalent in the diffusion of a sufficient degree of property throughout the whole fabric of society.

3

The Tragedy
of the Commons

Garrett Hardin
(1968)

At the end of a thoughtful article on the future of nuclear war, J.B. Wiesner and H.F. York concluded that: "Both sides in the arms race are . . . confronted by the dilemma of steadily increasing military power and steadily decreasing national security. *It is our considered professional judgment that this dilemma has no technical solution.* If the great powers continue to look for solutions in the area of science and technology only, the result will be to worsen the situation."[1]

I would like to focus your attention not on the subject of the article (national security in a nuclear world) but on the kind of conclusion they reached, namely that there is no technical solution to the problem. An implicit and almost universal assumption of discussions published in professional and semipopular scientific journals is that the problem under discussion has a technical solution. A technical solution may be defined as one that requires a change only in the techniques of the natural sciences, demanding little or nothing in the way of change in human values or ideas of morality.

In our day (though not in earlier times) technical solutions are always welcome. Because of previous failures in prophecy, it takes courage to assert that a desired technical solution is not possible. Wiesner and York exhibited this courage; publishing in a science journal, they insisted that the solution to the problem was not to be found in the natural sciences. They cautiously qualified their statement with the phrase, "It is our con-

Reprinted with permission from *Science,* **162:**1243–1248, 1968. Copyright 1968 by the American Association for the Advancement of Science.

sidered professional judgment. . . ." Whether they were right or not is not the concern of the present article. Rather, the concern here is with the important concept of a class of human problems which can be called "no technical solution problems," and more specifically, with the identification and discussion of one of these.

It is easy to show that the class is not a null class. Recall the game of tick-tack-toe. Consider the problem, "How can I win the game of tick-tack-toe?" It is well known that I cannot, if I assume (in keeping with the conventions of game theory) that my opponent understands the game perfectly. Put another way, there is no "technical solution" to the problem. I can win only by giving a radical meaning to the word "win." I can hit my opponent over the head; or I can falsify the records. Every way in which I "win" involves, in some sense, an abandonment of the game, as we intuitively understand it. (I can also, of course, openly abandon the game—refuse to play it. This is what most adults do.)

The class of "no technical solution problems" has members. My thesis is that the "population problem," as conventionally conceived, is a member of this class. How it is conventionally conceived needs some comment. It is fair to say that most people who anguish over the population problem are trying to find a way to avoid the evils of overpopulation without relinquishing any of the privileges they now enjoy. They think that farming the seas or developing new strains of wheat will solve the problem—technologically. I try to show here that the solution they seek cannot be found. The population problem cannot be solved in a technical way, any more than can the problem of winning the game of tick-tack-toe.

What Shall We Maximize?

Population, as Malthus said, naturally tends to grow "geometrically," or, as we would now say, exponentially. In a finite world this means that the per-capita share of the world's goods must decrease. Is ours a finite world?

A fair defense can be put forward for the view that the world is infinite; or that we do not know that it is not. But, in terms of the practical problems that we must face in the next few generations with the foreseeable technology, it is clear that we will greatly increase human misery if we do not, during the immediate future, assume that the world available to the terrestrial human population is finite. "Space" is no escape.[2]

A finite world can support only a finite population; therefore, population growth must eventually equal zero. (The case of perpetual wide fluctuations above and below zero is a trivial variant that need not be discussed.) When this condition is met, what will be the situation of mankind? Specifically, can Bentham's goal of "the greatest good for the greatest number" be realized?

No—for two reasons, each sufficient by itself. The first is a theoretical one. It is not mathematically possible to maximize for two (or more) variables at the same time. This was clearly stated by von Neumann and Morgenstern,[3] but the principle is implicit in the theory of partial differential equations, dating back at least to D'Alembert (1717–1783).

The second reason springs directly from biological facts. To live, any organism must have a source of energy (for example, food). This energy is utilized for two purposes: mere maintenance and work. For man, maintenance of life requires about 1600 kilocalories a day ("maintenance calories"). Anything that he does over and above merely staying alive will be defined as work, and is supported by "work calories" which he takes in. Work calories are used not only for what we call work in common speech; they are also required for all forms of enjoyment, from swimming and automobile racing to playing music and writing poetry. If our goal is to maximize population it is obvious what we must do: We must make the work calories per person approach as close to zero as possible. No gourmet meals, no vacations, no sports, no music, no literature, no art. . . . I think that everyone will grant, without argument or proof, that maximizing population does not maximize goods. Bentham's goal is impossible.

In reaching this conclusion I have made the usual assumption that it is the acquisition of energy that is the problem. The appearance of atomic energy has led some to question this assumption. However, given an infinite source of energy, population growth still produces an inescapable problem. The problem of the acquisition of energy is replaced by the problem of its dissipation, as J. H. Fremlin has so wittily shown.[4] The arithmetic signs in the analysis are, as it were, reversed; but Bentham's goal is unobtainable.

The optimum population is, then, less than the maximum. The difficulty of defining the optimum is enormous; so far as I know, no one has seriously tackled this problem. Reaching an acceptable and stable solution will surely require more than one generation of hard analytical work—and much persuasion.

We want the maximum good per person; but what is good? To one person it is wilderness, to another it is ski lodges for thousands. To one it is estuaries to nourish ducks for hunters to shoot; to another it is factory land. Comparing one good with another is, we usually say, impossible because goods are incommensurable. Incommensurables cannot be compared.

Theoretically this may be true; but in real life incommensurables *are* commensurable. Only a criterion of judgment and a system of weighting are needed. In nature the criterion is survival. Is it better for a species to be small and hideable, or large and powerful? Natural selection commensurates the incommensurables. The compromise achieved depends on a natural weighting of the values of the variables.

Man must imitate this process. There is no doubt that in fact he already does, but unconsciously. It is when the hidden decisions are made explicit that the arguments begin. The problem for the years ahead is to work out an acceptable theory of weighting. Synergistic effects, nonlinear variation, and difficulties in discounting the future make the intellectual problem difficult, but not (in principle) insoluble.

Has any cultural group solved this practical problem at the present time, even on an intuitive level? One simple fact proves that none has: there is no prosperous population in the world today that has, and has had for some time, a growth rate of zero. Any people that has intuitively identified its optimum point will soon reach it, after which its growth rate becomes and remains zero.

Of course, a positive growth rate might be taken as evidence that a population is below its optimum. However, by any reasonable standards, the most rapidly growing populations on earth today are (in general) the most miserable. This association (which need not be invariable) casts doubt on the optimistic assumption that the positive growth rate of a population is evidence that it has yet to reach its optimum.

We can make little progress in working toward optimum population size until we explicitly exorcise the spirit of Adam Smith in the field of practical demography. In economic affairs, *The Wealth of Nations* (1776) popularized the "invisible hand," the idea that an individual who "intends only his own gain," is, as it were, "led by an invisible hand to promote . . . the public interest."[5] Adam Smith did not assert that this was invariably true, and perhaps neither did any of his followers. But he contributed to a dominant tendency of thought that has ever since interfered with positive action based on rational analysis, namely, the tendency to assume that decisions reached individually will, in fact, be the best decisions for an entire society. If this assumption is correct it justifies the continuance of our present policy of *laissez faire* in reproduction. If it is correct we can assume that men will control their individual fecundity so as to produce the optimum population. If the assumption is not correct, we need to reexamine our individual freedoms to see which ones are defensible.

Tragedy of Freedom in a Commons

The rebuttal to the invisible hand in population control is to be found in a scenario first sketched in a little-known pamphlet in 1833 by a mathematical amateur named William Forster Lloyd (1794–1852).[6] We may well call it "the tragedy of the commons," using the word "tragedy" as the philosopher Whitehead used it[7]: "The essence of dramatic tragedy is not unhappiness. It resides in the solemnity of the remorseless working of things." He then goes on to say, "This inevitableness of destiny can only be illustrated in terms of human life by incidents which in fact involve unhappiness. For it is only by them that the futility of escape can be made evident in the drama."

The tragedy of the commons develops in this way. Picture a pasture open to all. It is to be expected that each herdsman will try to keep as many cattle as possible on the commons. Such an arrangement may work reasonably satisfactorily for centuries because tribal wars, poaching, and disease keep the numbers of both man and beast well below the carrying capacity of the land. Finally, however, comes the day of reckoning, that is, the day when the long-desired goal of social stability becomes a reality. At this point, the inherent logic of the commons remorselessly generates tragedy.

As a rational being, each herdsman seeks to maximize his gain. Explicitly or implicitly, more or less consciously, he asks, "What is the utility *to me* of adding one more animal to my herd?" This utility has one negative and one positive component.

1. The positive component is a function of the increment of one animal. Since the herdsman receives all the proceeds from the sale of the additional animal, the positive utility is nearly $+1$.

2. The negative component is a function of the additional overgrazing created by one more animal. Since, however, the effects of overgrazing are shared by all the herdsmen, the negative utility for any particular decision-making herdsman is only a fraction of -1.

Adding together the component partial utilities, the rational herdsman concludes that the only sensible course for him to pursue is to add another animal to his herd. And another. . . . But this is the conclusion reached by each and every rational herdsman sharing a commons. Therein is the tragedy. Each man is locked into a system that compels him to increase his herd without limit—in a world that is limited. Ruin is the destination toward which all men rush, each pursuing his own best interest in a society that believes in the freedom of the commons. Freedom in a commons brings ruin to all.

Some would say that this is a platitude. Would that it were! In a sense, it was learned thousands of years ago, but natural selection favors the forces of psychological denial.[8] The individual benefits as an individual from his ability to deny the truth even though society as a whole, of which he is a part, suffers. Education can counteract the natural tendency to do the wrong thing, but the inexorable succession of generations requires that the basis for this knowledge be constantly refreshed.

A simple incident that occurred a few years ago in Leominster, Massachusetts, shows how perishable the knowledge is. During the Christmas shopping season the parking meters downtown were covered with plastic bags that bore tags reading: "Do not open until after Christmas. Free parking courtesy of the mayor and city council." In other words, facing the prospect of an increased demand for already scarce space, the city fathers reinstituted the system of the commons. (Cynically, we suspect that they gained more votes than they lost by this retrogressive act.)

In an approximate way, the logic of the commons has been understood for a long time, perhaps since the discovery of agriculture or the invention of private property in real estate. But it is understood mostly only in special cases which are not sufficiently generalized. Even at this late date, cattlemen leasing national land on the Western ranges demonstrate no more than an ambivalent understanding, in constantly pressuring federal authorities to increase the head count to the point where overgrazing produces erosion and weed-dominance. Likewise, the oceans of the world continue to suffer from the survival of the philosophy of the commons. Maritime nations still respond automatically to the shibboleth of the "freedom of the seas." Professing to believe in the "inexhaustible resources of the oceans," they bring species after species of fish and whales closer to extinction.[9]

The National Parks present another instance of the working out of the tragedy of the commons. At present, they are open to all, without limit. The parks themselves are limited in extent—there is only one Yosemite Valley—whereas population seems to grow without limit. The values that visitors seek in the parks are steadily eroded. Plainly, we must soon cease to treat the parks as commons or they will be of no value to anyone.

What shall we do? We have several options. We might sell them off as private property. We might keep them as public property, but allocate the right to enter them. The allocation might be on the basis of wealth, by the use of an auction system. It might be on the basis of merit, as defined by some agreed-upon standards. It might be by lottery. Or it might be on a first-come, first-served basis, administered to long queues. These, I think, are all objectionable. But we must choose—or acquiesce in the destruction of the commons that we call our National Parks.

Pollution

In a reverse way, the tragedy of the commons reappears in problems of pollution. Here it is not a question of taking something out of the commons, but of putting something in—sewage, or chemical, radioactive, and heat wastes into water; noxious and dangerous fumes into the air; and distracting and unpleasant advertising signs into the line of sight. The calculations of utility are much the same as before. The rational man finds that his share of the cost of the wastes he discharges into the commons is less than the cost of purifying his wastes before releasing them. Since this is true for everyone, we are locked into a system of "fouling our own nest," so long as we behave only as independent, rational, free-enterprisers.

The tragedy of the commons as a food basket is averted by private property, or something formally like it. But the air and waters surrounding us cannot readily be fenced, and so the tragedy of the commons as a cesspool must be prevented by different means, by coercive laws or taxing devices that make it cheaper for the polluter to treat his pollutants than to discharge them untreated. We have not progressed as far with the solution of this problem as we have with the first. Indeed, our particular concept of private property, which deters us from exhausting the positive resources of the earth, favors pollution. The owner of a factory on the bank of a stream—whose property extends to the middle of the stream—often has difficulty seeing why it is not his natural right to muddy the waters flowing past his door. The law, always behind the times, requires elaborate stitching and fitting to adapt it to this newly perceived aspect of the commons.

The pollution problem is a consequence of population. It did not much matter how a lonely American frontiersman disposed of his waste. "Flowing water purifies itself every ten miles," my grandfather used to say, and the myth was near enough to the truth when he was a boy, for there were not too many people. But as population became denser, the natural chemical and biological recycling processes became overloaded, calling for a redefinition of property rights.

How to Legislate Temperance?

Analysis of the pollution problem as a function of population density uncovers a not generally recognized principle of morality, namely: *the morality of an act is a function of the state of the system at the time it is performed.*[10] Using the commons as a cesspool does not harm the general public under frontier conditions, because there is no public; the same behavior in a metropolis is unbearable. A hundred and fifty years ago a plainsman could kill an American bison, cut out only the tongue for his dinner, and discard the rest of the animal. He was not in any important sense being wasteful. Today, with only a few thousand bison left, we would be appalled at such behavior.

In passing, it is worth noting that the morality of an act cannot be determined from a photograph. One does not know whether a man killing an elephant or setting fire to the grassland is harming others until one knows the total system in which his act appears. "One picture is worth a thousand words," said an ancient Chinese; but it may take ten thousand words to validate it. It is as tempting to ecologists as it is to reformers in general to try to persuade others by way of the photographic shortcut. But the essence of an argument cannot be photographed: it must be presented rationally—in words.

That morality is system-sensitive escaped the attention of most codifiers of ethics in the past. "Thou shalt not . . ." is the form of traditional ethical directives which make no allowance for particular circumstances. The laws of our society follow the pattern of ancient ethics, and therefore are poorly suited to governing a complex, crowded, changeable world. Our epicyclic solution is to augment statutory law with administrative law. Since it is practically impossible to spell out all the conditions under which it is safe to burn trash in the back yard or to run an automobile without smog-control, by law we delegate the details to bureaus. The result is administrative law, which is rightly feared for an ancient reason —*Quis custodiet ipsos custodes?*—Who shall watch the watchers themselves? John Adams said that we must have a "government of laws and not men." Bureau administrators, trying to evaluate the morality of acts in the total system, are singularly liable to corruption, producing a government by men, not laws.

Prohibition is easy to legislate (though not necessarily to enforce); but how do we legislate temperance? Experience indicates that it can be accomplished best through the mediation of administrative law. We limit possibilities unnecessarily if we suppose that the sentiment of *Quis custodiet* denies us the use of administrative law. We should rather retain the phrase as a perpetual reminder of fearful dangers we cannot avoid. The great challenge facing us now is to invent the corrective feedbacks that are needed to keep custodians honest. We must find ways to legitimate the needed authority of both the custodians and the corrective feedbacks.

Freedom to Breed Is Intolerable

The tragedy of the commons is involved in population problems in another way. In a world governed solely by the principle of "dog eat dog" —if indeed there ever was such a world—how many children a family had would not be a matter of public concern. Parents who bred too exuberantly would leave fewer descendants, not more, because they would be unable to care adequately for their children. David Lack and others have found that such a negative feedback demonstrably controls the fecundity of birds.[11] But men are not birds, and have not acted like them for millenniums, at least.

If each human family were dependent only on its own resources; *if* the children of improvident parents starved to death; *if,* thus, over-breeding brought its own "punishment" to the germ line—*then* there would be no public interest in controlling the breeding of families. But our society is deeply committed to the welfare state,[12] and hence is confronted with another aspect of the tragedy of the commons.

In a welfare state, how shall we deal with the family, the religion, the race, or the class (or indeed any distinguishable and cohesive group) that adopts overbreeding as a policy to secure its own aggrandizement?[13] To couple the concept of freedom to breed with the belief that everyone born has an equal right to the commons is to lock the world into a tragic course of action.

Unfortunately this is just the course of action that is being pursued by the United Nations. In late 1967, some thirty nations agreed to the following: "The Universal Declaration of Human Rights describes the family as the natural and fundamental unit of society. It follows that any choice and decision with regard to the size of the family must irrevocably rest with the family itself, and cannot be made by anyone else."[14]

It is painful to have to deny categorically the validity of this right; denying it, one feels as uncomfortable as a resident of Salem, Massachusetts, who denied the reality of witches in the seventeenth century. At the present time, in liberal quarters, something like a taboo acts to inhibit criticism of the United Nations. There is a feeling that the United Nations is "our last and best hope," that we shouldn't find fault with it; we shouldn't play into the hands of the archconservatives. However, let us not forget what Robert Louis Stevenson said: "The truth that is suppressed by friends is the readiest weapon of the enemy." If we love the truth we must openly deny the validity of the Universal Declaration of Human Rights, even though it is promoted by the United Nations. We should also join with Kingsley Davis[15] in attempting to get Planned Parenthood–World Population to see the error of its ways in embracing the same tragic ideal.

Conscience Is Self-Eliminating

It is a mistake to think that we can control the breeding of mankind in the long run by an appeal to conscience. Charles Galton Darwin made this point when he spoke on the centennial of the publication of his grandfather's great book. The argument is straightforward and Darwinian.

People vary. Confronted with appeals to limit breeding, some people will undoubtedly respond to the plea more than others. Those who have more children will produce a larger fraction of the next generation than those with more susceptible consciences. The differences will be accentuated, generation by generation.

In C. G. Darwin's words: "It may well be that it would take hundreds of generations for the progenitive instinct to develop in this way, but if it should do so, nature would have taken her revenge, and the variety *Homo contracipiens* would become extinct and would be replaced by the variety *Homo progenitivus.*"[16]

The argument assumes that conscience or the desire for children (no matter which) is hereditary—but hereditary only in the most general formal sense. The result will be the same whether the attitude is transmitted through germ cells, or exosomatically, to use A. J. Lotka's term. (If one denies the latter possibility as well as the former, then what's the point of education?) The argument has here been stated in the context of the population problem, but it applies equally well to any instance in which society appeals to an individual exploiting a commons to restrain himself for the general good—by means of his conscience. To make such an appeal is to set up a selective system that works toward the elimination of conscience from the race.

Pathogenic Effects of Conscience

The long-term disadvantage of an appeal to conscience should be enough to condemn it; but it has serious short-term disadvantages as well. If we ask a man who is exploiting a commons to desist "in the name of conscience," what are we saying to him? What does he hear?—not only at the moment but also in the wee small hours of the night when, half asleep, he remembers not merely the words we used but also the nonverbal communication cues we gave him unawares? Sooner or later, consciously or subconsciously, he senses that he has received two communications, and that they are contradictory: 1. (intended communication) "If you don't do as we ask, we will openly condemn you for not acting like a responsible citizen"; 2. (the unintended communication) "If you *do* behave as we ask, we will secretly condemn you for a simpleton who can be shamed into standing aside while the rest of us exploit the commons."

Everyman then is caught in what Bateson has called a "double bind." Bateson and his co-workers have made a plausible case for viewing the double bind as an important causative factor in the genesis of schizophrenia.[17] The double bind may not always be so damaging, but it always endangers the mental health of anyone to whom it is applied. "A bad conscience," said Nietzsche, "is a kind of illness."

To conjure up a conscience in others is tempting to anyone who wishes to extend his control beyond the legal limits. Leaders at the highest level succumb to this temptation. Has any president during the past generation failed to call on labor unions to moderate voluntarily their demands for higher wages, or to steel companies to honor voluntary guidelines on prices? I can recall none. The rhetoric used on such occasions is designed to produce feelings of guilt in noncooperators.

For centuries it was assumed without proof that guilt was a valuable, perhaps even an indispensable, ingredient of the civilized life. Now, in this post-Freudian world, we doubt it.

Paul Goodman speaks from the modern point of view when he says: "No good has ever come from feeling guilty, neither intelligence, policy, nor compassion. The guilty do not pay attention to the object but only to themselves, and not even to their own interests, which might make sense, but to their anxieties."[18]

One does not have to be a professional psychiatrist to see the consequences of anxiety. We in the Western world are just emerging from a dreadful two centuries-long Dark Ages of Eros that was sustained partly by prohibition laws, but perhaps more effectively by the anxiety-generating mechanisms of education. Alex Comfort has told the story well in *The Anxiety Makers;*[19] it is not a pretty one.

Since proof is difficult, we may even concede that the results of anxiety may sometimes, from certain points of view, be desirable. The larger question we should ask is whether, as a matter of policy, we should ever encourage the use of a technique the tendency (if not the intention) of which is psychologically pathogenic. We hear much talk these days of responsible parenthood; the coupled words are incorporated into the titles of some organizations devoted to birth control. Some people have proposed massive propaganda campaigns to instill responsibility into the nation's (or the world's) breeders. But what is the meaning of the word conscience? When we use the word responsibility in the absence of substantial sanctions are we not trying to browbeat a free man in a commons into acting against his own interest? Responsibility is a verbal counterfeit for a substantial quid pro quo. It is an attempt to get something for nothing.

If the word responsibility is to be used at all, I suggest that it be in the sense Charles Frankel uses it.[20] "Responsibility," says this philosopher, "is the product of definite social arrangements." Notice that Frankel calls for social arrangements—not propaganda.

Mutual Coercion Mutually Agreed Upon

The social arrangements that produce responsibility are arrangements that create coercion, of some sort. Consider bank robbing. The man who takes money from a bank acts as if the bank were a commons. How do we prevent such action? Certainly not by trying to control his behavior solely by a verbal appeal to his sense of responsibility. Rather than rely on propaganda we follow Frankel's lead and insist that a bank is not a commons; we seek the definite social arrangements that will keep it from becoming a commons. That we thereby infringe on the freedom of would-be robbers we neither deny nor regret.

The morality of bank robbing is particularly easy to understand because we accept complete prohibition of this activity. We are willing to say "Thou shalt not rob banks," without providing for exceptions. But temperance also can be created by coercion. Taxing is a good coercive device. To keep downtown shoppers temperate in their use of parking space we introduce parking meters for short periods, and traffic fines for longer ones. We need not actually forbid a citizen to park as long as he wants to; we need merely make it increasingly expensive for him to do so. Not prohibition, but carefully biased options are what we offer him. A Madison Avenue man might call this persuasion; I prefer the greater candor of the word coercion.

Coercion is a dirty word to most liberals now, but it need not forever be so. As with the four-letter words, its dirtiness can be cleansed away by exposure to the light, by saying it over and over without apology or embarrassment. To many, the word coercion implies arbitrary decisions of distant and irresponsible bureaucrats; but this is not a necessary part of its meaning. The only kind of coercion I recommend is mutual coercion, mutually agreed upon by the majority of the people affected.

To say that we mutually agree to coerecion is not to say that we are required to enjoy it, or even to pretend we enjoy it. Who enjoys taxes? We all grumble about them. But we accept compulsory taxes because we recognize that voluntary taxes would favor the conscienceless. We institute and (grumblingly) support taxes and other coercive devices to escape the horror of the commons.

An alternative to the commons need not be perfectly just to be preferable. With real estate and other material goods, the alternative we have chosen is the institution of private property coupled with legal inheritance. Is this system perfectly just? As a genetically trained biologist I deny that it is. It seems to me that, if there are to be differences in individual inheritance, legal possession should be perfectly correlated with biological inheritance—that those who are biologically more fit to be the custodians of property and power should legally inherit more. But genetic recombination continually makes a mockery of the doctrine of "like father, like son" implicit in our laws of legal inheritance. An idiot can inherit millions, and a trust fund can keep his estate intact. We must admit that our legal system of private property plus inheritance is unjust

—but we put up with it because we are not convinced, at the moment, that anyone has invented a better system. The alternative of the commons is too horrifying to contemplate. Injustice is preferable to total ruin.

It is one of the peculiarities of the warfare between reform and the status quo that it is thoughtlessly governed by a double standard. Whenever a reform measure is proposed it is often defeated when its opponents triumphantly discover a flaw in it. As Kingsley Davis has pointed out,[21] worshipers of the status quo sometimes imply that no reform is possible without unanimous agreement, an implication contrary to historical fact. As nearly as I can make out, automatic rejection of proposed reforms is based on one of two unconscious assumptions: (1) that the status quo is perfect; or (2) that the choice we face is between reform and no action; if the proposed reform is imperfect, we presumably should take no action at all, while we wait for a perfect proposal.

But we can never do nothing. That which we have done for thousands of years is also action. It also produces evils. Once we are aware that the status quo is action, we can then compare its discoverable advantages and disadvantages with the predicted advantages and disadvantages of the proposed reform, discounting as best we can for our lack of experience. On the basis of such a comparison, we can make a rational decision which will not involve the unworkable assumption that only perfect systems are tolerable.

Recognition of Necessity

Perhaps the simplest summary of this analysis of man's population problems is this: the commons, if justifiable at all, is justfiable only under conditions of low-population density. As the human population has increased, the commons has had to be abandoned in one aspect after another.

First we abandoned the commons in food gathering, enclosing farm land and restricting pastures and hunting and fishing areas. These restrictions are still not complete throughout the world.

Somewhat later we saw that the commons as a place for waste disposal would also have to be abandoned. Restrictions on the disposal of domestic sewage are widely accepted in the Western world; we are still struggling to close the commons to pollution by automobiles, factories, insecticide sprayers, fertilizing operations, and atomic energy installations.

In a still more embryonic state is our recognition of the evils of the commons in matters of pleasure. There is almost no restriction on the propagation of sound waves in the public medium. The shopping public is assaulted with mindless music, without its consent. Our government has paid out billions of dollars to create a supersonic transport which would disturb 50,000 people for every one person whisked from coast to coast 3 hours faster. Advertisers muddy the airwaves of radio and television and pollute the view of travelers. We are a long way from outlawing the commons in matters of pleasure. Is this because our Puritan inheritance makes us view pleasure as something of a sin, and pain (that is, the pollution of advertising) as the sign of virtue?

Every new enclosure of the commons involves the infringement of somebody's personal liberty. Infringements made in the distant past are accepted because no contemporary complains of a loss. It is the newly proposed infringements that we vigorously oppose; cries of "rights" and "freedom" fill the air. But what does "freedom" mean? When men mutually agreed to pass laws against robbing, mankind became more free, not less so. Individuals locked into the logic of the commons are free only to bring on universal ruin; once they see the necessity of mutual coercion, they become free to pursue other goals. I believe it was Hegel who said, "Freedom is the recognition of necessity."

The most important aspect of necessity that we must now recognize, is the necessity of abandoning the commons in breeding. No technical solution can rescue us from the misery of overpopulation. Freedom to breed will bring ruin to all. At the moment, to avoid hard decisions many of us are tempted to propagandize for conscience and responsible parenthood. The temptation must be resisted, because an appeal to independently acting consciences selects for the disappearance of all conscience in the long run, and an increase in anxiety in the short.

The only way we can preserve and nurture other and more precious freedoms is by relinquishing the freedom to breed, and that very soon. "Freedom is the recognition of necessity"—and it is the role of education to reveal to all the necessity of abandoning the freedom to breed. Only so, can we put an end to this aspect of the tragedy of the commons.

Notes

1. J. B. Wiesner and H. F. York, *Scientific American* 211 (No. 4), 27 (1964).
2. G. Hardin, *Journal of Heredity* 50, 68 (1959), S. von Hoernor, *Science* 137, 18, (1962).
3. J. von Neumann and O. Morgenstern, *Theory of Games and Economic Behavior* (Princeton University Press, Princeton, N.J., 1947), p. 11.
4. J. H. Fremlin, *New Scientist,* No. 415 (1964), p. 285.

5. A. Smith, *The Wealth of Nations* (Modern Library, New York, 1937), p. 423.
6. W. F. Lloyd, *Two Lectures on the Checks to Population* (Oxford University Press, Oxford, England, 1833).
7. A. N. Whitehead, *Science and the Modern World* (Mentor, New York, 1948), p. 17.
8. G. Hardin, Ed., *Population, Evolution, and Birth Control* (Freeman, San Francisco, 1964), p. 56.
9. S. McVay, *Scientific American* 216 (No. 8), 13 (1966).
10. J. Fletcher, *Situation Ethics* (Westminster, Philadelphia, 1966).
11. D. Lack, *The Natural Regulation of Animal Numbers* (Clarendon Press, Oxford, England, 1954).
12. H. Girvetz, *From Wealth to Welfare* (Stanford University Press, Stanford, Calif., 1950).
13. G. Hardin, *Perspectives in Biology and Medicine* 6, 366 (1963).
14. U Thant, *International Planned Parenthood News,* No. 168 (February 1968), p. 3.
15. K. Davis, *Science* 158, 730 (1967).
16. S. Tax, Ed., *Evolution After Darwin* (University of Chicago Press, Chicago, 1960), vol. 2, p. 469.
17. G. Bateson, D. D. Jackson, J. Haley, J. Weakland, *Behavioral Science* 1, 251 (1956).
18. P. Goodman, *New York Review of Books* 10 (8), 22 (23 May 1968).
19. A. Comfort, *The Anxiety Makers* (Nelson, London, 1967).
20. C. Frankel, *The Case for Modern Man* (Harper & Row, New York, 1955), p. 203.
21. J. D. Roslansky, *Genetics and the Future of Man* (Appleton-Century-Crofts, New York, 1966), p. 177.

4

Intuition First, Then Rigor

Garrett Hardin

From the remarks made by Aristotle in the fourth century B.C., to the quasi-mathematical developments of the theory of the commons in 1833 and 1968 it should be apparent that a working understanding of the world can be reached without resort to formal, rigorous mathematics. It must certainly be true that millions of people with diverse experience have "intuitively" understood the suicidal threat of political systems based on the commons, rejecting such systems in favor of others that may be demonstrably deficient in justice but which are at least capable of enduring without further degradation or collapse. What excites our wonder is not that so many people can understand the commons without mathematics but that so many apparently cannot understand it at all. Perhaps "will not" is closer to the truth: "From each according to his ability, to each according to his needs" is not an argument but an appeal to envy and wishful thinking. Such appeals are seductive.

In the thinking that expands the frontiers of knowledge, intuition generally outruns mathematics. No apology need be offered for this fact. Even in the mind of Isaac Newton intuition led the way. On one occasion the great man was discussing a fundamental property of the motion of planets with his admirer Edmund Halley (of Halley's Comet fame). "Yes," agreed Halley, "but how do you know that? Have you proved it?" Though taken aback Newton promptly replied: "Why, I've known it for years. If you will give me a few days I'll certainly find you a proof." And he did.[1]

But lesser mortals should be wary of proceeding as cavalierly as the inventor of the calculus. Intuition can be wrong. Equally important, language can deceive. As Bronowski and Mazlish have put the matter:

> Mathematics is no more than a symbolism. But it is the only symbolism invented by the human mind which steadfastly resists the constant attempts of the mind to shift and smudge the meaning. It is the only exact symbolism and, by being exact, it is self-correcting.
>
> This is why, to this day, our confidence in any science is roughly proportional to the amount of mathematics it employs—that is, to its ability to formulate its concepts with enough precision to allow them to be handled mathematically.[2]

Lewis Richardson has made the same point somewhat more succinctly:

> Another advantage of a mathematical statement is that it is so definite that it might be definitely wrong. . . . Some verbal statements have not this merit; they are so vague that they could hardly be wrong, and are correspondingly useless.[3]

That those whose professions require the use of mathematics should testify in its favor is no surprise. More impressive is the testimony of a "reluctant witness." The words of Malcolm X merit attention. His short life of "hustling" and fighting for minority rights, a life ended by violence, offered little scope for mathematics; yet recalling his childhood days in school he once remarked:

> I'm sorry to say that the subject I most disliked was mathematics. I have thought about it. I think the reason was that mathematics leave no room for argument. If you made a mistake, that was all there was to it.[4]

A major strength of mathematics, then, is that it is transparent to error. In this property we see a reason for the wide utility of mathematics in the pursuit of science, in keeping with the modern view of scientific method, principally deriving from the work of Karl Popper.[5] We no longer think that scientific hypotheses can be *proved;* the most we can hope for is that they can be *falsified.* Always we seek the "falsifiable hypothesis," a hypothesis that can then be assiduously tested against the world. If a hypothesis, as stated, is not falsifiable by some empirical test then it is not a *scientific* hypothesis. On the other hand, if it *is* falsifiable, and if the most rigorous tests we can think of fail to prove it false, then we tentatively assume it to be true. We don't call it true; we just assume it to be so because we need something to base action on.

The needs of scientific testing are well served by the mathematization of hypotheses, since (as Richardson said) a mathematical statement is so definite that it might be definitely wrong, unlike ordinary rhetoric which easily smudges meaning (to quote Bronowski and Mazlish). Two different mathematizations of the theory of the commons follow. Those who have a taste for mathematics should find these statements superior to the ones given earlier. Mathematical statements suggest empirical tests. Moreover, they open the way to the further development of theory.

Notes

1. John Maynard Keynes, *Essays in Biography* (London: Hart-Davis, 1951). The passage occurs in the essay on "Newton, the Man," p. 313.
2. J. Bronowski and Bruce Mazlish, *The Western Intellectual Tradition* (New York: Harper & Row, 1960), p. 218.
3. Lewis Fry Richardson, "Mathematics of War and Foreign Politics," in James R. Newman, *The World of Mathematics*, vol. 2 (New York: Simon & Schuster, 1956), p. 1248.
4. Malcolm X (assisted by Alex Haley), *The Autobiography of Malcolm X* (New York: Grove Press, 1966), p. 29.
5. Karl R. Popper, *The Logic of Scientific Discovery* (New York: Basic Books, 1959).

5

An Algebraic Theory
of the Commons

H. V. Muhsam
(1973)

The tragedy of the commons is concerned with the consequences of introducing grazing animals, e.g., cattle, onto the commons, beyond its grazing capacity. We shall assume in the following, that the loss in value of each head of cattle kept on the overgrazed pasture increases in straight proportion to the number of heads of cattle introduced beyond grazing capacity, although this is certainly an oversimplification. Let the number of herdsmen be h, the average number of cattle belonging to each of them at the limit of the grazing capacity of the commons n, and the number of the herd at this limit $N = nh$. If the value of each head of cattle with no overgrazing is taken as unity and the percentage loss in value of each head of cattle due to one head of overgrazing cattle is a, and x is the number of heads of cattle introduced beyond grazing capacity, the value of each head of cattle under overgrazing becomes $1 - ax$ and the total value of the herd $(N + x)(1 - ax)$. Overgrazing can be said to occur, if the introduction of one or more head of cattle decreases the total value of the herd, i.e. if this last expression is smaller than the value of the herd at the limit of the grazing capacity of the commons, which is exactly N. This will be so if $a > 1/N$.

In the following it will be assumed that a is large enough to fulfill this condition, but that a is not too large. The importance of the latter assumption will appear below. If, for example, the number of herdsmen is

This is the Appendix of Muhsam's "A World Population Policy for the World Population Year," *Journal of Peace Research*, vol. 1-2, 97–99, 1973. Reprinted with permission of the author and publisher, Universitetsforlaget, Oslo.

$h = 50$, the average number of cattle per herdsman $n = 20$ and the total herd $N = 1000$, we may assume the loss on each head of the cattle due to each head of overgrazing cattle to be, for instance, one percent, i.e. $a = 0.01$. We shall now analyze by game-theory approach the strategy of the individual herdsman. For this purpose, the situation of the tragedy of the commons will be considered as a non-zero-sum two-person game. The two players are (1) one of the herdsmen, to whom we shall refer in the following as 'our individual herdsman' and (2) all the other herdsmen. Each player has one move to make and he has two choices: our individual herdsman, those of adding or not one head of cattle; and all the other herdsmen, those of adding one head of cattle each, or of not adding any cattle. It is true that even if we maintain our basic restriction that each herdsman can add only one head of cattle at one time, all the other herdsmen have in fact much more choices: they may add, together, any number of cattle between zero and $h - 1$; but it will be shown in the following that such a differentiation would not affect our results.

The pay-off matrix of our individual herdsman is as shown in Table 5.1. For example, the upper lefthand element of this matrix is obtained by comparing the value of the herd of our individual herdsman, after all have added one head of cattle to their herd with the value of his initial herd. The former numbers $n + 1$ heads, if we assume that our individual herdsman had an initial herd of average size and the value of each head of cattle is $1 - ah$; thus, the total value of this final herd is $(n + 1)$ $(1 - ah)$ as against the value of his initial herd of n. His pay-off is therefore $(n + 1) (1 - ah) - n = 1 - a(N + h)$, if we remember that $nh = N$. The other elements are obtained correspondingly.

Now it is obvious that if all the other herdsmen do not add any cattle (right-hand column of the pay-off matrix) it is worthwhile for our individual herdsman to add a head of cattle as long as $a < 1/n + 1$, i.e. the loss due to the introduction of one additional head of cattle is not too large; we mentioned above that it should be assumed that a is in fact not too large. We see now, what should be taken as 'not too large' and shall see further instances later on. If all the other herdsmen add a head of cattle

TABLE 5.1

Our Individual Herdsman	All the Other Herdsmen	
	Add	Do Not Add
Adds	$1 - a(N + h)$	$1 - a(n + 1)$
Does Not Add	$- a(N - n)$	0

each, it is still worthwhile for our individual herdsman to add a head of cattle too, because his loss is thereby decreased. If in fact all the other herdsmen add a head of cattle and he does not, his loss is $a(N - n)$, while it is $a(N + h) - 1$ if he does, the loss being the absolute value of the negative entries of the pay-off matrix. Now the former loss is larger than the latter loss because $a(N - n) - [a(N + h) - 1] = 1 - a(n + h)$ which is positive, if it is again assumed that a, i.e. the loss due to the introduction of one head of cattle beyond grazing capacity is not large, now the condition being $a < 1/(n + h)$. This shall also be assumed. Thus, whatever the action of all the other herdsmen, our individual herdsman will always have an advantage in adding a head of cattle to his herd. Obviously, each of the herdsmen will put himself in the position of our individual herdsman and come to the same conclusion: whatever the others do, it is worthwhile for himself to add a head of cattle to his herd.

This is the *tragedy of the commons:* Each individual herdsman who wishes to optimize his strategy will add a head of cattle to his herd, and this leads necessarily to the disaster for the community as a whole. But before we consider the moral of the parable with regard to the population problem, a few remarks should be made with respect to the result of our game-theory analysis.

It will first be noted that our individual herdsman is able to make a profit by adding a head of cattle to his herd only if all the other herdsmen do not do so. If they also add to their herds, our individual herdsman can only decrease his loss by adding to his herd. It would therefore be to the advantage of the individual herdsman to convince all the others not to add any cattle to their herds, and to do so only himself. It is also easily seen by considering the pay-off matrix of all the other herdsmen that, whatever the move of our individual herdsman, all the others are better off, if they do not add to their herds. Indeed, the pay-off matrix of all the other herdsmen is as shown in Table 5.2. Looking at the table line by line, we see that if our individual herdsman does not add to his herd (lower line), all the other herdsmen have certainly a loss by adding to their herds, while they have none if they also refrain from adding cattle. This is so because we assume that $a > 1/N$ thus, we have, in general, also

TABLE 5.2

Our Individual Herdsman	All the Other Herdsmen	
	Add	Do Not Add
Adds	$(h - 1) [1 - a(N + h)$	$- a(N - n)$
Does Not Add	$(h - 1) [1 - a(h - 1)(n + 1)]$	0

$$a > \frac{1}{(h - 1)\, (n + 1)}$$

and the lower left-hand element of the matrix is negative. Comparing the two elements of the upper row of the matrix, we see that the left-hand one is, in absolute value, larger than the right-hand element, because $(h - 1)\, [a(N + h) - 1] + a(N - n) = (h - 1)\, [a(N + h - n) - 1]$ which, under our assumptions, is in general certainly negative; i.e., the righthand element is larger, or in other words the loss of all the other herdsmen is larger, when they also add a head of cattle each to their herd.

We recall that it would be of advantage to our individual herdsman if all the others do not add to their herds, and now we see that this is also the best strategy for themselves. This makes it easier for our individual herdsman to convince his fellows not to add any cattle to their herds.

Secondly, we see that it is of advantage to our individual herdsman to add a head of cattle to his herd, whether all the others together add zero or $h - 1$ heads of cattle: it is therefore obvious that this is also true for any other number of cattle added by the other herdsmen—between zero and $h - 1$. Thus, for our present purpose, we may (as we claimed before) disregard the many different moves among which all the other herdsmen, taken as a group, can in fact choose.

Finally, we note that our individual herdsman obtains a bigger advantage from adding a head of cattle to his herd if all the other herdsmen do not add to their herds than otherwise. It was shown, indeed, that in the former case his profit is $1 - a(n + 1)$ while in the latter case his loss is decreased by $1 - a(h + n)$. Obviously, $1 - a(n + 1) - 1 - a(n + h) = a(h - 1) > 0$, as long as our individual herdsman is not the only herdsman in the community. It is true, that in our parable, this does not contribute very much to the interest of our individual herdsman in convincing the others not to add to their herds—he has enough reason to do so, and all the others have enough reason to accept his advice, as long as they act as a group.

Thus, as long as each herdsman selects the strategy most advantageous to himself as an individual, he will add a head of cattle to his herd, and so they will act all, as individuals—as long as the community of herdsmen is unable or unwilling to convince its members that it is worthwhile to act in cooperation, and force them to do so. This is now the exact formulation of the 'tragedy of the commons.' It may be mentioned that the situation resembles that of the famous 'prisoner's dilemma.' Here, as there, it would be in the interest of all players to maximize their joint utility. But to each individual player, game theory attributes an optimal strategy which consists of convincing the other player—or players—to act so as to maximize their joint utility, while he himself obtains a special advantage by acting differently.

6

A Model of the Commons

Jay M. Anderson
(1974)

Garrett Hardin's seminal paper, "The Tragedy of the Commons," describes in general terms the problems surrounding the depletion of common-property resources. He then applies his analysis to the population problem in particular. The model proposed here offers no results not already anticipated by Hardin; it does, however, exhibit Hardin's assumptions and conclusions in a formal way, laying each open to examination and criticism.

Let us consider the "tragedy" in general terms. Men use common-property resources such as space, water, air, etc. In a system where these resources are free, the gain to the resource user is not reduced by a resource cost. Normally, therefore, the user will be induced to use yet more of the "commons."

Let us consider this economic-ecological system (truly an *eco*system) as being made up of two interwoven parts: capital and commons. "Commons" will represent any renewable common-property resource, and "capital" will represent any means of production of goods. Table 6.1 shows some examples. Figure 6.1 shows the cause-and-effect relationships between the elements of the system. Capital is regulated by investment and depreciation, and commons by natural regeneration and usage. One can deduce the behavior of the system by examining the feedback loops (closed circuits of causal relationships) which characterize the system. The stability of the commons-capital system hangs on the balance

Reprinted, with permission, from *IEEE Transactions on Systems, Man, and Cybernetics,* Vol. SMC-4, No. 1, pp. 103–105. Copyright 1974 by the Institute of Electrical and Electronics Engineers, Inc. Here we have omitted the last section of the original, "Dynamic Models: Systems Dynamics," in which there is an incomplete description of the DYNAMO program used for the model, together with the curves resulting from a few scenarios.

TABLE 6.1
Capital and Commons

Problem	Commons	Capital	Product
Overgrazing the Village-Green	Grass	Sheep	Wool
Polluting Water	Water	Factory	Gadgets
Overuse of Wilderness	Wilderness	Men	Recreation

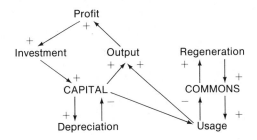

FIGURE 6.1
Cause-and-effect relationships between capital and commons in "The Tragedy of the Commons." Tail of arrow is at cause and arrowhead at effect. Sign at arrowhead indicates sense of relationship; for example, regeneration increases commons but usage depletes commons.

between the positive driving forces of investment and regeneration and the negative restraining forces of depreciation and usage.

In this correspondence we shall develop a model for "The Tragedy of the Commons" and formally examine Hardin's assumptions and conclusions.

Dynamic Models: The Calculus

A model is nothing more than statements about cause and effect. Models can be carried in one's mind, but mental models often suffer from incompleteness and inaccuracy. Formal models exhibit cause-and-effect relationships explicitly, and dynamic models illustrate the time dependence of these relationships as well.

In fact, one simple explicit language for the expression of dynamic models is the calculus. The model then appears as a system of differential equations. For example, we could write

$$\frac{dC}{dt} = \frac{C}{\tau_r} - \min{(\alpha K, C)} \tag{1}$$

where C represents commons, τ_r is the regeneration time constant for the commons, and K represents capital. Here we assume that the regeneration of commons follows first-order kinetics (a rate proportional to the remaining commons) and that the commons is depleted at a rate proportional to working capital, but no more than the existing commons.

In the logistic growth curve often used by ecologists, however, the regeneration rate of a species tends toward zero as the population of the species approaches the carrying capacity of the environment for that species. Accordingly, we represent the regeneration time constant for the commons not as a constant, but as a monotonically increasing function of commons*

$$\tau = \frac{\tau_0 C_0}{C_0 - C} \qquad (2)$$

so that

$$\frac{dC}{dt} = 0.4C \, \frac{C_0 - C}{C_0} - \min(\alpha K, C).$$

The rate of change of capital depends on investment and depreciation

$$\frac{dK}{dt} = (a - b)K$$

where a and b represent investment and depreciation, respectively. As long as $a > b$, K grows; if K grows enough, the commons usage rate may become total, that is, $\min(\alpha K, C) = C$. Then

$$\frac{dC}{dt} = -0.6C - \frac{0.4C^2}{C_0}$$

which is necessarily negative, leading ultimately to no commons.

What is the effect of regulation? Suppose that a limit of annual commons use is imposed and that that limit is some fraction of the original commons, say, βC_0. Then $dC/dt = 0$ establishes a condition for minimum stable commons

$$C = \frac{-0.4 \pm \sqrt{0.16 - 1.6\beta}}{-0.8}$$

Clearly $\beta \leq 0.1$. That is, the commons will always decrease to zero—there will be a "tragedy"—unless a firm limit of no more than 10 percent of the commons used annually is imposed. For this, the most generous limit,

---

*In the program actually used, this equation appears as $\tau = 2.5[C_0/(C_0 - C + 1)]$ to avoid a singularity.

C (at equilibrium) $= C_0/2$, or half the commons will remain. This conclusion, representing the ultimate or equilibrium state of the system, is independent of the speed by which that equilibrium is reached (the constant $0.4 = \tau_0$ in Equation 2.

Consider an alternative solution: the taxation of industry at a rate proportional to used commons. This solution admits, by analysis analogous to that just undertaken, of a range of possibilities for equilibria of both commons and capital. One can choose from a range extending from little capital and much commons to much capital and little commons.

It is, therefore, clear that coercive solutions are required to save the commons. Merely technological solutions, changing the relationship between capital and commons or the regeneration rate of the commons (the constants α in Equation 1 or τ_0 in Equation 2) are of no avail.

The Growing Awareness

7

Denial and Disguise

Garrett Hardin

The theory of the commons was first developed as a way of understanding human population problems. In the process of explaining the human situation Lloyd also threw light on problems of land management and grazing practice. That the logic of the commons had very wide application should have been apparent from the beginning, but it is only recently that these other applications have become explicit.[1]

One of the seminal ideas of psychology is that failure usually results from more than a mere lack of something. Failing to "remember" is usually a failure to recall something that is jolly well remembered but which our subconscious elects not to bring up to the level of consciousness. "Forgetting" is most often a positive act. Likewise, failure to *see* an obvious fact is often an act of wilfull blindness to something we subconsciously fear may be unpleasant. *Denial,* as Freud has taught us, is the process our subconscious uses to keep us from coming to grips with unpleasant reality. But of course denial is almost never explicitly acknowledged by the ego: an acknowledgement of denial would threaten its continuance.

The hypothesis of denial as stated above looks perilously like a "waterproof hypothesis"—a hypothesis stated in such terms that it cannot possibly be refuted, and which consequently is useless as a scientific explanation. The situation is not quite as bad as it at first seems. Sometimes the unselfconscious denier also unconsciously reveals his inner resistance by the language he uses. Others can see through his language. Malthus, for example, quaintly expressed his emotional resistance to the idea of mechanical contraception in language that revealed more than he intended. Condoms were well known in Malthus' day. Condorcet recommended that artificial methods be used to meet the difficulty created by the exponential growth of population. Referring to this suggestion, Malthus said that Condorcet "proceeds to remove the difficulty in a manner which I profess not to understand."[2] The key word here is *profess*. If Malthus had really not understood what Condorcet was referring to he would surely have said ". . . which I do not understand," or he would have said nothing. But Malthus' innate honesty broke through the crust of denial and hypocritically inserted the revealing word "profess," thus giving the show away. So the hypothesis of denial is not always a waterproof hypothesis.

It is our contention that the ignoring of the idea of the commons for more than a century was in part due to subconscious denial. Lloyd's analysis came at a time when concern for social justice was growing stronger every day. Proposals to do away with the commons were no doubt often suspected to be the attempts of greedy groups to fatten themselves at the expense of the people, to subvert justice. There was ample cause for this suspicion.

Consider the way the common pasture lands of England were converted to private property. This was accomplished by the passage of parliamentary Enclosure Acts, a process that accelerated during the eighteenth and nineteenth centuries. More often than not the land that was enclosed and turned into private property was given to the richest land owner in the district. It would be hard to find a justification for this under any acceptable definition of social justice. The moral meaning of the Enclosure Acts was well summarized by an anonymous jingle of the time:

> They clap in gaol the man or woman
> Who steals the goose from off the common;
> But let the bigger knave go loose
> Who steals the common from the goose.

Unjust though the Enclosure Acts were, they did put an end to the tragedy of the commons in this aspect of agriculture. A balanced view of history would surely discuss both aspects of the change; but the Hammonds, in their classic work *The Village Labourer,* resolutely closed their eyes to half the truth. In the first paragraph they primly announce that: "We are not concerned to corroborate or to question the contention that enclosure made England more productive. . . ." And later:

> We are not concerned at this juncture to inquire into the truth of the view that the sweeping policy of enclosure increased the productivity and resources of the State: we are concerned only to inquire into the way in which the aristocracy gave shape and effect to it.[3]

And they condemn the governing class of England for having no care "for its reputation for justice"—as apparently it did not, if we are to judge from its actions.

Works like the Hammonds' have created a climate of opinion in which the search for justice has been preeminent. Such a concern is admirable, but the consistent emphasis on justice has probably contributed to a widespread insensitivity to the evils of the commons. In the name of justice people have laid claim to the most outlandish rights. Jerry Rubin, one of the youthful radicals of the 1960s, justified thievery in this way: "All money represents theft. To steal from the rich is a sacred and religious act. To take what you need is an act of self-love, self-liberation. While looting, a man is true to himself."[4]

Rubin was not, of course, being very original: justice has been offered as a rationalization for crime countless times in the past. Jean-Paul Marat, for instance, nearly two centuries earlier justified his theft of gold coins from the Ashmolean Museum in much the same terms.[5] He admitted that stealing from a person is a crime, but he maintained that stealing from a public institution is not. One Boston radical in our own time summarizing the moral situation as he saw it in these words: "To steal from the A & P is fine, but to steal from a little grocery store run by on old couple is unthinkable."[6]

What is common to these assertions is the view that whatever is owned by many people should be free for the taking by anyone who feels a need for it. This is precisely the idea of the commons. Unfortunately, the idea of the commons, and a knowledge of its tragic tendencies, are unknown to most of the people who call for justice.

Let us not be contemptuous of radicals, however; at worst they may be merely expressing more blatantly what conservative members of society frequently practice without verbal justification. There is always a tendency to pervert a useful social institution into a commons. for example, the development of data banks has revealed that many a "straight" member of society is no more moral or perceptive than Marat or Rubin. A shared data bank is a computer in which many business concerns can store their data, each one retrieving its own data by calling for it with a secret code. Ingenious computer specialists can often figure out other people's codes and retrieve valuable data to which they have no legal claim. A recent survey made at a gathering of 56 computer specialists revealed that 23 percent saw no ethical objection to retrieving data other than their own, with 18 percent admitting that they had already committed such thefts.[7] We are willing to bet that none of these specialists would be willing to steal from the "little grocery store run by an old couple."

It must not be supposed that all commons are bad in all situations. Before agriculture, when there were only a few million people in the world, it was all right to run the hunting grounds as a commons, though even then an area was no doubt often managed as tribal property to prevent its being overrun by other tribes. In our time we manage the streets as a commons paid for by all taxpayers and used "by each according to his needs." As long as streets are only streets-for-walking the system creates no danger from overuse. A person, after all, can walk only one street at a time. Streets-for-autos, however, can easily be overburdened: parking and the demands of commercial vehicles sooner or later compel us to manage access to this public property.

Insurance, which begins as a wager between the insured and the insurer, ends as a commons in which the losses of some are paid from the common pool of premium receipts. The odds of the wager are often shaded on an actuarial basis, e.g., a person who has been in several auto accidents is required to pay bigger premiums. But because of their passion for fairness many people oppose such risk-related discrimination. An insurance commissioner in New York, for example, argued that auto insurance companies should not be allowed to charge higher rates to young drivers, old drivers, inner-city residents, bartenders "and other arbitrarily designated bad risks."[8] This use of the word arbitrary is typical of politically motivated statements. The actuary of an insurance company can easily prove that the risk of accidents by the named groups is greater than that of certain others, such as married women between the ages of 25 and 50 who work in offices. Left to their own devices, actuaries would *discriminate* between many groups, and base the premiums for each group on its empirically determined risk figure, thus substituting many different commons for one big commons. But "discriminate," like "arbitrary," is a dirty word in our society. The insurance commissioner in our example went so far as to say that he did not believe that bartenders were poor risks. He cited no evidence: he just did not believe it. As he put the matter: "I don't believe that people should be discriminated against because they choose to work at a job where there is drink around. It's ridiculous to say that every bartender is a drunk."

To our knowledge, no one ever has said that "every bartender is a drunk." The word "every" is almost never used by actuaries; they deal only with frequencies, and they almost never encounter the extreme frequencies of 0 and 1. That an insurance commissioner—a public official —should seek to make regulatory law on the basis of so gross an error shows how far we are from a general understanding of the commons problem.

The dangers of insurance as a commons would not be so great if people acted only selfishly. It is our generous, sharing impulses that create the greatest danger of a destructive runaway process, particularly in the area of malpractice insurance. A jury is faced with a plaintiff who appears to be in wretched physical shape. It is asserted that the condition is irremediable, that it causes grievous physical and mental anguish, and that it is the doctor's fault. The jury may have some doubts on all these points, but their sympathies are with the plaintiff; and they *know* (even though the evidence for this fact cannot be presented in court) that the doctor carries malpractice insurance. For the same reason that a radical will not steal from an old couple but will from the A&P, the jury, which perhaps would not rule against an uninsured doctor, will almost certainly do so against an insured one, recommending high damages. It's just a matter of dipping into the commons. Next year the premium on malpractice insurance goes up, doctors raise their fees, lawyers demand larger payments, and court judgments rise to still greater heights. Round and round it goes: a real vicious circle in the commons.

Since all this happens within the jurisdiction of a sovereign state we should be able to do something about it. Perhaps some day we will. More serious are the commons that fall between the cracks of sovereignty, the international commons of air and water. The problems created here can only be solved by abolishing the commons themselves. Either we must create private property in air and water, or the common property must be managed by a legitimated regulatory agency. In either case, the traditional boundaries of national sovereignty are infringed upon. How can that be done peacefully? We don't know, and so we thresh about, wasting time and money in ways that will surely seem grotesque to posterity. The boundary conditions set (implicitly and explicitly) when a conference on the "law" of the sea is called, insure that no solutions will be found. We should not, therefore, be surprised when the actions of the delegates, as described by Barry Newman in *The Wall Street Journal,* seem grossly inappropriate to the gravity of the problem. What else are people to do when they are handed a problem that is, by the definition of its boundaries, insoluble?

The 'Law of the Sea' Is Still Unwritten

The United Nations' Law of the Sea Conference, [in Caracas, Venezuela], which winds up Thursday, has produced a certain amount of petty bickering (China called Cambodian leaders a "handful of national scum"), hours of irrelevant grandiloquence (an entire morning devoted to praise of Simon Bolivar), some slapstick crisis (a flood the Caracas fire department had to clean up), and some unfortunate accidents (the president of the conference broke a kneecap playing tennis).

But as far as the subject at hand is concerned—an international law that will define who owns what in the oceans—concrete accomplishments are elusive. In 10 full weeks the representatives of 150 countries at the biggest international meeting in history haven't even gotten down to hard negotiations. They've just been stating and restating their positions.

"Progress has been made not in bringing the sides closer together," says C. W. Pinto, the representative of Sri Lanka, "but in clearly defining where they are farthest apart." Without such diplomatic delicacy, a member of the United States delegation says: "The reality is that nobody has made any concessions that hurt."

Their Lives' Work

So after 70 days of talk about a law to govern use of the oceans and their resources, the conference is making only one firm decision: to hold more conferences. But this isn't discouraging the 5,000 diplomats and experts who have passed through this brassy Latin capital over the summer. Drafting a treaty acceptable to the myriad national and business interests involved is a task of monumental complexity, and many of the conference participants seem resigned to making the law of the sea their lives' work. Many of them say the conference has been a moderate success; in any event, life at this giant meeting hasn't been entirely agonizing.

The site is the Parque Central, a brand new set of 43-story, concrete-slab condominiums sitting on several layers of meeting halls, conference rooms, supermarkets, boutiques and restaurants, all set off by warm sunlight, palm trees, waterfalls and art exhibits. Granted, the place is being guarded by what seems to be at least half the Venezuelan military, the terrazzo floors are buffed slick as a skating rink, the elevators don't work and the air conditioning works too well. But despite all this it is hard to imagine a more spectacular setting.

Venezuela, moreover, is a land of many holidays, and they have been respected by the international community in this springlike climate. (When Venezuela didn't provide a holiday one week, the UN declared a special one.) There has been time to take jaunts to places like the racetrack and the oil fields of Lake Maracaibo, and hotel pools and Caribbean beaches haven't been off limits either. "Diplomats can best learn of the oceans and can become 'diplonauts,' " says a sign near a conference room, "by getting into the water."

Caracas "night life" has gained some favor at the conference too, driving up prices of certain services. A conference official eagerly recommends a plush bar called Les Robles. "You'll find delegates there —shopping," he says. Les Robles turns out to be as multilingual as the plenary hall, and the call girls there say they've been kept busy the last two months. "After *la conferencia*," says Marta, a silver-blonde woman gulping scotches at the bar, "business will drop."

A Happier Bunch

Some diversion also has been available at the conference itself. "It's a much happier lot than the bunch of sourpusses you see at the General Assembly in New York," says another official. "There has been and continues to be," he adds, "a lot of sexual activity at this conference." Whether or not that's the case, there certainly have been a lot of parties here.

"We're having so much fun, you have no idea," says a young female secretary. "There are so many parties. I love it. I love to go dancing." At which point she hands over an invitation to a huge cocktail party set for that evening, sponsored by the president of the conference, who is the ambassador from Sri Lanka. About 1,800 elegantly appointed people showed up, jamming a broad patio. Dozens of white-coated waiters carrying silver trays offer shrimp, smoked salmon, small egg rolls and large drinks to an assemblage babbling loudly in any number of languages while a musician plays rhumbas on an electric piano. "All talk," shouts a young diplomat from Kuwait above the din. "All talk and no communication."

He might be talking about the cocktail party, but he isn't. He is talking about the conference.

The volume of verbiage is staggering. There are actually three meetings—one dealing with coastal waters, one with the deep sea and one with pollution and ocean research—and each is struggling with several issues that would each merit conferences of their own. The UN has 90 mimeograph operators grinding away at 27 machines around the clock, spewing forth 250,000 pages of documents a day. Each is prepared in three, and sometimes five, languages by teams of translators and typists, (Chinese is an exception: the UN didn't bring any Chinese typewriters, so all the Chinese documents are laboriously inscribed by hand.) The list of documents produced so far is itself 160 pages long.

Most of these are records of formal public meetings at which, almost everybody agrees, almost nothing ever happens. After weeks of reading position papers, a semblance of debate began about three weeks ago. But that tends to get bogged down in diplomatic niceties as well.

The committee concerned with ocean pollution holds a typical public meeting in a big room with rows of white-plastic desks interrupted by mirrored columns. The soberly dressed delegates (with the exception of a man at San Marino's desk who doesn't have any shoes on) plug in their earphones and receive an earful from speaker after speaker who deeply regret an oil tanker accident near Chile. Finally the chairman asks everyone to dispense with the condolences and get down to business. He then recognizes the representative from Spain, who procedes at length to express his sympathies to "our brother country, Chile" over the accident. . . .

For all the confusion, though, there has been a little movement at the conference that may some day result in a treaty to govern the seas. The U.S. and the Soviet Union, for example, are both backing a crucial compromise that would create a 200-mile "economic zone" off the shores of coastal countries, giving them control of ocean resources but falling short of absolute sovereignty.

Compromise hasn't even been suggested on other hotly contested issues, such as a face-off between industrialized and developing states over how deep-sea minerals should be mined. But the countries have at least arrived, after all the talk, at the jumping-off point for what one diplomat calls "the most rough-and-tumble, sophisticated, tactically involved international negotiation that has ever taken place."[9]

Two days later the editors of *The Wall Street Journal* gave their personal reaction to this charade:

On to Calcutta

Nathan Detroit, you will recall, conducted the oldest established permanent floating crap game in New York. The United Nations' Law of the

Sea Conference, which floats from spa to shining spa, has brought to the world what Mr. Detroit gave New York.

With the United States footing a large part of the bill, through its contribution to the UN, 5,000 bureaucrats from 150 nations are now departing sunny Caracas after 70 days of predictably inconclusive blather. A charming debate on whether the next should be in Geneva, Vienna or back in Caracas ended in compromise. There will be two conferences in 1975, one in Geneva, one in Caracas.

Granted, the hundreds of millions of dollars it costs to keep this fiesta afloat each year keeps out of circulation 5,000 bureaucrats who might otherwise be making mischief. But even wars eventually come to some conclusion; the Law of the Sea Conference may go on forever.

The only solution may be to take from the conferees the ability to make the only decision they seem capable of, i.e., where they will next meet. Finance ministers around the world should be given that job. For the next five meetings, the U.S. Treasury Secretary should propose the following: (1) Calcutta; (2) Katmandu; (3) Phnom Penh; (4) Ulan Bator; (5) Philadelphia.[10]

Notes

1. Many of these applications will be found in Garrett Hardin, 1972. *Exploring New Ethics for Survival: The Voyage of the Spaceship Beagle.* New York: Viking. This is a book-length elaboration of "The Tragedy of the Commons." As of 1976, this essay had been reprinted more than fifty times, principally in anthologies. The fact that these anthologies are devoted not only to ecology and the environment, but also to political science, sociology, economics, ethics, and the law shows that Lloyd's insight is at last entering the mainstream of scholarship.
2. From Chapter VIII of the first edition of Malthus' *Essay on Population.*
3. J. L. Hammond and Barbara Hammond, 1927. *The Village Labourer,* 4th ed. London: Longmans, Green. pp. 19, 34.
4. Jerry Rubin, 1970. *Do It!* New York: Simon & Schuster.
5. William C. Gibson, "Wilderness—A Psychiatric Necessity," in Bruce M. Kilgore, ed.; 1966. *Wilderness in a Changing World* (San Francisco: Sierra Club, p. 230).
6. *Time,* 22 June 1970, p. 52.
7. *Mosaic* (National Science Foundation), **6** (1):19 (1975).
8. *New York Times,* 21 October 1974.
9. *The Wall Street Journal,* 27 August 1974. Reprinted with permission of The Wall Street Journal, © Dow Jones & Company, Inc. 1974. All Rights Reserved.
10. *The Wall Street Journal,* 29 August 1974. Reprinted with permission of The Wall Street Journal, © Dow Jones & Company, Inc. 1974. All Rights Reserved.

8

The Tragedy
of the Commons
Revisited

Beryl L. Crowe
(1969)

There has developed in the contemporary natural sciences a recognition that there is a subset of problems, such as population, atomic war, and environmental corruption, for which there are no technical solutions.[1,2] There is also an increasing recognition among contemporary social scientists that there is a subset of problems, such as population, atomic war, environmental corruption, and the recovery of a livable urban environment, for which there are no current political solutions.[3] The thesis of this article is that the common area shared by these two subsets contains most of the critical problems that threaten the very existence of contemporary man.

The importance of this area has not been raised previously because of the very structure of modern society. This society, with its emphasis on differentiation and specialization, has led to the development of two insular scientific communities—the natural and the social—between which there is very little communication and a great deal of envy, suspicion, disdain, and competition for scarce resources. Indeed, these two communities more closely resemble tribes living in close geographic proximity on university campuses than they resemble the "scientific culture" that C. P. Snow placed in contrast to and opposition to the "humanistic culture."[4]

Reprinted with permission from *Science,* **166**:1103–1107, 1969. Copyright 1969 by the American Association for the Advancement of Science.

Perhaps the major problems of modern society have, in large part, been allowed to develop and intensify through this structure of insularity and specialization because it serves both psychological and professional functions for both scientific communities. Under such conditions, the natural sciences can recognize that some problems are not technically soluble and relegate them to the nether land of politics, while the social sciences recognize that some problems have no current political solutions and then postpone a search for solutions while they wait for new technologies with which to attack the problem. Both sciences can thus avoid responsibility and protect their respective myths of competence and relevance, while they avoid having to face the awesome and awful possibility that each has independently isolated the same subset of problems and given them different names. Thus, both never have to face the consequences of their respective findings. Meanwhile, due to the specialization and insularity of modern society, man's most critical problems lie in limbo, while the specialists in problem-solving go on to less critical problems for which they can find technical or political solutions.

In this circumstance, one psychologically brave, but professionally foolhardy soul, Garrett Hardin, has dared to cross the tribal boundaries in his article "The Tragedy of the Commons."[1] In it, he gives vivid proof of the insularity of the two scientific tribes in at least two respects: first, his "rediscovery" of the tragedy was in part wasted effort, for the knowledge of this tragedy is so common in the social sciences that it has generated some fairly sophisticated mathematical models;[5] second, the recognition of the existence of a subset of problems for which science neither offers nor aspires to offer technical solutions is not likely, under the contemporary conditions of insularity, to gain wide currency in the social sciences. Like Hardin, I will attempt to avoid the psychological and professional benefits of this insularity by tracing some of the political and social implications of his proposed solution to the tragedy of the commons.

The commons is a fundamental social institution that has a history going back through our own colonial experience to a body of English common law which antedates the Roman conquest. That law recognized that in societies there are some environmental objects which have never been, and should never be, exclusively appropriated to any individual or group of individuals. In England the classic example of the commons is the pasturage set aside for public use, and the "tragedy of the commons" to which Hardin refers was a tragedy of overgrazing and lack of care and fertilization which resulted in erosion and underproduction so destructive that there developed in the late 19th century an enclosure movement. Hardin applies this social institution to other environmental objects such as water, atmosphere, and living space.

The cause of this tragedy is exposed by a very simple mathematical model, utilizing the concept of utility drawn from economics. Allowing the utilities to range between a positive value of 1 and a negative value of 1, we may ask, as did the individual English herdsman, what is the utility to me of adding one more animal to my herd that grazes on the commons? His answer is that the positive utility is near 1 and the negative utility is only a fraction of minus 1. Adding together the component partial utilities, the herdsman concludes that it is rational for him to add another animal to his herd; then another, and so on. The tragedy to which Hardin refers develops because the same rational conclusion is reached by each and every herdsman sharing the commons.

Assumptions Necessary to Avoid the Tragedy

In passing the technically insoluble problems over to the political and social realm for solution, Hardin has made three critical assumptions: (1) that there exists, or can be developed, a "criterion of judgment and a system of weighting . . ." that will "render the incommensurables . . . commensurable . . ." in real life; (2) that, possessing this criterion of judgment, "coercion can be mutually agreed upon," and that the application of coercion to effect a solution to problems will be effective in modern society; and (3) that the administrative system, supported by the criterion of judgment and access to coercion, can and will protect the commons from further desecration.

If all three of these assumptions were correct, the tragedy which Hardin has recognized would dissolve into a rather facile melodrama of setting up administrative agencies. I believe these three assumptions are so questionable in contemporary society that a tragedy remains in the full sense in which Hardin used the term. Under contemporary conditions, the subset of technically insoluble problems is also politically insoluble, and thus we witness a full-blown tragedy wherein "the essence of dramatic tragedy is not unhappiness. It resides in the remorseless working of things."

The remorseless working of things in modern society is the erosion of three social myths which form the basis for Hardin's assumptions, and this erosion is proceeding at such a swift rate that perhaps the myths can neither revitalize nor reformulate in time to prevent the "population bomb" from going off, or before an accelerating "pollution immersion," or perhaps even an "atomic fallout."

Eroding Myth of the Common Value System

Hardin is theoretically correct, from the point of view of the behavioral sciences, in his argument that "in real life incommensurables *are* commensurable." He is, moreover, on firm ground in his assertion that to fulfill this condition in real life one needs only "a criterion of judgment and a system of weighting." In real life, however, values are the criteria of judgment, and the system of weighting is dependent upon the ranging of a number of conflicting values in a hierarchy. That such a system of values exists beyond the confines of the nation-state is hardly tenable. At this point in time one is more likely to find such a system of values within the boundaries of the nation-state. Moreover, the nation-state is the only political unit of sufficient dimension to find and enforce political solutions to Hardin's subset of "technically insoluble problems." It is on this political unit that we will fix our attention.

In America there existed, until very recently, a set of conditions which perhaps made the solution to Hardin's problem subset possible: we lived with the myth that we were "one people, indivisible. . . ." This myth postulated that we were the great "melting pot" of the world wherein the diverse cultural ores of Europe were poured into the crucible of the frontier experience to produce a new alloy—an American civilization. This new civilization was presumably united by a common value system that was democratic, equalitarian, and existing under universally enforceable rules contained in the Constitution and the Bill of Rights.

In the United States today, however, there is emerging a new set of behavior patterns which suggest that the myth is either dead or dying. Instead of believing and behaving in accordance with the myth, large sectors of the population are developing life-styles and value hierarchies that give contemporary Americans an appearance more closely analogous to the particularistic, primitive forms of "tribal" organizations living in geographic proximity than to that shining new alloy, the American civilization.

With respect to American politics, for example, it is increasingly evident that the 1960 election was the last election in the United States to be played out according to the rules of pluralistic politics in a two-party system. Certainly 1964 was, even in terms of voting behavior, a contest between the larger tribe that was still committed to the pluralistic model of compromise and accommodation within a winning coalition, and an emerging tribe that is best seen as a millennial revitalization movement directed against mass society—a movement so committed to the revitalization of old values that it would rather lose the election than compromise its values. Under such circumstances former real-life commensurables within the Republican Party suddenly became incommensurable.

In 1968 it was the Democratic Party's turn to suffer the degeneration of commensurables into incommensurables as both the Wallace tribe and the McCarthy tribe refused to play by the old rules of compromise, accommodation, and exchange of interests. Indeed, as one looks back on the 1968 election, there seems to be a common theme in both these camps—a theme of return to more simple and direct participation in decision-making that is only possible in the tribal setting. Yet, despite this similarity, both the Wallaceites and the McCarthyites responded with a value perspective that ruled out compromise, and they both demanded a drastic change in the dimension in which politics is played. So firm were the value commitments in both of these tribes that neither (as was the case with the Goldwater forces in 1964) was willing to settle for a modicum of power that could accrue through the processes of compromise with the national party leadership.

Still another dimension of this radical change in behavior is to be seen in the black community where the main trend of the argument seems to be, not in the direction of accommodation, compromise, and integration, but rather in the direction of fragmentation from the larger community, intransigence in the areas where black values and black culture are concerned and the structuring of a new community of like-minded and like-colored people. But to all appearances even the concept of color is not enough to sustain commensurables in their emerging community as it fragments into religious nationalism, secular nationalism, integrationists, separationists, and so forth. Thus those problems which were commensurable, both interracial and intraracial, in the era of integration become incommensurable in the era of Black Nationalism.

Nor can the growth of commensurable views be seen in the contemporary youth movements. On most of the American campuses today there are at least ten tribes involved in "tribal wars" among themselves and against the "imperialistic" powers of those "over 30." Just to tick them off, without any attempt to be comprehensive, there are: the uptight protectors of the status quo who are looking for middle-class union cards; the revitalization movements of the Young Americans for Freedom; the reformists of pluralism represented by the Young Democrats and the Young Republicans; those committed to New Politics; the Students for a Democratic Society; the Yippies; the Flower Children; the Black Students Union; and the Third World Liberation Front. The critical change in this instance is not the rise of new groups; this is expected within the pluralistic model of politics. What is new are value positions assumed by these groups which lead them to make demands, not as points for bargaining and compromise with the opposition, but rather as points which are "not negotiable." Hence, they consciously set the stage for either confrontation or surrender, but not for rendering incommensurables commensurable.

Moving out of formalized politics and off the campus, we see the remnants of the "hippie" movement which show clear-cut tribal overtones in their commune movements. This movement has, moreover, already fragmented into an urban tribe which can talk of guerrilla warfare against the city fathers, while another tribe finds accommodation to urban life untenable without sacrificing its values and therefore moves out to the "Hog Farm," "Morning Star," or "Big Sur." Both hippie tribes have reduced the commensurables with the dominant WASP tribe to the point at which one of the cities on the Monterey Peninsula felt sufficiently threatened to pass a city ordinance against sleeping in trees, and the city of San Francisco passed a law against sitting on sidewalks.

Even among those who still adhere to the pluralistic middle-class American image, we can observe an increasing demand for a change in the dimension of life and politics that has disrupted the elementary social processes: the demand for neighborhood (tribal?) schools, control over redevelopment projects, and autonomy in the setting and payment of rents to slumlords. All of these trends are more suggestive of tribalism than of the growth of the range of commensurables with respect to the commons.

We are, moreoever, rediscovering other kinds of tribes in some very odd ways. For example, in the educational process, we have found that one of our first and best empirical measures in terms both of validity and reproducibility—the I. Q. test—is a much better measure of the existence of different linguistic tribes than it is a measure of "native intellect."[6] In the elementary school, the different languages and different values of these diverse tribal children have been rendered the commensurables that obtained in the educational system suddenly incommensurable.

Nor are the empirical contradictions of the common value myth as new as one might suspect. For example, with respect to the urban environment, at least seven years ago Scott Greer was arguing that the core city was sick and would remain sick until a basic sociological movement took place in our urban environment that would move all the middle classes to the suburbs and surrender the core city to the ". . . segregated, the insulted, and the injured."[7] This argument by Greer came at a time when most of us were still talking about compromise and accommodation of interests, and was based upon a perception that the life styles, values, and needs of these two groups were so disparate that a healthy, creative restructuring of life in the core city could not take place until pluralism had been replaced by what amounted to geographic or territorial tribalism; only when this occurred would urban incommensurables become commensurable.

Looking at a more recent analysis of the sickness of the core city, Wallace F. Smith has argued that the productive model of the city is no longer viable for the purposes of economic analysis.[8] Instead, he develops a model of the city as a site for leisure consumption, and then seems to suggest that the nature of this model is such that the city cannot regain its health because it cannot make decisions, and that it cannot make decisions because the leisure demands are value-based and, hence, do not admit of compromise and accommodation; consequently there is no way of deciding among these various value-oriented demands that are being made on the core city.

In looking for the cause of the erosion of the myth of a common value system, it seems to me that so long as our perceptions and knowledge of other groups were formed largely through the written media of communication, the American myth that we were a giant melting pot of equalitarians could be sustained. In such a perceptual field it is tenable, if not obvious, that men are motivated by interests. Interests can always be compromised and accommodated without undermining our very being by sacrificing values. Under the impact of the electronic media, however, this psychological distance has broken down and we now discover that these people with whom we could formerly compromise on interests are not, after all, really motivated by interests but by values. Their behavior in our very living room betrays a set of values, moreover, that are incompatible with our own, and consequently the compromises that we make are not those of contract but of culture. While the former are acceptable, any form of compromise on the latter is not a form of rational behavior but is rather a clear case of either apostasy or heresy. Thus, we have arrived not at an age of accommodation but one of confrontation. In such an age "incommensurables" remain "incommensurable" in real life.

Erosion of the Myth of the Monopoly of Coercive Force

In the past, those who no longer subscribed to the values of the dominant culture were held in check by the myth that the state possessed a monopoly on coercive force. This myth has undergone continual erosion since the end of World War II owing to the success of the strategy of guerrilla warfare, as first revealed to the French in Indochina, and later conclusively demonstrated in Algeria. Suffering as we do from what Senator Fulbright has called "the arrogance of power," we have been extremely slow to learn the lesson in Vietnam, although we now realize that war is political and cannot be won by military means. It is apparent that the myth of the monopoly of coercive force as it was first qualified in the civil rights conflict in the South, then in our urban ghettos, next on the streets of Chicago, and now on our college campuses has lost its hold over the minds of Americans. The technology of guerrilla warfare has made it evident that, while the state can win battles, it cannot win wars of values. Coercive force which is centered in the modern state cannot be sustained in the face of the active resistance of some 10 percent of its population unless the state is willing to embark on a deliberate policy of genocide directed against the value dissident groups. The factor that sustained the myth of coercive force in the past was the acceptance of a common value system. Whether the latter exists is questionable in the modern nation-state. But, even if most members of the nation-state remain united around a common value system which makes incommensurables for the majority commensurable, that majority is incapable of enforcing its decisions upon the minority in the face of the diminished coercive power of the governing body of the nation-state.

Erosion of the Myth of Administrators of the Commons

Hardin's thesis that the administrative arm of the state is capable of legislating temperance accords with current administrative theory in political science and touches on one of the concerns of that body of theory when he suggests that the ". . . great challenge facing us now is to invent the corrective feedbacks that are needed to keep the custodians honest."

Our best empirical answers to the question—*Quis custodiet ipsos custodes?*—"Who shall watch the watchers themselves?"—have shown fairly conclusively that the decisions, orders, hearings, and press releases of the custodians of the commons, such as the Federal Communications Commission, the Interstate Commerce Commission, the Federal Trade Commission, and even the Bureau of Internal Revenue, give the large but unorganized groups in American society symbolic satisfaction and assurances.[9] Yet, the actual day-to-day decisions and operations of these administrative agencies contribute, foster, aid, and indeed legitimate the special claims of small but highly organized groups to differential access to tangible resources which are extracted from the commons. This has been so well documented in the social sciences that the best answer to the question of who watches over the custodians of the commons is the regulated interests that make incursions on the commons.

Indeed, the process has been so widely commented upon that one writer has postulated a common life cycle for all of the attempts to develop regulatory policies.[10] This life cycle is launched by an outcry so widespread and demanding that it generates enough political force to bring about the establishment of a regulatory agency to insure the equitable, just, and rational distribution of the advantages among all holders of interest in the commons. This phase is followed by the symbolic reassurance of the offended as the agency goes into operation, developing a period of political quiescence among the great majority of those who hold a general but unorganized interest in the commons. Once this political quiescence has developed, the highly organized and specifically interested groups who wish to make incursions into the commons bring sufficient pressure to bear through other political processes to convert the agency to the protection and furthering of their interests. In the last phase even staffing of the regulating agency is accomplished by drawing the agency administrators from the ranks of the regulated.

Thus, it would seem that, even with the existence of a common value system accompanied by a viable myth of the monopoly of coercive force, the prospects are very dim for saving the commons from differential exploitation or spoliation by the administrative devices in which Hardin places his hope. This being the case, the natural sciences may absolve themselves of responsibility for meeting the environmental challenges of the contemporary world by relegating those problems for which there are no technical solutions to the political or social realm. This action will, however, make little contribution to the solution of the problem.

Are the Critical Problems of Modern Society Insoluble?

Earlier in this article I agreed that perhaps until very recently, there existed a set of conditions which made the solution of Hardin's problem subset possible; now I suggest that the concession is questionable. There is evidence of structural as well as value problems which make comprehensive solutions impossible and these conditions have been present for some time.

For example, Aaron Wildavsky, in a comprehensive study of the budgetary process, has found that in the absence of a calculus for resolving "intrapersonal comparison of utilities," the governmental budgetary process proceeds by a calculus that is sequential and incremental rather than comprehensive. This being the case ". . . if one looks at politics as a process by which the government mobilizes resources to meet pressing problems"[11] the budget is the focus of these problem responses and the responses to problems in contemporary America are not the sort of comprehensive responses required to bring order to a disordered environment. Another example of the operation of this type of rationality is the American involvement in Vietnam; for, what is the policy of escalation but the policy of sequential incrementalism given a new Madison Avenue euphemism? The question facing us all is the question of whether incremental rationality is sufficient to deal with twentieth-century problems.

The operational requirements of modern institutions make incremental rationality the only viable form of decision-making, but this only raises the prior question of whether there are solutions to any of the major problems raised in modern society. It may well be that the emerging forms of tribal behavior noted in this article are the last hope of reducing political and social institutions to a level where incommensurables become commensurable in terms of values *and* in terms of comprehensive responses to problems. After all, in the history of man on earth we might well assume that the departure from the tribal experience is a short-run deviant experiment that failed. As we stand "on the eve of destruction," it may well be that the return to the face-to-face life in the small community unmediated by the electronic media is a very functional response in terms of the perpetuation of the species.

There is, I believe, a significant sense in which the human environment is directly in conflict with the source of man's ascendancy among the other species of the earth. Man's evolutionary position hinges, not on specialization, but rather on generalized adaptability. Modern social and political institutions, however, hinge on specialized, sequential, incremental decision-making and not on generalized adaptability. This being the case, life in the nation-state will continue to require a singleness of purpose for success but in a very critical sense this singleness of purpose becomes a straightjacket that makes generalized adaptation impossible. Nowhere is this conflict more evident than in our urban centers where there has been a decline in the livability of the total environment that is almost directly proportionate to the rise of special purpose districts. Nowhere is this conflict between institutional singleness of purpose and the human dimension of the modern environment more evident than in the recent warning of S. Goran Lofroth, chairman of a committee studying pesticides for the Swedish National Research Council, that many breast-fed children ingest from their mother's milk "more than the recommended daily intake of DDT"[12] and should perhaps be switched to cow's milk because cows secrete only 2 to 10 percent of the DDT they ingest.

How Can Science Contribute to the Saving of the Commons?

It would seem that, despite the nearly remorseless working of things, science has some interim contributions to make to the alleviation of those problems of the commons which Hardin has pointed out.

These contributions can come at two levels:

1. Science can concentrate more of its attention on the development of technological responses which at once alleviate those problems and reward those people who no longer desecrate the commons. This approach would seem more likely to be successful than the ". . . fundamental extension in morality . . ." by administrative law; the engagement of interest seems to be a more reliable and consistent motivator of advantage-seeking groups than does administrative wrist-slapping or constituency pressure from the general public.

2. Science can perhaps, by using the widely proposed environmental monitoring systems, use them in such a way as to sustain a high level of "symbolic disassurance" among the holders of generalized interests in the commons—thus sustaining their political interest to a point where they would provide a constituency for the administrator other than those bent on denuding the commons. This later approach would seem to be a first step toward the ". . . invention of the corrective feedbacks that are needed to keep custodians honest." This would require a major change in the behavior of science, however, for it could no longer rest content with development of the technology of monitoring and with turning the technology over to some new agency. Past administrative experience suggests that the use of technology to sustain a high level of "disassurance" among the general population would also require science to take up the role and the responsibility for maintaining, controlling, and disseminating the information.

Neither of these contributions to maintaining a habitable environment will be made by science unless there is a significant break in the insularity of the two scientific tribes. For, if science must, in its own insularity, embark on the independent discovery of "the tragedy of the commons," along with the parameters that produce the tragedy, it may be too slow a process to save us from the total destruction of the planet. Just as important, however, science will, by pursuing such a course, divert its attention from the production of technical tools, information, and solutions which will contribute to the political and social solutions for the problems of the commons.

Because I remain very suspicious of the success of either demands or pleas for fundamental extensions in morality, I would suggest that such a conscious turning by both the social and the natural sciences is, at this time, in their immediate self-interest. As Michael Polanyi has pointed out, ". . . encircled today between the crude utilitarianism of the philistine and the ideological utilitarianism of the modern revolutionary move-ment, the love of pure science may falter and die."[13] The sciences, both social and natural, can function only in a very special intellectual environment that is neither universal nor unchanging, and that environ-ment is in jeopardy. The questions of humanistic relevance raised by the students at M.I.T., Stanford Research Institute, Berkeley, and wher-ever the headlines may carry us tomorrow, pose serious threats to the maintenance of that intellectual environment. However ill-founded *some* of the questions raised by the new generation may be, it behooves us to be ready with at least some collective, tentative answers—if only to maintain an environment in which both sciences will be allowed and fostered. This will not be accomplished so long as the social sciences continue to defer the most critical problems that face mankind to future technical advances, while the natural sciences continue to defer those same problems which are about to overwhelm all mankind to false ex-pectations in the political realm.

Notes

1. Garrett Hardin, *Science,* Vol. 162 (1968), p. 1243.
2. J. B. Weisner and H. F. York, *Scientific American,* Vol. 211, No. 4 (1964), p. 27.
3. C. Woodbury, *American Journal of Public Health,* Vol. 45 (1955), p. 1; S. Marquis, *American Behavioral Scientist,* Vol. 11 (1968), p. 11; W. H. Ferry, *Center Magazine,* Vol. 2 (1969), p. 2.
4. C. P. Snow, *The Two Cultures and the Scientific Revolution* (New York: Cambridge University Press, 1959).
5. M. Olson, Jr., *The Logic of Collective Action* (Cambridge, Mass.: Harvard University Press, 1965).
6. G. A. Harrison, et al., *Human Biology* (New York: Oxford University Press, 1964), p. 292; W. W. Charters, Jr., in *School Children in the Urban Slum* (New York: The Free Press, 1967).
7. Scott Greer, *Governing the Metropolis* (New York: John Wiley & Sons, 1962), p. 148.
8. Wallace F. Smith, "The Class Struggle and the Disquieted City," paper presented at 1969 annual meeting of Western Economic Association, Oregon State University, Corvallis.
9. M. Bernstein, *Regulating Business by Independent Commissions* (Princeton, N.J.: Princeton University Press, 1955); E. P. Herring, *Public Administration and the Public Interest* (New York: McGraw-Hill Book Co., 1936); E. M. Redford, *Administration of National Economic Control* (New York: Mac-millan, 1952).

10. M. Edelman, *The Symbolic Uses of Politics* (Urbana: University of Illinois Press, 1964).
11. Aaron Wildavsky, *The Politics of the Budgetary Process* (Boston: Little, Brown, 1964).
12. Corvallis, Ore., *Gazette-Times,* May 6, 1969, p. 6.
13. Michael Polanyi, *Personal Knowledge* (New York: Harper & Row, 1964), p. 182.

9

An Operational Analysis of "Responsibility"

Garrett Hardin

The word "responsible" is often used irresponsibly. Glaser and Strauss[1] tell a story that admirably illustrates the "heads I win, tails you lose" strategy with which this word is so often employed. A woman had just given birth to a grossly deformed child. It was within the power of medical science to keep it alive but the mother, foreseeing the heartache its continued existence would bring to both its parents and to itself (and probably to others), pleaded with the doctor to let the child die. He refused, bluntly telling her that it was his responsibility as a physician to keep the child alive, and her responsibility to take care of it.

Note that the physician did not suggest an interchange of roles; he did not for a moment entertain the thought that he should be responsible for taking care of the child ever after. Obviously the physician was merely using the *word* responsibility as a means of personally evading the *fact* of responsibility.

We need a definition of the concept of responsibility that transcends mere rhetoric and is *operational,* in the sense made clear by the physicist Percy Bridgman.[2] The philosopher Charles Frankel[3] has given such a definition: *"A decision is responsible when the man or group that makes it has to answer for it to those who are directly or indirectly affected by it."* By this definition it is clear that the physician discussed above was behaving irresponsibly, since he was not proposing to take over any fraction of the lifelong burden of childcare created by his refusal to let the deformed baby die.

Not all examples of professional irresponsibility are as blatant as this. The techniques of rhetorical camouflage are beyond cataloging. Consider, for example, the way in which Nicholas, the last Tsar of Russia, used the word to evade the burden.[4] An intermediary had pleaded with him to change the laws so as to remove some of the disabilities suffered by the Jews. He refused, justifying his decision to the supplicant in the following words:

> Up to now my conscience has never led me astray, or been mistaken. On that account, I am going, once more, to obey its dictates. I know that you, as well as myself, believe that the heart of the Tsar is in the hands of God. Let it therefore remain so. I am bearing in the sight of the Almighty a terrible responsibility in regard to the power which I possess and wield, but I stand always ready to render Him an account.

It would be difficult to imagine a more convenient way to escape Frankelian responsibility on earth than by asserting responsibility solely to an unearthly god, whose voice is heard only after passing through the filter of self interest. Tsar Nicholas was not the last person to choose this route for escaping personal responsibility.

The word "God" is no longer as fashionable as it once was, but that fact has not put an end to the claims of non-Frankelian responsibility. Many an unwanted burden is now imposed on the general public with the assertion that "You can't stop Progress." Obviously Progress (with a capital P) has become a new God who confers immunity from responsible cost accounting. As President Nixon once said,[5] in justifying the building of nuclear breeder reactors despite expressed doubts of their safety, "We must always explore the unknown. We must never be afraid of it. That is why we have to go to space. That is why we should have built the SST." That he should have cited the space effort is particularly significant because the arguments supporting it have been notable for their elevated religious tone and general irresponsibility.[6]

"Responsibility" is clearly a term of relationship between two or more agents. The actions of any man can most easily be explained on the basis of his own self interest. Self-interest necessarily includes a person's desire for the good opinion of others. Admittedly, defining self-interest in this extended way runs the danger of creating a waterproof hypothesis of the sort Popper[7] has warned us about, but the risk must be taken. We are, after all (like most animals) social by nature: we have been programmed by evolution to esteem the good opinion of our fellow men. But we have also been programmed by evolution to place that esteem second to personal survival. Natural selection could not have acted otherwise: individuals motivated by "pure" altruism would be at a disadvantage in competition with those moved by self-interest (which can include some quasi-altruism, when actions which benefit others also benefit the self). The question of altruism is still a controversial one. On the biological level the reviews of Robert Trivers[8] and W. D. Hamilton[9] should be consulted. Thomas Nagel[10] has discussed some of the philosophical underpinnings, while Kenneth Boulding[11] and a number of other authors[12] have tried to put the concept on a firm economic foundation.

For the present, our conservative policy will be to regard altruism as a marginal motive (to use a favorite adjective of the economists). Our question is this: in a finite universe—one in which people must economize, must choose—how will one social, egoistic human being relate to others, who are also egoistic and social? In other words, how will they compete? The rules of competition are obviously simplest when there are only two people involved. With more than two people competing, alliances inevitably develop. Much of the behavior of each individual is determined by the perceived opposition between himself and others (the group). If the group does not include the individual in question, no difficult logical problem is posed. A man confronted by a band of robbers may have trouble surviving, but the logic of the situation is no part of his problem. But when the group *does* include the individual the analysis becomes more difficult. Self interest is then divisible into two parts: narrow self interest, and the interest of the self as a member of the group. It must never be presumed that the same action will bring benefits to the individual through both routes, though that is the casual assumption of Adam Smith's "invisible hand" and a number of other melioristic schemes.

In utilizing the environment for his own benefit, social man has several possibilities open to him. The operational analysis that follows is slightly modified from *Exploring New Ethics for Survival*[13] and is designed especially to show the way in which Frankelian responsibility predicts the viability of the various systems. The heuristic image to keep in mind is the familiar one of a pasture land from which individuals can benefit by using cattle to convert grass to beef.

The utilization of the pasture land may be controlled by individuals or by the group as a whole—which makes *two* possibilities. Independently of this, the proceeds resulting from the operation can go either to the individuals or to the groups—again *two* possibilities.

This means there are $2 \times 2 = 4$ possible ways to benefit from the environment—four possible politico-economic systems (or, more briefly, political systems). These four—which exhaust the possibilities of pure systems—are shown in the accompanying Table 9.1. The names of the systems are given in the center column. The first three systems are well recognized. The fourth, something of a special case, is not ordinarily recognized as a political system. It is included here primarily for logical completeness; its significance will be discussed later.

In a resource-rich, sparsely populated world it might not matter which system we followed. But problems arise when the population has grown

TABLE 9.1
The Four Possible Systems of Environmental Utilization

| | Rules of the Game | | | | | Results of the Game | | | |
| | Utilization of Environment by: | | Proceeds Go to: | | | Gain From Stressing the System: | | | |
Case	Individual (1)	Group (2)	Individual (3)	Group (4)	Politico-Economic System	Overall Gain (5)	Gain to the Decision Maker (6)	Intrinsic Responsibility (7)	Temptation to Sabotage Information (8)
I	✓		✓		Private Enterprise	−	−	+	0
II		✓		✓	Socialism	−	0	0	+
III		✓	✓		System of the Commons	−	+	−	(0)
IV	✓			✓	Private Philanthropy	−	0	0	0

to such an extent that it is pressing against the limit of the carrying capacity of the environment. By the definition of "carrying capacity," if one more animal is added to the herd the aggregate gain will be negative. Column 5 indicates that this is the state of the system under discussion; the aggregate gain is negative whatever the political system: Put another way, the gain to the individual *as a member of the goup* is negative. But the *direct* gain to the individual decision maker depends on the system being followed. The two gains (columns 5 and 6) must be identical to produce operational responsibility (column 7).

Under private enterprise (Case I), the owner who decides to overload his own pasture will eventually suffer for it in a number of different ways. Total beef production may fail; his malnourished cattle may be more susceptible to disease; overgrazing may result in the replacement of "sweet grass" by "weeds": and overgrazing and trampling may produce soil erosion and reduction in the growth of grass in subsequent years. Whatever happens, the decision maker loses if he makes a bad decision; he is responsible in the Frankelian sense. We can say that he is *intrinsically* responsible (column 7).

Given intelligent decision makers who are keen observers, private enterprise works admirably *for those who are in the system.* Political instability is likely to develop, however, if there are many people who are effectively disenfranchised, i.e., who have no pasture lands of their own to manage. There is no simple, quantitative relation between the degree of disenfranchisement and the probability of a revolt against the system. The potential for dissatisfaction is always present because of envy, the ubiquity and disguises of which have been admirably described by Helmut Schoeck.[14] Among its many disguises—though it is not wholly a disguise—is a passion for justice. With this thought in mind, a careful study of John Rawls' modern classic[15] is well worth the time invested. In any particular situation the power of envy or of a passion for justice (take your pick) is mitigated by the extent to which the disenfranchised have achieved psychological freedom as defined by Hegel's aphorism, "Freedom is the recognition of necessity." Historical systems that we now regard as unjust, but which managed to endure for a considerable time, did so because the disenfranchised were successfully imbued with the idea of the necessity of the status quo. Consider the following two stanzas from a Victorian hymn,[16] "All Things Bright and Beautiful," which is still to be found in some church hymnals (though it is difficult to believe that many of today's young accept the sentiment):

> All things bright and beautiful,
> All creatures great and small,
> All things wise and wonderful,
> The Lord God made them all.

> The rich man in his castle,
> The poor man at his gate,
> God made them, high or lowly,
> And ordered their estate.

Ironically, this was first published in 1848, the year of Marx and Engels' *Communist Manifesto.*

The rebel who does not accept his "estate" may seek to move himself up on the politico-economic ladder. He may be successful, but if the game in which he has triumphed is a zero-sum game,[17] his personal success does not diminish whatever pressures there may be that work toward changing the system.

If pressures against the system of private enterprise are great enough to change the system, the change will most likely be to that diagrammed as Case II, which we call "socialism." In a very small socialistic group all the decisions could be made in a "town meeting." In this case socialism would not differ essentially from private enterprise, and the functional relationships would be adequately described by Case I on the first line. But town meetings become unmanageable when the size of the group is more than a few hundred and a different sort of organization must be adopted, leading to Case II. Decision making must be delegated by the community to one or more managers. What then happens to a socialistic decision maker when he mades a bad decision?

The group loses, by definition; and since the decision maker is a member of the group, he loses, too. But his share of the loss resulting from a bad decision is very small—so small that we can safely call it zero (column 6). It follows that his intrinsic responsibility is also essentially zero (column 7), contrasting with that of the decision maker (owner) under private enterprise.

This won't do, of course. An axiom of psychology is that *we get the behavior we reward for.* Since the intrinsic responsibility of the simplest conceivable socialistic system is negligible, it is always augumented by various sorts of *contrived responsibility*—which make the system more complex. The decision maker is enmeshed in a network of laws and customs that punish him for bad performance and perhaps reward him for good. (It should be noted that the envy of those who have not the power of decision makes them reluctant to establish much in the nature of rewards. In the typical socialistic system the administrator must have a thick skin.)

With luck, decision making under socialism, with its contrived responsibility, may be as good as it is under private enterprise with its intrinsic responsibility, and the public interest may be served better. But there is always an appreciable possibility that it may become much worse. Contrived responsibilities can be effectively applied to the decision maker only if the community is well informed of the consequences of his decisions. But the person who makes the decisions is generally in the most favorable position to control the flow of information about the consequences of his decisions. If he makes a bad decision he is then tempted to falsify the information about the consequences. In other words, he is tempted to sabotage the information system, as the private enterpriser is not (column 8). He is in a specially favorable position to do so if his reports can be classified as national defense secrets, or if they can be suppressed as a matter of "executive privilege."

It should be obvious that the generalizations made here apply only to pure systems in their simplest form. Introducing even so slight a complication as high interest rates can, as Fife has shown,[18] make some nominally private enterprise systems act like one of the other systems. Moreover, no major nation today operates wholly under one system or another. The Soviet Union is a mixed economy; so is the United States. The relative merits of the various mixed economies is a matter of great interest and importance, but it is not our concern here. Our immediate concern is rather with the third great system, the system of the commons. We especially want to focus on its responsibility aspects.

Case III shows the properties of the system of the commons. Most noteworthy is the plus in column 6. When the system is already at its carrying capacity it is actually to the advantage of the individual herdsman to add one more cow to his herd. Whatever loss this produces is shared among all the herdsmen, whereas the gain is wholly his. Even with perfect knowledge of the ultimately destructive effects of overloading the pasture, the individual herdsman cannot rationally refrain from making the "wrong" decision. The aberrant herdsman who does refrain will be at a competitive disadvantage vis-à-vis the herdsmen who overload the commons. It is not too much to say that each herdsman in a commons enjoys a *negative responsibility* (column 7), for he is systematically rewarded (in short term) for making the "wrong" decision.

The situation can also be categorized in terms of rights and responsibilities. Herdsmen have the right to pasture their cattle in the commons, but this right is unmatched by a corresponding responsibility. The resulting tragic evolution of the system shows that the concept of absolute right is intolerable. If the concept of right is to be used at all, a right must surely always be regarded as conditional. Right must always be matched with an appropriate responsibility. The classic commons leads to tragedy because it allows unconditional rights.

Case IV still remains to be discussed. In this case, the individual utilizes the environment and the proceeds go to the group. This arrangement violates the assumption of self-interest theory since there is (apparently) no quid pro quo for the individual, hence no obvious motivation. It is not surprising then to hear that no nation is run by a political system of this sort. In spite of this, the class of arrangements defined by Case IV is not a completely null class: its principal (and perhaps only important) member is private philanthropy.

A Rockefeller or a Ford makes a fortune out of the environment (or out of his fellow men?), and then in old age gives most of his money to a foundation (without a conventional quid pro quo to him), which in turn, disburses the money to others (also without obvious quid pro quos). The motivation of the philanthropist seems obscure until we learn about what psychoanalysts call "secondary gains." The quid pro quo of the private philanthropist is the knowledge of what he has done—"the contemplation" (in the ringing words of Condorcet[19] of "the joy of having performed a lasting service, which no fatality can ever destroy. . . . This contemplation is for him a place of refuge. . . [where] he forgets him whom greed, fear, or envy torment and corrupt. . . . There it is that he exists in . . . an elysium which his reason has been able to create for him, and which his love for humanity enhances with the purest enjoyments."

By postulating secondary gains we can save the theory of universal self interest from its apparent disproof by the existence of private philanthropy. A critical historian of science might wonder whether this saving were no better than the various versions of "saving the hypothesis" that supported the Ptolemaic system of the universe for too long. We think otherwise. The psychoanalytical concept of secondary gains meshes perfectly with the inescapably social nature of humankind. We *do* care what our fellow men and women think. For some, the anticipation of posterity's opinion is a very powerful motive.

Philanthropic endeavors are started and continued for two reasons, both based on self interest. For the founder, the self-interest of secondary gains is usually the crucial factor. For those who carry out his plans, philanthropy is a job much like any job, and the hypothesis of self-interest is sufficient to explain their devotion (though it may not, in truth, tell the whole story).

A very important characteristic of private philanthropy, which is seldom noted, is that *it is essentially irresponsible* (column 7). 'Irresponsible" is usually so pejorative a word that this statement may shock the reader. But saying that philanthropy is irresponsible does not necessarily condemn it: the results may be either good or bad. We must not forget that, operationally speaking, private philanthropy does not meet the criterion of Frankelian responsibility. The decision makers (i.e., the foundation executives) are not answerable for their actions to the society for whose benefits their decisions are supposedly made.

The lack of corrective feedback in Case IV sometimes leads to a bizarre distribution of resources. In 1959, for instance, a philanthropic organization called Seeing Eye, Inc., stopped soliciting money for buying and training seeing-eye dogs because it had more money than it knew what to do with.[20] At the same time the National Society for the Prevention of Blindness was struggling along on a budget of scarcely more than a million dollars a year.

Perhaps a worse example is that of the "Green Revolution" in agriculture. Seeking to put an end to the "shortage" of food by increasing agricultural productivity, the Rockefeller Foundation financed a technically successful effort to increase the yield of crops. There is still at least as great a shortage of food, for the fundamental reason that was pointed out by one of the Foundation's own vice presidents, and which is now called "Gregg's Law."[21] Alan Gregg saw the continued growth of the human population on an already overpopulated earth as a form of cancer, and reminded us that *You can't cure a cancer by feeding it.* Dr. Gregg's own institution has ignored his advice for twenty years, for two quite understandable reasons: first, being a Case IV institution it can with impunity do just about anything it wishes to; and second, whatever it does gives employment to its own people who have developed an immense emotional investment in what they are doing, no matter how dubious its value may appear to outsiders. The combination of operational irresponsibility with emotional investment creates a powerful and conservative force. Philanthropic organizations sometimes cling to the status quo far more strongly than the most conservative business organizations.

It is, no doubt, a realization of the essential irresponsibility of private philanthropy that partially accounts for recent congressional attempts to restrict the power and limit the life-span of philanthropic foundations. Perhaps nothing should be immortal, no matter how "good," so we can support this attempt of Congress, even though it is hard to see exactly what the length of life of a foundation should be.

But something needs to be said on the other side. Looking back over the history of philanthropy we see that, time after time, philanthropy has started what a responsible politico-economic organization seemed incapable or unwilling to do: free libraries, low-cost health services for the poor, family planning clinics, etc. That the public sector later takes over what philanthropy started does not diminish our admiration for philanthropy. A political system of total responsibility is apt to be an inflexible system. Until Utopia, we would be wise to retain the loose-jointedness in the system that irresponsible, poorly controllable, private philanthropy furnishes.

Notes

1. Barney G. Glaser and A. L. Strauss, 1965. *Awareness of Dying.* Chicago: Aldine. (p. 100)
2. P. W. Bridgman, 1927. *The Logic of Modern Physics.* New York: Macmillan.
3. Charles Frankel, 1955. *The Case for Modern Man.* New York: Harper & Row. (p. 203)
4. Bertrand Russell, 1965. *Freedom Versus Organization, 1776–1914.* London: Allen & Unwin. (p. 225)
5. Allen L. Hammond, 1972. [News report.] *Science,* **176:**393.
6. Garrett Hardin, 1973. *Stalking the Wild Taboo,* Los Altos, Calif.: Kaufmann. (Chap. 16).
7. Karl R. Popper, 1959. *The Logic of Discovery.* New York: Basic Books.
8. Robert L. Trivers, 1971. The evolution of reciprocal altruism. *Quarterly Review of Biology,* **46:**35–57.
9. W. D. Hamilton, 1972. "Altruism and related phenomena, mainly in social insects." *Annual Review of Ecology and Systematics,* **3:**193–232.
10. Thomas Nagel, 1970. *The Possibility of Altruism.* Oxford: Clarendon Press.
11. Kenneth Boulding, 1973. *The Economy of Love and Fear: A Preface to Grants Economics.* Belmont, Calif.: Wadsworth.
12. Edmund S. Phelps, ed., 1975. *Altruism, Morality, and Economic Theory.* New York: Russell Sage Foundation.
13. Garrett Hardin, 1972. *Exploring New Ethics for Survival: The Voyage of the Spaceship Beagle.* New York: Viking. (p. 184)
14. Helmut Schoeck, 1969. *Envy.* New York: Harcourt Brace Jovanovich.
15. John Rawls, 1971. *A Theory of Justice.* Cambridge, Mass.: Harvard University Press.
16. Cecil Frances Alexander, 1848. "All Things Bright and Beautiful." (Stanzas 1, 3)
17. Duncan Luce and Howard Raiffa, 1958. *Games and Decisions.* New York: Wiley.
18. Daniel Fife, 1971. "Killing the Goose." *Environment,* **13**(3):20–27. (Reprinted as chap. 10 of this volume.)
19. Frederick J. Teggert, ed., 1949. *The Idea of Progress. A Collection of Readings.* Berkeley: University of California Press. (p. 358)
20. Louis Cassels, United Press report, 1 February 1968.
21. Garrett Hardin, 1975. "Gregg's Law." *BioScience,* **25:**415.

10

Killing the Goose

Daniel Fife
(1971)

There are three important assumptions in [Hardin's] description of the tragedy of the commons: One, each herdsman (entrepreneur) acts essentially alone for his own good without regard for the good of the others; there is no community. Two, each herdsman (entrepreneur) when faced with a chance to increase profits is under great pressure to do so and will eventually act in accordance with that pressure. Three, the ruining of the commons causes ruin for the entrepreneurs.

The first two assumptions fit many areas of the business world rather well. However, there are many situations in the business world where the third assumption might seem to apply, but where in fact ruining the commons does not bring ruin to the entrepreneurs. [The line in Hardin's essay that reads "Freedom in a commons brings ruin to all," should read: "Freedom in a commons brings death to the commons."] If death to the commons brings ruin to the entrepreneurs then we have the tragedy of the commons. However, we can write a mathematical statement of the conditions under which death coming to the commons *does not* bring ruin to all entrepreneurs. Where these conditions apply, the tragedy of the commons may appear to be occurring but in fact something quite different is really happening. The commons is being killed but someone is getting rich. The goose that lays golden eggs is being killed for profit.

Reprinted from *Environment,* **13** (3):20 27 (1971) by permission of the author and The Committee for Environmental Information. Copyright ©1971 by The Committee for Environmental Information. The first five paragraphs, which summarize the theory of the commons, have been omitted here to minimize repetition. Material in brackets has been inserted by the editors of this volume for clarification.

The Inequality

I have no pretensions to neutrality, so the notation will be a little pro-
pagandistic. Let us say that a business is run *responsibly* if it is run in
such a way that it could continue to run indefinitely. In many businesses
profits can be raised for a period by running the business in a way which
is not responsible. For example, a farmer might double profits for a period
by overuse of the land. When a business abandons responsible tactics
as defined above in favor of higher temporary profits we will say it is
running *irresponsibly* or *fast*.

Let us imagine a business which derives its profit from the exploitation
of some natural resource which renews itself—a whale fishery, perhaps.
When this business is being run responsibly, it makes a certain profit.
For a limited period of time, until the resource is depleted, it can be run
irresponsibly at a higher rate of profit. This profit can then be invested,
and a regular dividend collected from the investment. It is clear that,
if the available investments provide sufficient return at no greater risk
than that of a responsible business, and if the increased profits from irresponsible operation are great enough, the return from the investment
of these profits will be greater than the businessman could obtain from
responsible operation of his business.

That is, if the ratio of profits from an irresponsible business to the
profits of a business responsibly run is great enough under given conditions of investment, it pays to run irresponsibly and invest the higher
profits as fast as they come in. It pays for the businessman to kill
his business.

The conditions under which it pays to be irresponsible are stated in
the form of an inequality given as Equation 1 at the end of this article.
The inequality defines the conditions under which a businessman can
expect to be at least as rich from running his business fast as by running
it responsibly, at every time from the beginning of the process onward
(no matter how long). He can expect to be ahead not merely for the next
five years. He can expect to be ahead forever. In addition, he no longer
has to run the business.

For the convenience of any businessmen reading this paper, I have
compiled Table 10.1. In order to use the table, first estimate the rate of
profit you might receive if you ran your business irresponsibly, and then
calculate the ratio of this rate of profit to that derived from responsible
operation. If the value of this ratio is greater than the "golden number"
in the right hand column of the table, then it pays to run your business
fast. To find your golden number, estimate the number of years (m) the
business can run fast before the resource you depend on is depleted, and

TABLE 10.1

sm	Golden Number $e^{sm}/(e^{sm} - 1)$
0.1	10.5
0.2	5.5
0.3	3.7
0.4	3.0
0.5	2.5
0.6	2.2
0.7	2.0
0.8	1.8
0.9	1.7
1.0	1.6
1.1	1.5
1.2	1.4
1.3	1.4
1.4	1.3
1.5	1.3

multiply it by the rate of investment return (s) available to you at a risk similar to the risk involved in your business run responsibly. Locate the product (sm) of these two numbers in the left hand column of the table; your golden number will then be the corresponding one in the right hand column. (The symbols at the head of the columns are those used in the derivation of the inequality.)

Approximations

In writing this article I have made several rather coarse approximations. I have assumed that in an irresponsibly run business money will come in at a fixed rate and then suddenly stop. Perhaps one could get a better approximation by assuming a linear or exponential decrease beginning after some period of income at a fixed rate. I have also written in the inequality a condition under which running irresponsibly leaves the businessman ahead for all time. This is perhaps stronger than necessary. A businessman could profitably decide to run irresponsibly if it would put him ahead at *some* future time rather than at all future time. If a more careful version of the inequality were derived using either of these ideas we might find several businesses in which, using the above table, it appeared that it did not pay to run irresponsibly, but using the sharper version it would turn out to pay after all. In mathematical language, the inequality stated here gives a sufficient condition, but *not* a necessary condition, for killing the goose profitably.

Throughout this paper I have ignored two major effects, namely the effect of taxes and the problem of extracting invested capital. Large corporations can often deal efficiently with tax problems. For a business which cannot do so, the inequality may have to be applied by computing after taxes. The second problem, extracting invested capital, may cause a business which appears to be able to run irresponsibly to have to run responsibly after all. This would be especially true in a business involving a large capital investment in a physical plant which is not readily modified.

Conclusions

A condition has been described under which a business depending on a renewable resource may be run irresponsibly (destroying the resource) and not result in loss of income to all of the businessmen involved. Taking advantage of such a situation has been termed "killing the goose" and is different from the tragedy of the commons. The characteristic difference is that the long-term economic interests of at least one of the entrepreneurs are not harmed by destroying the resource. As there are businesses which have demonstrably depleted the resources on which they depend (whaling, for instance), killing the goose is not purely hypothetical. There may be businesses doing it now.

It is a common practice of conservationists to issue warnings of the coming tragedy of the commons to businessmen engaged in destroying a renewable resource. It is a common practice for businessmen to ignore them. Perhaps this article has shed light on the reason. The businessman may have realized more or less explicitly that he is in a position to kill the goose and that the conservationists' economic arguments are simply false. Further economic argument by the conservationists is then pointless. He must go back to his real reason for arguing and try to convince society to protect the resource. If he cannot do so he fails and the resource will be destroyed.

This article also indicates that in certain situations, namely those where it may pay to kill the goose, "industrial self-regulation" is not merely questionable, it is farcical. It is in fact equivalent to a policy of destroying the resource in question. In such situations society is the only possible protector of the resource, and any efforts directed to protecting the resource without government intervention are doomed to fail in the long run.

Deriving the Inequality

We define the following terms:

N_r = profit rate for responsibly run business (dollars per year).

N_i = profit rate for irresponsibly run business (dollars per year).

s = dividend (interest) rate on available investments (dollars per dollar years).

m = time business can be run at profit N_i (years).

We will show that if

$$\frac{N_i}{N_r} \geq \frac{e^{sm}}{e^{sm} - 1} \tag{1}$$

then it pays to run irresponsibly and invest the (higher) profits at the rate s as fast as they come in.

Let N be a profit either N_i or N_r. Let t represent time and $T(t)$ the total money accumulated at time t under the profit N. Thus T_r corresponds to N_r and T_i to N_i. dT/dt is the rate of accumulation of money. Money comes in from profit at a rate N and from investments at a rate $sT(t)$ [since $T(t)$ is the total that is invested at time t]. Let us assume $T(O) = 0$. Then we have

$$\frac{dT}{dt} = N + sT \tag{2}$$

$$T(O) = 0.$$

It is well known that such a system has only one solution, $T(t)$. Since

$$T(t) = \frac{N}{s}(e^{st} - 1) \tag{3}$$

solves system (2) it must be the (only) solution.

Therefore, if we assume a responsible business, the total money accumulated by time t will be given by

$$T_r(t) = \frac{N_r}{s}(e^{st} - 1). \tag{4}$$

If we assume an irresponsibly run business, then at the end of m years the total will be

$$T_i(m) = \frac{N_i}{s}(e^{st} - 1). \tag{5}$$

After $t > m$ the only income will be from interest and equation (2) must be replaced.

$$\frac{dT_i}{dt} = sT_i$$

$$T_i(m) = \frac{N_i}{s}(e^{sm} - 1) \tag{6}$$

whose solution is

$$T_i(t) = \frac{N_i}{s}(e^{sm} - 1)e^{s(t-m)} \ (t > m). \tag{7}$$

We are interested in finding out under what conditions $T_i(t) \geq T_r(t)$ for all t. If $t \leq m$ clearly $T_i(t) \geq T_r(t)$, so we need only consider $t > m$. Then subtracting (4) from (7)

$$T_i(t) - T_r(t) = \frac{N_i}{s}(e^{sm} - 1)e^{s(t-m)} - \frac{N_r}{s}(e^{st} - 1)$$

$$T_i(t) - T_r(t) = \frac{1}{s}e^{s(t-m)} \{N_i(e^{sm} - 1) - N_r e^{sm} + N_r e^{s(m-t)}\}. \tag{8}$$

Since $N_r e^{s(m-t)}$ is never negative,

$$T_i(t) - T_r(t) \geq \frac{1}{s}e^{s(t-m)} \{N_i(e^{sm} - 1) - N_r e^{sm}\}. \tag{9}$$

The right side of (9) is positive if $N_i(e^{sm} - 1) - N_r e^{sm} \geq 0$, i.e., if

$$\frac{N_i}{N_r} \geq \frac{e^{sm}}{e^{sm} - 1}$$

which is inequality (1).

11

The Economics
of Overexploitation

Colin W. Clark
(1973)

Renewable resources, by definition, possess self-regeneration capacities and can provide man with an essentially endless supply of goods and services. But man, in turn, possesses capacities both for the conservation and for the destruction of the renewable resource base.

Indeed, man's increasing capacity to seriously deplete the world's natural resources appears to be reaching a critical stage;[1] if this is not imminent for the nonrenewable resources,[2] it certainly appears so for many of the renewable ones.[3] The problems of environmental pollution that loom so large today, for example, often result from a process of overexploitation of the regenerative capacity of our atmospheric and water resources. Economists lately have devoted much attention to environmental questions,[4] and most are agreed that "externalities"—that is, effects not normally accounted for in the cost-revenue analyses of producers—are the leading economic cause of pollution and the destruction of natural beauty.

Animate resources, or biological resources, are also subject to serious misuse by man. An accelerating decline has been observed in recent years in the productivity of many important fisheries,[5] particularly the great whale fisheries and the famous Grand Banks fisheries of the western Atlantic, as well as the spectacularly productive Peruvian anchovy fishery.[6] As technology improves and demand increases, so the pressure

Reprinted with permission from *Science*, **181**:630–634, 1974. Copyright 1974 by the American Association for the Advancement of Science.

on renewable resources grows more severe. The long-recognized need for effective international regulation of fisheries has never been so pressing as it is today.

A prerequisite for effective regulation is a clear understanding of the basic reasons for overexploitation, and in this regard the outstanding article by Hardin[7] on "The tragedy of the commons" has been a positive asset, even though economists have long been aware of the common property problem in fisheries.[8] Indeed, in concentrating their attention on the problems of competitive overexploitation of fisheries, economists appear to have largely overlooked the fact that a corporate owner of property rights in a biological resource might actually prefer extermination to conservation, on the basis of maximization of profits.[9] In this article I argue that overexploitation, perhaps even to the point of actual extinction, is a definite possibility under private management of renewable resources.

The implications of this argument for successful international regulation would seem to be that, if it is assumed that society wishes to preserve the productivity of the oceans and to prevent the extermination of valuable commercial species, control of the physical aspects of exploitation is essential. In particular the popular idea of maximum sustainable yield should be generally adopted, at least in the sense of setting an upper limit on the allowable degree of exploitation. Only a dire emergency in local food supply should be considered as a valid reason for temporarily running down the basic stock of a biological resource.

Antarctic Blue Whale Fishery

In developing the economic theory of a biological resource, I take as an example the Antarctic blue whale population. No economic analysis of whaling as such has yet been published, to my knowledge. Certainly, the complete failure of the International Whaling Commission to carry out its mandate to protect and preserve the whale stocks has not been convincingly explained on economic grounds.

A committee appointed by the International Whaling Commission[10] estimated in 1964 the net reproductive capacity, in terms of net recruitment of 5 year-old blue whales, as a function of the breeding stock of this species. Their graph, which except for the lower end from 0 to 30,000 whales was little more than an educated guess, is shown in Figure 11.1. It appears to indicate a maximum sustainable yield of about 6000 blue whales per annum, but more recent information suggests that this estimate may have been somewhat too high.[11]

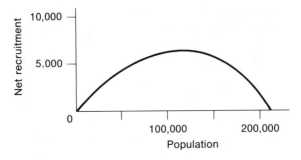

FIGURE 11.1

Recruitment curve for blue whale population.

Figure 11.2 shows the annual blue whale catch,[12] which expanded rapidly in 1926 following the construction of the first modern stern-slipway factory ships, and ended officially in 1965 when the International Whaling Commission agreed to protect the species. At that time the remaining population was believed to be less than 200 whales, but later estimates have been more optimistic, with the stock in 1972 estimated at about 6000 blue whales.[11] I return to the case of the blue whales after a general analysis of the economics of biological resources.

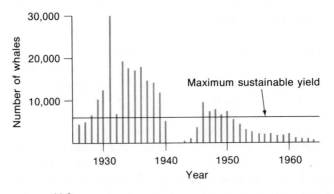

FIGURE 11.2

Annual blue whale catch, 1925 to 1965. [Data compiled from Committee for Whaling Statistics, *International Whaling Statistics, Nos. 1-49* (Oslo: Norwegian Whaling Council, 1930-1963).]

Economic Rent

The most commonly encountered proposal for managing a biological resource is to maximize the sustained yield. Indeed, this was the management scheme suggested by the committee to the Whaling Commission:[10] "The greater the reduction of the present quota, the more rapidly will whale stocks rebuild to the level of maximum sustainable productivity." Economists, however, have taken exception to such proposals:[8] "Focusing attention on the maximization of the catch neglects entirely the inputs of other factors of production which are used up in fishing and must be accounted for as costs."

Indeed, economists have generally suggested adopting the maximization of economic rent as a management policy. The term economic rent refers to the regular income derived from an endurable resource; it refers to net income, or excess of revenue over costs. Since there is a variety of management possibilities for most resources, it is worthwhile to enquire which policy will produce the maximum rent.

In order to obtain a simple mathematical model, suppose that the net recruitment to a particular resource stock of size x is given by a quadratic expression:

$$y = f(x) = Ax(\bar{x} - x) \qquad (1)$$

where $A > 0$ is a constant, and $\bar{x} > 0$ represents the natural equilibrium population. The blue whale curve (Figure 11.1) has roughly this form, which is related to the logistic equation of theoretical biology:

$$dx/dt = Ax(\bar{x} - x)$$

where t is time.

We also suppose that the net recruitment is the same as (or proportional to) the sustainable yield from a population of size x.

The economic components of our model consist of a constant price $p > 0$ per unit of harvested stock, and a unit harvesting cost $C(x)$ that depends on the population size x. The simplest assumption is that this unit harvesting cost is proportional to the density of the population; in the case of pelagic or demersal fish that are more or less uniformly distributed over their range, this assumption would mean simply that $C(x)$ varies inversely with x. Thus, the total cost of harvesting the sustainable yield $y = f(x)$ would be (approximately)

$$C = By/x = AB(\bar{x} - x) \qquad (2)$$

where B is the unit cost coefficient. More general forms of the cost function are considered below.

What sustainable yield, at what population x, gives rise to the maximum rent? Since rent is the difference between revenue R and cost C, the problem is to maximize the expression

$$R - C = pAx(\bar{x} - x) - AB(\bar{x} - x) \qquad (3)$$

The maximum occurs when $x = \hat{x}$, where (see Figure 11.3).

$$\hat{x} = \frac{\bar{x}}{2} + \frac{B}{2p} \qquad (4)$$

provided this expression is less than the equilibrium level $\bar{x}$. (The case $\hat{x} > \bar{x}$ corresponds to the case of negative rent $R - C$ for all populations x; in this case the resource is of no economic value.)

It is clear from Equation 4 that the rent-maximizing population $\hat{x}$ is greater than the level $\bar{x}/2$ of maximum sustained yield. It is this observation that seems to have led to the belief that a private resource owner would necessarily attempt to conserve his resource stock. I return to this question after discussing the common-property problem.

Since maximizing rent appears to be the same thing as maximizing profits, the question now arises, why in practice do fisheries and other resource industries never seem to attain this result? Economists have studied this question in detail; their solution was described by Gordon:[8]

> In sea fisheries the natural resource is not private property; hence the rent it may yield is not capable of being appropriated by anyone. The individual fisherman is more or less free to fish wherever he pleases. The result is a pattern of competition among fishermen which culminates in the dissipation of the rent . . .

To summarize the argument for dissipation of rent, suppose first (see Figure 11.3) that the fishery is actually operating at the rent-maximizing

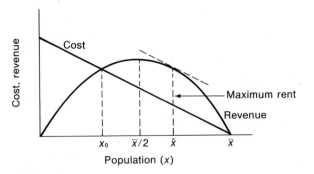

FIGURE 11.3
Economic rent.

level $\hat{x}$. Then, observing that the working fishermen are making a profit, new fishermen will be attracted to the industry. Fishing intensity will increase and the fish population will decrease, as will the total rent. As long as any rent remains, the process continues. The fishery will expand until in the end the population reaches the level x_0 of zero economic rent. Thus, in a competitive situation, the rent will be entirely dissipated and economic efficiency will vanish.

In practice, fishermen will no longer be attracted to a fishery when they can earn a greater income in some alternative employment. This alternative income determines what economists call the opportunity costs of labor in fishing, and these costs are normally included in the total cost function. In cases of high unemployment, opportunity costs for fishermen may be nearly zero, so that the rent dissipation argument would be particularly forceful in explaining the overexploitation of fisheries.

So runs the standard economic argument for the overexploitation of resources, neatly laying the blame on open competition, particularly among the impoverished and the powerless. Yet the most spectacular and threatening developments of today, such as the reduction of the whale stocks and of the demersal fisheries on the Grand Banks, can by no means be attributed to impoverished local fishermen. On the contrary, it is the large, high-powered ships and the factory fleets of the wealthiest nations that are now the real danger. Poor and wealthy nations alike, however, may suffer unless successful control is soon achieved.

Economists themselves have begun to question the adequacy of the rent-dissipation argument to explain current developments.[13] The fact that (as in the above model) extinction is theoretically impossible has been called "one of the more serious deficiencies of the received doctrine."[14] But the principal shortcoming of the existing theories is their disregard of the time variable, both biologically and economically.

On the one hand, biological populations take time to respond to harvesting pressures, and only approach a new equilibrium after several seasons. On the other hand, but equally important, the value of monetary payments also possesses a time component due to the discounting of future payments. It denies the fundamental principles of economics itself to overlook the latter effect, and that is just what the rule of maximizing economic rent does.

The fact that maximization of rent and maximization of present value are not equivalent has long been recognized in agriculture[15] and forestry,[16] and some analyses of fishing have also recognized the difference.[17] The latter, however, have invariably utilized advanced mathematical techniques from the calculus of variations and optimal control theory, and are consequently somewhat beyond the level of intuitive understanding.

In the remainder of this article, I first show how the possibility of extinction can easily be included in the analysis, and then discuss the question of maximization of present value in resource management. The principal outcome will be that if extinction is economically feasible, then it will tend to result not only from common-property exploitation, but also from the maximization of present value, whenever a sufficiently high rate of discount is used.[18] Generally, high rates of discount have the effect of causing biological overexploitation whenever it is commercially feasible.

The question of the cause of high discount rates is a complex one; it is sufficient to remark that at any time the discount rate adopted by exploiters will be related to the marginal opportunity cost of capital in alternative investments. In a technologically expanding economy, this rate could be quite large.

When applied to the Antarctic blue whale, the analysis indicates that an annual discount rate between 10 and 20 percent would be sufficient for extinction to result from maximization of the present value of harvests, assuming that extinction is commercially feasible. Such rates are by no means exceptional in resource development industries.

The question of the feasibility of extermination of the whale stocks is an interesting one. Gulland[19] has pointed out to me that fishing for the Antarctic blue whale probably would have become uneconomical several years earlier had it not been for the simultaneous occurrence of finback whales in the same area. It appears likely that the whalers agreed to a moratorium on blue whales in 1965 because they did not anticipate any significant further profits from the species.

These considerations raise serious doubts, in my opinion, about the wisdom of assuming that corporate resource exploiters will automatically behave in a socially desirable manner.[20] There is no reason to suppose that the fishing corporations themselves desire regulations designed to conserve the world's fisheries. The governments of the world will fail in their responsibility to their citizens unless they succeed in formulating effective international conservation treaties in spite of pressures from these corporations.

Possibility of Extinction

The fact that populations can be driven to extinction by commercial hunting hardly needs to be emphasized. Only a minor change in the model described above is required in order to include the possibility of extinction in a reasonable way.

In Equation 2 we made the assumption that harvesting costs vary inversely with population x. It thus appears that costs become infinite as x approaches zero. The variable x, however, is in reality restricted to integral values ($x = 1, 2, 3, \ldots$), and the cost of extinction is actually the cost of a unit harvest when $x = 1$. The simplest way to adjust the model to admit the possibility of extinction is to replace Equation 2 by

$$C = \frac{By}{x + 1} = \frac{ABx(\bar{x} - x)}{x + 1} \qquad (2')$$

In this formula, the coefficient B represents the cost of extinction, that is, the cost of a unit harvest which reduces the breeding population from one to zero. If B is less than the price p, then the cost curve C will lie below the revenue curve $R = pAx(\bar{x} - x)$ for all values of x, as in Figure 11.4. In this case the zero rent population x_0 equals zero, and rent dissipation will lead to extinction.

In practice, extinction may not require the actual extermination of the last member of the population. Biologists speak of a minimum viable population such that survival is impossible, or highly improbable, once the population falls below this level.[21] Such a possibility is easily included in our model by replacing Equation 1 for the net recruitment by

$$y = A(x - \underline{x})(\bar{x} - x) \qquad (1')$$

when x represents the minimal viable population. Note that there is no sustainable yield when $x < \underline{x}$. In this case extinction is again economically feasible provided the cost coefficient B of Equation 2 or $2'$ is small.[22]

Henceforth for the sake of definiteness I adopt the model described by Equations 1 and $2'$, so that extinction is feasible if the extinction cost B is

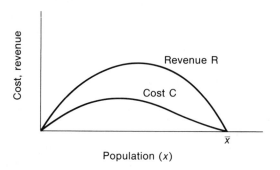

FIGURE 11.4

Cost-revenue curves (extinction feasible).

less than the price p. (The more general case of Equation 1' can be treated by a similar analysis, or can be reduced to the previous case by shifting the origin of the population axis to the point $\underline{x}$ below which extinction becomes automatic.) Hence the rent function $R - C$ is given by

$$F(x) = pAx(\bar{x} - x) - \frac{ABx(\bar{x} - x)}{x + 1} = f(x)\left[p - \frac{B}{x + 1}\right] \quad (5)$$

Maximization of Present Value

The concept of economic rent as discussed so far is time-independent. A more general understanding of the concept, as it applies to agricultural land economics, has been given by Gaffney,[15] who identifies several categories of economic rent. Some of these do not apply to the case of fisheries or other wild animal resources, but his categories of conservable flow and expendable surplus are relevant in general.

In Gaffney's words, the expendable surplus is "that portion of virgin fertility whose emplaced value is less than its liquidation value." In other words, the immediate profit obtained from expending this surplus exceeds the present value of revenues that could be obtained in perpetuity by conserving it. Conversely the conservable flow refers to that portion of fertility whose emplaced value is greater than its liquidation value.

The expendable surplus thus provides a temporary contribution to rent, and disappears once it is expended, leaving the conservable flow as the enduring rent. Obviously, the expendable surplus and the conservable flow are complementary quantities; how much of virgin fertility is assigned to each category depends critically, as we shall see, on the rate of discount utilized in computing present values.

In our own case, let $\hat{x}$ now denote the economically conservable breeding population. The problem is to determine the value of $\hat{x}$. The conservable flow equals the rent $F(\hat{x})$ from Equation 5, and the emplaced value of this rent is just the present value of a (continuous) annuity $F(\hat{x})$, namely

$$P_1(\hat{x}) = \int_0^\infty F(\hat{x}) e^{-\delta t} dt = \frac{1}{\delta} F(\hat{x}) \quad (6)$$

where $\delta > 0$ is the adopted discount rate. A high discount rate corresponds to a low emplaced value, and vice versa.

To derive the value of the expendable surplus, suppose that the population is originally at its natural equilibrium level $\bar{x}$. The surplus is therefore $\bar{x} - \hat{x}$, and this can produce an immediate gross revenue of $p(\bar{x} - \hat{x})$, at a harvesting cost given by

$$\int\limits_{x}^{\bar{x}} C(x)\, dx$$

where, as in Equation 2′, $C(x) = B/(x + 1)$ is the unit harvest cost at the population level x. Thus, the value of the surplus is equal to

$$P_2(\hat{x}) = p(\bar{x} - \hat{x}) - B\log\frac{\bar{x} + 1}{\hat{x} + 1} \qquad (7)$$

The value of $\hat{x}$ is now determined by maximizing the total present value $p_1(\hat{x}) + P_2(\hat{x})$.[23] From Equations 6 and 7 we obtain, except in the end-point cases ($\hat{x} = 0$ or $\bar{x}$), the necessary condition

$$\frac{1}{\delta}F'(\hat{x}) = p - \frac{B}{\hat{x} + 1} = p - C(\hat{x}) \qquad (8)$$

Equation 8 is a marginal condition of the type familiar in economic analysis. The right-hand expression, $p - C(\hat{x})$, represents the additional, or marginal, net revenue obtained by harvesting one unit from the population $\hat{x}$. The left-hand expression, $\delta^{-1}F'(\hat{x})$, is the marginal increase in the present value of the annuity $F(\hat{x})$ that results from leaving this additional unit of population to contribute to net recruitment. Neglecting exceptional cases, we must have equality of these marginal values at the optimal population $\hat{x}$.

Since by Equation 5 we have $F(x) = f(x)[p - C(x)]$, a simple calculation reduces Equation 8 to

$$\delta - f'(\hat{x}) = \frac{-C'(\hat{x})f(\hat{x})}{p - C(\hat{x})} \qquad (9)$$

[Equation 9 can be derived generally for an arbitrary recruitment function $f(x)$ and unit cost function $C(x)$.]

In analyzing Equation 9 there are two cases to consider, depending on whether extinction is feasible or not. If $p < B = C(0)$, then extinction is not feasible. Let

$$p = C(x_0) \qquad (10)$$

so that x_0 represents the population at which price equals unit harvesting cost. Thus $F(x_0) = 0$, that is, x_0 is the "zero rent" level, which we found would be the level resulting from common-property dissipation of rent. Since $F(x) < 0$ for $x < x_0$, it is clear that the desired equilibrium population $\hat{x}$ must be $\geqslant x_0$.

Let $H(x)$ denote the expression on the right side of Equation 9. Then (Figure 11.5) $H(x) > 0$ for $x > x_0$ and the graph of $H(x)$ is asymptotic to the line $x = x_0$. The left side of Equation 9 is a linear function with a

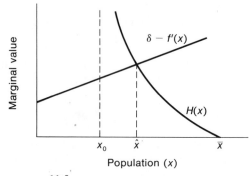

FIGURE 11.5

Maximization of present value (extinction not feasible).

positive slope. Consequently Equation 9 has a solution $\hat{x}$ lying between x_0 and $\bar{x}$. The value $\hat{x}$ is the conservable population.

The two special cases $\delta = 0$ and $\delta = +\infty$ deserve comment. When $\delta = 0$, Equation 8 implies that $F'(\hat{x}) = 0$. Thus, a zero discount rate corresponds to the maximization of economic rent and results in the largest possible conservable flow. When δ is infinite, on the other hand, we see from Figure 11.5 that $\hat{x} = x_0$. In this case $F(\hat{x}) = 0$ and there is no conservable flow; the entire profitable portion of the virgin population is expendable surplus: it is completely dissipated. Rent maximization and rent dissipation thus occur mathematically as two extreme cases of maximization of present value.

Let us turn to the case $p > B$, in which extinction is feasible. In this case $H(x)$ is a positive bounded function (Figure 11.6). Depending on the value of δ, there may be one, several, or no solutions to Equation 9. As before, the case $\delta = 0$ corresponds to the maximization of rent. Now, however, the rent will be dissipated (and the population exterminated) not only for an infinite discount rate, but also for any sufficiently high rate. The following theorem is proved in the Appendix.

THEOREM. *Assume extinction is feasible ($p > B$). Then extinction will indeed occur as a result of the maximization of present value, whenever $\delta > 2f'(0)$.*

Note that $f'(0)$ represents the maximum reproductive potential of the population.

Let us return at last to the blue whales. Figure 11.1 indicates a maximum reproductive potential of about 10 percent per annum (and more

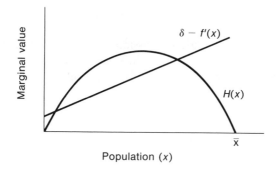

FIGURE 11.6

Maximization of present value (extinction feasible.

recent reports indicate an even smaller rate, perhaps 4 to 5 percent[11]). If in their calculations of profit and loss, the owners of the whaling fleets were to utilize an annual rate of discount of 20 percent or greater, they would therefore opt for complete extermination of the whales—at least as long as whaling remained profitable. This would occur whether they were competing, or cooperating, in the slaughter.

Summary

The general economic analysis of a biological resource presented in this article suggests that overexploitation in the physical sense of reduced productivity may result from not one, but two social conditions: common-property competitive exploitation on the one hand, and private-property maximization of profits on the other. For populations that are economically valuable but possess low reproductive capacities, either condition may lead even to the extinction of the population. In view of the likelihood of private firms adopting high rates of discount, the conservation of renewable resources would appear to require continual public surveillance and control of the physical yield and the condition of the stocks.[25]

Appendix

To prove the theorem stated above, we will show that Equation 9 has no solution in cases $\delta > 2f'(0)$ and $p > B$; this implies that $\hat{x} = 0$ maximizes the total present value, since $\hat{x} = \bar{x}$ would give both zero rent and zero present value.

Since $H(x)$, the right-side expression in Equation 9, is a decreasing function of p, it suffices to consider the case $p = B$. Then by the generalized mean value theorem of elementary calculus,

$$H(x) = -C'(x)\frac{f(x)}{C(0) - C(x)}$$

$$= \frac{C'(x)f'(\xi)}{C'(\xi)}\,(0 < \xi < x) < f'(\xi) < f'(0)$$

Thus $\delta - f'(x) > 2f'(0) - f'(x) > f'(0) > H(x)$, so Equation 9 has no solution as claimed.

Notes

1. Forrester, *World Dynamics* (Wright-Allen, Cambridge, Mass., 1971); D. H. Meadows, D. L. Meadows, J. Randers, and W. W. Behrens III, *The Limits to Growth* (Universe, New York, 1972).
2. R. Gillette, *Science* **175**, 1088 (1972).
3. E. F. Murphy, *Governing Nature* (Quadrangle, Chicago, 1967), pp. 8–11.
4. For a recent survey, see R. M. Solow, *Science* **173**, 498 (1971).
5. F. T. Christy and A. D. Scott, *The Common Wealth in Ocean Fisheries* (Johns Hopkins Press, Baltimore, 1965), pp. 80–86.
6. T. Loftas, *New Scientist* **55** (No. 813), 583 (1972).
7. G. Hardin, *Science* **162**, 1243 (1968).
8. H. S. Gordon, *Journal of Political Economy* **62**, 124 (1954).
9. See J. Crutchfield and A. Zellner, *Economic Aspects of the Pacific Halibut Fishery* (Government Printing Office, Washington, D.C., 1963), pp. 19–20.
10. *International Whaling Commission, 14th Annual Report* (International Whaling Commission, London, 1964), appendix 5, pp. 32–83.
11. J. Gulland, *New Scientist* **54** (No. 793), 198 (1972).
12. Committee for Whaling Statistics, *International Whaling Statistics, Nos. 1–49* (Norwegian Whaling Council, Oslo, 1930–1963).
13. See, for example, S. N. S. Cheung, in *Economics of Fisheries Management: A Symposium*, A. Scott, Ed. (Institute of Animal Resource Ecology, University of British Columbia, Vancouver, 1970), pp. 97–108.
14. V. L. Smith, *Journal of Political Economy* **77**, 181 (1969).
15. M. M. Gaffney, *Natural Resources Journal* **4**, 537 (1964).
16. A. D. Scott, *Natural Resources: The Economics of Conservation* (University of Toronto Press, Toronto, 1955).

17. C. G. Plourde, *American Economic Review* **60**, 518 (1970); *Western Economic Journal* **9**, 256 (1971); A. Zellner, in *Economic Aspects of Fishery Regulation* (Food and Agriculture Organization of the United Nations, Rome, 1962), pp. 497–510; see also Note 13.
18. C. W. Clark, *Journal of Political Economy* **81**, 950 (1973).
19. J. Gulland, personal communication.
20. That oligopolistic development of resources may be the most destructive of all possibilities has been recognized in the conservation literature. See S.V. Ciriacy-Wantrup, *Resource Conservation: Economics and Policies* (University of California Press, Berkeley, 1952), pp. 190–198.
21. For further details, see K. E. F. Watt, *Ecology and Resource Management* (McGraw-Hill, New York, 1968), pp. 54–73.
22. J. R. Gould, *Journal of Political Economy* **80**, 1031 (1972).
23. The Pontrjagin maximum principle [L.S. Pontrjagin, V. S. Boltjanskii, R. V. Gamkrelidze, E. F. Mishchenko, *The Mathematical Theory of Optimal Processes* (Pergamon, Oxford, 1964), pp. 18–19] can be invoked to prove that maximization of the present-value integral

$$\int \exp\left(-\delta t\right) h\left(t\right) \{ p - C\left[x\left(t\right)\right] \} \, dt$$

for $h(t) \geq 0$ is equivalent to maximization of the simple expression $P_1(x) + P_2(x)$ described here.
24. This possibility was also suggested by D. Fife [*Environment* **13** (No. 3), 20 (1971)].
25. Among the many friends and colleagues whose ideas have contributed to this article, I would especially like to thank P. Bradley, P. Pearse, A. Scott, and all other economists who have patiently suffered my errors.

12

A Test
of the Tragedy
of the Commons

James A. Wilson

Introduction

The phrase, "the tragedy of the commons" came into widespread use
following the publication of Garrett Hardin's article of that title. Hardin
used the phrase to dramatize the fact that, with a growing population,
uncontrolled access to commonly owned replenishable resources usually
results in the depletion or disappearance of those resources. Commercial
fish, whales, grazing areas, fresh water supplies, and even the air in our
larger industrial and urban centers are the kinds of non-owned, or commonly owned, resources Hardin mentions. Oceanic fisheries particularly
seem to be subject to the tragedy of the commons because of the lack of
controls on the resource dictated by the tradition of the freedom of
the seas.

Though the hypothesis of the tragedy of the commons has an immediate intuitive appeal, which the recent concern for the environment
serves to dramatize, there is no strong evidence that we know of, other
than that supplied by hindsight, which tends to support the notion. Recently we came across a situation in the inshore lobster *(Homarus
americanus)* fishery in the State of Maine in which social and economic
arrangements contribute to a nearly controlled experiment for testing
the hypothesis of the tragedy of the commons. Briefly, some small areas
of the fishery have been effectively appropriated by groups of fishermen
for their own use; that is, the fishermen have virtually created extralegal

group property rights for themselves in the midst of the oceanic common property. In each case in which such property rights exist, the fishermen have chosen to exercise their rights of property through both the exclusion of other men from their property and controls on the fishing effort of the group itself. The investigation we undertook was to measure and compare the biological and economic characteristics of the areas in which property rights and limits on fishing effort exist (controlled access areas) with similar measurements in adjacent areas where no such property rights and limits on fishing effort exist (uncontrolled access areas). The results of our investigation tend to confirm the tragedy hypothesis though some ambiguity of interpretation is introduced by uncertainty concerning the stock/recruit relationships of the lobster population.

A Restatement of the "Tragedy" Hypothesis

The economic theory of common property resource exploitation appears to be the most precise theoretical formulation of the tragedy phenomenon. In Hardin's analysis, the problem is symptomatic of a breakdown in Adam Smith's rule that an individual who "intends only his own gain" is, as it were, "led by an invisible hand to promote . . . the public interest." In the language of more recent economic theory: "In the absence of exclusive rights to the use of the fishing ground, the right to contract so as to stipulate its use does not exist."[1] Applied to a fishery, the economic analysis proceeds from the observation that the common property nature of the resource creates a situation in which the individual fisherman has no incentive to conserve resources, since his inability to withhold the resource from others in the future means that he will not be able to reap the rewards of his conservationist (waiting) action. As Hardin points out, the social costs of this resource exploitation do not become apparent until population pressure—to the economist, the effective demand for the product—rises to the point where one producer's activity on the commons affects the activity of all producers on the commons. In the fishery commons these social costs[2] become manifest in the following three distinct ways.

Crowding
At a given time it is possible for the level of fishing intensity to be so great that congestion of gear, boats, and so on, results in inefficiency, a decline in fishermen's income, and possibly unacceptably high rates of exploitation of the species in question. In a trap fishery like the inshore lobster fishery, crowding becomes most apparent in the numbers of and reasons for laying traps. In many areas of the Maine coast crowding has

reached the point where many traps are employed not to catch lobsters but to reserve areas of the bottom where current catch rates are low because of present water temperatures but are expected to become greater in the near future. Thus an optimal fishing technique requiring that traps be moved with changes in water temperature and other variable factors is displaced by an almost random placement and greatly increased number of traps. In addition to the greater capital cost, random placement also results in larger numbers of lost traps due to gear entanglements during hauling, snarls of gear during heavy weather with strong currents, increased time spent searching for gear—because a fisherman often cannot keep track of the locations of 600-plus individual traps —time and fuel spent hauling less than optimally placed traps, and an increased probability of traps lost to the propellors of passing vessels. Crowding also results in more pronounced seasonality in fisheries like the lobster fishery where growth to the legally mandated minimum size is discrete (i.e., associated with the annual molt). The sudden increase in the number of legal-size animals at molting time produces a sudden rush by fishermen to place gear in the water. Consequently a greater part of each year's catch is obtained in the period immediately during or after the seasonal molt. For the remainder of the year gear, and often men as well, are idle or relatively unproductive.

Age or Size of Harvest

For each fish species there is a socially optimal age or size for harvesting. This optimum is given by individual growth rates over the lifespan of the fish and economic variables such as the market price of the species and cost of harvesting (if they vary by the age of the species), and the appropriate discount rate. The individual fisherman, however, is not able to choose the socially optimal age of harvesting because a delay in harvesting on his part will not be respected by his competitors. Hence, he attempts to harvest as early in the life of the fish as feasible,[3] resulting in a lower catch in weight per unit of fishing effort expended for the fishery as a whole.

Size of Reproducing Stock

For each species of fish it is felt that there is an optimum, or at least a range of, population size of the reproducing stock, which is compatible with a maximum sustained biological or economic yield. Since the level or intensity of fishing effort is a major determinant of the size of the reproducing stock it follows that there is a socially optimal level or range of fishing effort. The common property nature of the fishery again creates a situation in which the individual fisherman does not have the incentive to harvest in a manner consistent with a social optimum. If he does attempt to act in a way that conforms to society's interests, reducing his level of effective fishing effort in order to increase the size of the reproducing stock, he has no guarantee that the future benefits of such action—a larger harvestable population—will in fact materialize for him. It is more likely his competitors will merely catch what he did not; even if they don't, they will share proportionately with him the benefits of his action. In other words, the individual fisherman individually pursuing a policy in line with society's long run interests will find that his costs exceed his benefits.

In its most extreme manifestation, the tragedy of the commons results in the reduction of the reproducing stock to a level of near or complete extinction. More commonly, the tragedy is simply a reduction of reproducing stock to a level not capable of sustaining economically viable activity.[4] It should be noted that crowding and age/size of capture aspects of the fishing problem are merely short run symptoms of the same cause—uncontrolled exploitation of the resource.

Working Hypothesis

Given this analysis of the common property resource problem in a fishery, it is possible to restate the tragedy hypothesis in the form of hypotheses about observable differences between similar fisheries with uncontrolled access (i.e. common property) and with controlled access.

From the analysis of crowding effects it follows that:

1. A controlled access fishery should exhibit a larger average number of lobsters per trap haul than an uncontrolled access fishery because of the frequent non-optimal placement of traps in the latter.

2. Greater capital and variable costs (gas, bait, etc.) in the uncontrolled access fishery should lead to a lower net income per lobster caught than in the controlled access fishery.

3. A controlled access fishery should exhibit less seasonality than an uncontrolled access fishery.

From the analysis of age of capture effects it follows that:

1. Average weight and value produced per trap haul should be greater in the controlled access than in the uncontrolled access fishery.

2. The length frequency distribution of the catch in controlled fisheries should exhibit a greater mean and a larger standard deviation than that in uncontrolled fisheries if fishing activity in both is constrained by the same legal minimum size. (Higher exploitation

rates will lead to a high proportion of the catch being near the legal minimum and low exploitation rates to a greater dispersion of lengths at capture.)

From the analysis of size of reproducing stock effects it follows that:

1. The probability of a female reaching mature age or size is greater in the controlled than in the uncontrolled access fishery.

2. If lobsters were completely sedentary during their entire life span —if there were no interchange of stocks between the two fisheries —the controlled fishery should exhibit a greater stock density than the uncontrolled fishery. (Because of larval drift during the surface feeding stages this is not the case in the fisheries studied here.)

The Circumstances of the Experiment

In the bottom dwelling stage, lobsters in northern waters appear to be relatively sedentary creatures, unlike schooling fish which must be hunted over a wide expanse of the ocean. This characteristic has made possible a year-round inshore fishery consisting of small boats exploiting relatively small inshore areas.[5] Inshore area lobsters are caught in wooden traps which are baited and left on the bottom for a period of one day to a week or more. Each trap, or sometimes a trawl[6] of traps, is marked by buoys in the distinctive colors of each fisherman. These characteristics of the fishery—almost daily access to the fishing area and the ready identification of gear—have made possible the practice of a kind of territoriality by the fisherman.[7]

Two distinguishable forms of territoriality exist in the Maine fishery;[8] the purpose of both is the exclusion of other fishermen from a given area of the ocean bottom. In its major attributes, one form closely resembles a typical uncontrolled fishery and the second, a fishery with carefully controlled access. In the first and most common form, a group of men (usually operating from the same harbor) share the fishery resource in a particular area and cooperate in the *short run* exclusion of fishermen from other harbors. The degree of exclusion varies extensively from harbor to harbor. In most areas of the coast, territorial boundaries are more or less subject to intrusion by men from other harbors. Generally, the factors defining which outsiders are permitted access are dependent on blood relationships; friendships; historical "rights" to a particular area (e.g., a man whose family fished a certain area may still be accorded access to that area even after he has moved to another harbor area); and an assessment of the costs and benefits of boundary line defense, the costs of which can usually be stated in terms of expected gear losses.[9]

Over much of the coast, exclusion is practiced *only toward men "from away."* Entry into a particular area through the establishment of residence at the appropriate harbor is generally easily accomplished. In addition, entry of younger men who have grown up in the harbor is almost totally unrestricted. Thus, the effect of this form of exclusion is limited, especially in that over a period of time it does not constrain the number of men fishing in a particular area. For this reason we have taken the social and economic characteristics of this fishing mode to be an approximation of the uncontrolled access typical of a common property resource.

A second form of territoriality found along the coast combines a very strong form of short-run exclusion of men from away, with the ability of the group to control the total number of men engaged in the fishery in a particular area over a period of time. In other words, *growth of the group itself is controlled.* This second form of territoriality is of extreme interest because as long as group membership remains stable or controllable, exclusion implies that individual members of the fishing group should receive benefits proportionate to any conservationist measures they take, if all other members of the group practice similar restraints. Voluntary agreements among fishermen with respect to the size of the group having access to the resource would appear to confer on the group the potential benefits of ownership and control. The fact that such group ownership is subject to the problems of voluntary agreements, however, does flaw the comparison with rational control implied by the tragedy hypothesis.

There is one particular aspect of group management which strains the comparison with the rationalized control situation implied by the tragedy hypothesis. In situations of uncertainty about the optimum level of short and long-run fishing effort rational management could conceivably experiment with various levels of fishing effort in order to find an optimum. The group arrangements we have observed are then severely constrained. For example, when the current level of fishing effort appears satisfactory to the members of the group, long-run fishing effort could be increased or decreased in either of two ways.

First, the number of men fishing the area could be altered. In the case of a decrease in fishing effort, this would mean the exclusion of one or more currently participating members of the group; this would, of course, place severe political and social strains on the voluntary agreement. If fishing effort were increased, the inclusion of new members in the group would be a threat to future benefits expected by long-time members of the group; the increase would likely be opposed by them. Moreover, such a change in the numbers of men in a given area would not be easily reversible, as it should be to achieve efficiency in searching for traps and gear. This is not to say that any change in numbers is impossible; a variety of social conditions cause change (e.g., retirement, sickness, etc.). But such changes are not likely to be undertaken consciously to identify the optimum level of fishing effort which would be the goal of a rational control system.

Secondly, a long-run fishing effort could be increased or decreased by altering the level of fishing effort expended by all current members of the group. This is the more probable course because it is reversible, though the degree of change is limited. Essentially, trap or gear limits are feasible when gear crowding has caused the optimum fishing technique to be replaced by a random placement technique. In such situations fishermen are generally willing to return to optimum trap placement techniques (provided, of course, that all fishermen do the same), but they are not willing to cut their trap numbers to the point at which they expect a loss of income.

In other words, it is possible to set the trap limit at that used by a boat fishing with the optimum technique (optimum from the myopic point of view of the individual fisherman), but not to go below that number. Trap and gear limits set below the optimum impose an immediate economic loss on the fisherman and thus create a situation in which each fisherman has an incentive to violate the provisions of the agreement. On the other hand, trap and gear limitations set at about the optimum number do not create an incentive to violate the agreement and consequently do not require the group to undertake substantial enforcement costs. It is especially difficult to justify enforcement costs where economic gains are uncertain, which is a common situation.

These reasons, then, lead us to believe that group ownership or voluntary arrangements are not likely to efficiently locate an optimum level of fishing effort. Nevertheless, we do feel that the use of controlled access areas as a surrogate for a system of rational control is justified. The reason is simple: in the absence of a perceived benefit from controlled access, the social mechanisms controlling access would break down. Thus we postulate that group cohesion is based upon perceived benefits even though the level of benefits may not be at the optimum because of the social, and perhaps biological, constraints on efficient search.

Design of the Experiment and Data

The goal of the experimental design was to obtain economic and biological measures of controlled and uncontrolled access areas, that is, to isolate the effect of controls on access. Consequently, we obtained data in both areas from full-time fishermen with at least ten years experience in the commercial fishery in order to eliminate as much as possible bias resulting from differences in fishing skill. We chose fishermen who fished similar types of bottom and conditions; specifically, men who fished in relatively deep, unprotected waters, and men who used the same design of gear. In all cases, the men in uncontrolled areas fished territories whose boundaries immediately abutted the controlled areas from which we obtained data.[10]

The total number of fishermen involved in the experiment was 15: 7 from controlled areas and 8 from uncontrolled areas. Each fisherman was instructed in the collection of the following data for each trap haul:[11] (1) the number of legal-sized lobsters; (2) the carapace measure of legal-sized lobsters; (3) whether the lobster was punched,[12] carrying eggs, or neither; (4) the approximate depth of the trap;[13] (5) the location of the trap vis-à-vis the territorial boundary; and (6) the number of days the trap had been in the water. Data collection took place over 75 fishing days, involved 10,734 individual trap hauls and measurements of 9,089 individual legal sized lobsters.

Results

Table 12.1 and Figure 12.1 summarize the data collected from both the controlled and uncontrolled access fisheries. Though interpretation of these results is subject to a certain amount of ambiguity and speculation owing to unknown characteristics of the lobster population stock/recruit relationships it would seem that the following could be stated.

TABLE 12.1
Catch Effort Characteristics by Area[a]

	Controlled	Uncontrolled
Number Trap Hauls	5896	4837
Number of Lobsters	5762	2951
Weight of Lobsters (kgm)	3106	1568
Number/Trap Haul	.98	.61
Weight/Trap Haul	.54	.32
Weight/Lobster	.55	.53

[a]Differences in calculated means are all significant at the 0.005 level of confidence (t-test).

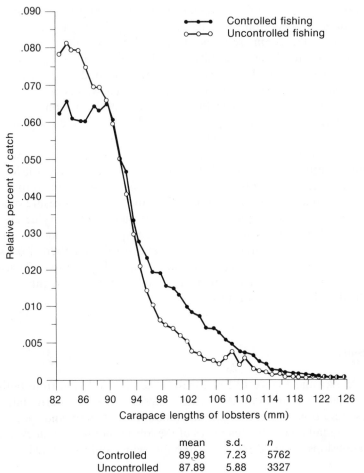

	mean	s.d.	n
Controlled	89.98	7.23	5762
Uncontrolled	87.89	5.88	3327

(*t*-value for differences in sample means = 12.55, significant at 0.005 level of confidence.)

FIGURE 12.1

Distribution of catch in controlled and uncontrolled access fisheries (81 mm is legal minimum size).

Crowding

Average catch in numbers per trap haul (C/TH) indicates that this measure of productivity is more than 60 percent greater in the controlled than in the uncontrolled access areas (Table 12.1) We would take this to be very strong evidence of the uneconomic effects of the crowding and non-optimal trap placement which results from uncontrolled access.

Seasonality

Table 12.2 breaks down the data according to the three seasons observed in the lobster fishery. The figures show that in season 1 (during which the annual molt occurs and there is a significant increase in availability) there is a relatively small but significant difference in C/TH between controlled and uncontrolled areas. In seasons 2 and 3 C/TH falls off rather drastically in uncontrolled areas while remaining relatively stable in controlled areas. This difference in the characteristics of the two fisheries exhibits the greater seasonality expected in an uncontrolled access fishery.

Age/Size of Capture

Differences in size of capture appear to be less marked than differences in crowding effects. Measures of each lobster caught indicate that lobsters in the controlled areas are caught at only slightly larger weights and sizes (2 mm) than those in the uncontrolled areas.[14] Nevertheless, to the fishermen in the controlled areas, these slight differences are responsible for substantial increases in the relative productivity per trap haul, which was 60 percent greater in controlled areas. When the greater weight of the lobsters in the controlled areas is taken into account relative productivity jumps to 69 percent greater in the controlled areas (Table 12.1).

This same effect is observable in the length frequency distributions presented in Figure 12.1. The curves clearly show that the limits on fishing effort in the controlled fishery result in a greater probability of escape from capture at sizes close to the legal minimum size of 88 mm and correspondingly greater probabilities of capture at sizes above 90 mm.

Size of Reproducing Stock

Perhaps the most important effect of controlled fishing is on sustained yield or future recruitment. Using estimates of female maturity by length (derived from Krouse[15]), we have calculated that the probability of a female being mature at time of capture is 1.52 times greater in the controlled than in the uncontrolled areas.[16] (See Figure 12.2.) These rather large differences may seem surprising at first given the small differences in average size/age of capture. The explanation lies in the fact that the onset of maturity appears to take place in the 90–100 mm length range.[17,18] This is the size range associated with one molt beyond the legal minimum length and, more importantly, is the size range associated with the greatest relative differences in the frequency of catch in the controlled and uncontrolled fisheries. (See Figure 12.1.) Viewed another

TABLE 12.2

Catch Effort Characteristics by Season by Area[a]

	Season 1[b]		Season 2[b]		Season 3[b]	
	Controlled	Uncontrolled	Controlled	Uncontrolled	Controlled	Uncontrolled
Number of Trap Hauls[c]	2536	1961	605	1018	1140	1560
Number of Lobsters[c]	2486	1373	551	601	981	639
Weight (kgm)[c]	1358	738	294	316	562	339
Number/Trap Haul	.98	.70	.91	.59	.86	.41
Weight/Trap Haul	.54	.38	.49	.31	.49	.22
Number/THSOD[d]	.36	.21	.10	.04	.29	.11
Weight/THSOD[d]	.19	.11	.05	.02	.17	.05
Weight/Lobster	.55	.54	.53	.52	.57	.53

[a]Differences between calculated sample means are a-1 significant at 0.01 level except for weight/lobster for seasons 1 and 2.
[b]Season 1 = August 1 to December 31, Season 2 = January 1 to April 30, Season 3 = May 1 to July 31.
[c]Numbers do not add to all year sample totals because some data were excluded for lack of set-over-day information and because one of the controlled areas has a legal season and therefore data are inappropriate for seasonal comparisons.
[d]THSOD = Trap haul times set over days.

way, the slightly lower level of fishing effort in the controlled areas produces rather large differences in the probability of escape until female maturity is attained.

Whether or not this attribute of the controlled fishery is beneficial depends upon the stock/recruit relationships at work in the lobster population. An abundant body of work in economics and fish population dynamics shows that a reduction in fishing effort or an increase in the size of the reproducing stock is beneficial only when the size of the reproducing stock is below optimal economic or biological yield.[19] Our investigation throws no light on this particular matter, but work by others, specifically Bell[20] and Thomas,[21] indicates that the size of the reproducing stock throughout the lobster fishery appears to be well below the optimum. If this is in fact the case we conclude that observed limits on fishing effort in the controlled fishery do have positive economic and biological consequences. It should be noted that since the controlled access fisheries represent only small enclaves in the total fishery, and since lobster larvae float with surface currents and winds during the

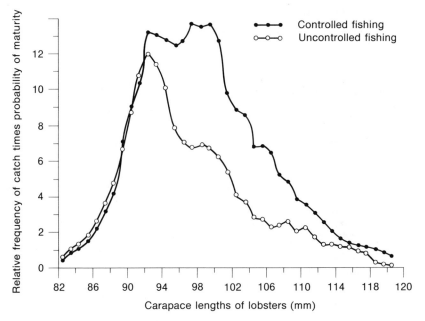

FIGURE 12.2

Estimated catch of mature females by length and type of area.

early stages of development (4–8 weeks), it is not possible to directly measure the impact of female maturity. Possible benefits generated by the fishing mode in controlled areas are just as likely to be received by fishermen in the uncontrolled areas.

Income Effects

The income differentials implied by differences in productivity per trap haul are corroborated by gross income figures obtained from 8 fishermen in controlled areas and 19 in uncontrolled areas. Unfortunately, the accounting methods used by most fishermen and their reluctance to release such information do not allow for the certain attribution of income differentials to crowding and age of capture effects. Table 12.3 summarizes the income data. Income figures for the controlled access areas have been standardized in order to eliminate the effect of higher prices which occur during seasons 2 and 3, when the greatest productivity differentials favor the controlled areas. Since this price effect is directly attributable to declining supply from the rest of the fishery, the extra income accruing to controlled area fishermen cannot be seen as a benefit of controls (i.e., if the entire fishery were controlled this income benefit would not appear). Even though the sample sizes are rather small, a two tailed t-test indicates less than .005 probability that the differences in the means could have arisen from the same population.

Conclusions and Qualifications

Though the Maine lobster fishery has yet to reach the depleted state of so many of the world's common property resources, the dynamics of

TABLE 12.3
Fishermen's Gross Income by Area

	Controlled	Uncontrolled
Number of Fishermen	8	19
Average Income[b]	$22,929[a]	$16,449
(Standard Deviation)	(4,112)	(5,213)

[a]Income of men in controlled areas was corrected in order to take out the effect of higher prices in seasons 2 and 3. This procedure reduced observed gross incomes by 16% for men in the controlled areas.
[b]The t-value for differences in sample means is calculated at 5.54.

common property resource exploitation appears to be working its inexorable, tragic course in the fishery. Biologic and economic indicators of the state of the uncontrolled fishery (which comprises probably well over 90 percent of the entire fishery) are markedly different from those same indicators in the controlled part of the fishery. The most apparent and most easily measured differences are short-term productivity effects. Catch in numbers per trap haul (C/TH), which we used as a measure of the short-term crowding manifestations of the tragedy phenomenon, indicates that crowding in the uncontrolled fishery has proceeded to the point where productivity is only 62 percent of that in controlled areas. When the fisheries are compared in terms of weight per trap haul, the measure we used to estimate the common property effect on size/age of capture, productivity in the uncontrolled fishery declines to only 59 percent of that in the controlled areas. Long term economic and biologic benefits of the controlled mode of fishing also appear to be greater, though this effect cannot be measured directly and is subject to the assumption that the current size of the reproducing stock is below the level compatible with maximum economic or biologic yield. If this benefit is positive, however, it would be logical to state that the larval drift of the lobster life cycle leads to an underestimate of the benefits of controlled fishing effort in a situation such as encountered in this experiment. This further implies that institutionalization of controls over the *entire* fishery would yield the long term biologic benefit of a greater size of sustainable future harvests.

It is apparent that, at least in the lobster fishery, advocates of rational control can point not only to long term but also to short term benefits to the fisherman himself. These benefits, of course, cannot be achieved without cost. If controls on fishing effort are to be instituted in the Maine lobster fishery undoubtedly the major cost will be in terms of the exclusion of potential entrants into the fishery. In the rural areas of the state where economic opportunities are very limited this indeed may be a costly policy. Yet if the choice is between controls of one sort or another and loss of the fishery, it is clear that from society's point of view the costs of controls are preferable.

In contrast with Hardin's conclusion, our work with the fishermen of Maine has given us reason to be somewhat optimistic about our chances of dealing with the tragedy of the commons. Maine fishermen are reputed to be excessively independent, the last of a dying breed, and yet they are fully conscious of the tragedy they are playing out. The question fishermen address themselves to now, is not whether there should be controls on the fishery but whether proposed controls will be effective and equitable—will controls achieve the benefits claimed and how will the costs and benefits of control be shared by current and potential users of the resource? At the moment, the prevention of tragedy on the Maine coast appears to be dependent upon our ability to negotiate a new social contract for the use of this resource.

Notes

1. S. N. S. Cheung, 1970. *Journal of Law and Economics,* **8**:49.
2. J. Crutchfield, 1964. *American Economic Review,* **54**:207. V. L. Smith, 1969. *Journal of Political Economy,* **77**:181.
3. Feasibility is usually defined by legally set minimum sizes or permissible net mesh sizes.
4. F. T. Christy and A. D. Scott, 1965. *The Common Wealth in Ocean Fisheries.* Pp. 9–12. Baltimore: Johns Hopkins Press.
5. Generally within the 3-mile limit.
6. A trawl is a number of connected traps, usually ten or more, marked by two buoys one on the first and one on the last trap.
7. Significantly, when lobster fishermen participate in the shrimp, scallop, or herring fisheries, none of which are fixed gear fisheries, they recognize no territorial boundaries whatsoever.
8. James M. Acheson, 1975. *Human Ecology,* **3**:183.
9. See M. Olson, 1971. *The Logic of Collective Action.* Pp. 36–43. Cambridge, Mass.: Harvard University Press.
10. The choice of immediately adjacent territories was made to assure as much comparability of fishing grounds as possible. On the other hand this choice endangered the experiment to the extent that interchanges of the two fishing stocks takes place. Significant interchange would, of course, tend to erase any noticeable differences in the lobster population on the two fishing grounds.
11. About 30 percent of the data was actually collected by project members or assistants working with the fishermen. There is no statistical difference between data collected by the fishermen working alone and that collected by project members working with the fishermen.
12. "Punched female" refers to a knife cut made in the tail flipper of an egged lobster. A lobster so marked, even if legal sized and without eggs, must be returned to the bottom. A change in the legislatively mandated definition of a "punched" female caused this data to be collected in a somewhat erratic and inconsistent fashion by fishermen involved in the project. Consequently the data were discarded.
13. Recorded depths were approximate for each string of traps set out by the fishermen. A "string" is a set of traps usually placed at the same depth around a ledge or along a bottom contour.

14. Measurements of a sample of each fisherman's traps indicated no statistically discernable difference in lath spacing which could have caused the differences in average size of capture.

15. J. Krouse, 1973. *Fishery Bulletin,* **71:**165.

16. Actual catch data (n = 191) for egg-carrying females indicates that the percent of egg-carrying females per catch is more than twice as great in the controlled areas (controlled = 2.7 percent; uncontrolled = 1.2 percent).

17. J. Thomas. NOAA Tech. Rep. NMFS, SSRF-667; and J. Krouse, note 15.

18. Maturity is defined here as the state of being capable of reproduction.

19. See, for example, R. J. H. Beverton and S. J. Holt *On the Dynamics of Exploited Fish Populations.* Fish. Invest. Ministry Agric., Fish. Food (G. B.) Ser. II, 19; Smith, note 2; Christy and Scott, note 4.

20. F. Bell, 1972. *Journal of Political Economy,* **80:**148.

21. J. Thomas, note 17.

13

Ethical Implications of Carrying Capacity

Garrett Hardin

It should be clear by now that the idea of the commons did not suddenly arise out of nothing in the year 1968. Passing references to the problem occur as far back as Aristotle, and Lloyd certainly saw it clearly in 1833. H. Scott Gordon's work in 1954 saw the beginning of a new concern with the problems presented by this politico-economic system. Yet the fact remains that a widespread recognition of these problems did not develop until after 1968. Why the delay? Two reasons are apparent.

First, a favorable climate of opinion was needed for remarks about the commons to be noticed. This was created in the 1960's by the rapid growth of the environmental movement, which alerted people to the consequences of distributional systems. Second, it was necessary that the properties of the commons be stated in no uncertain terms if people were to consider the matter seriously. It was necessary that the human tragedy of adhering to a commons-type distribution be emphasized. A good, solid fortissimo minor chord had to be sounded. Before 1968 most of the sounds were either mere grace notes or extended passages played pianissimo. The down-playing was for good reason, of course: the clear message of the commons threatened cherished beliefs and practices. Abandoning any traditional practice requires a political upset (though revolution may be too strong a word).

We have seen how the problem of the commons has been evaded in the exploitation of ocean fisheries. Understandably, it is evaded even more in the question of human populations. Both problems require for their rational resolution a clear understanding of the concept of carrying capacity and a willingness to fashion laws that take this concept into account.

Let us first look at the concept as it applies to other animals and plants, to the non-human populations we would like to exploit for our own benefit.

The carrying capacity of a particular area is defined as *the maximum number of a species that can be supported indefinitely by a particular habitat, allowing for seasonal and random changes, without degradation of the enviornment and without diminishing carrying capacity in the future.* There is some redundancy in this definition, but redundancy is better than inadequacy. Using deer as an example, the true carrying capacity of a region must allow for the fact that food is harder to get in winter than in summer and scarcer in drought years than in "normal years." If too many head of deer are allowed in the pasture they may overgraze it to such an extent that the ground is laid bare, producing soil erosion followed by less plant growth in subsequent years. Always, by eating the grasses that appeal to them, herbivores selectively favor the weed grasses that are not appealing, thus tending to diminish the carrying capacity for themselves and for their progeny in subsequent years.

The concept of carrying capacity is a time-bound, posterity-oriented concept. This is one of the reasons that it threatens the "conventional wisdom" (Galbraith's term) of the present time, which leans heavily on short term economic theory. The theory of discounting, using commercially realistic rates of interest, virtually writes off the future.[1] The consequences have been well described by Fife and Clark. Devotion to economic discounting in its present form is suicidal. How soon is it so? "In the long run," an economist would say, since disaster is more than five years off. "In the short run," according to biologists, since disaster occurs in much less than the million or so years that is the normal life expectancy of a species. Here we see a standing issue of dispute between economists and biologists, with their different professional biases in reckoning time.

Game management methods of maintaining the carrying capacity of a habitat impinge upon ethical theory. Officially, Judeo-Christian ethics is absolutist in form, rich in proscriptions such as "Thou shalt not kill." Can we base game management on such principles? Obviously we cannot. Time after time, in an area where men have eliminated such "varmints" as coyotes and wolves, prey species (e.g., deer) have multiplied far beyond the carrying capacity of their habitat, which they then severely damage thus reducing its carrying capacity in the future.[2] Taking for granted the legitimacy of human desire to maximize gains from the deer-pasture, is "Thou shalt not kill" a good ethical rule? *It depends.* If the herd size is less than the carrying capacity we might insist on this rule; but if the herd has grown beyond carrying capacity we should deliberately kill animals, until the size of the herd is brought to a safe level.

For the maximum yield of venison we should keep the herd at that level at which the first derivative of the population function is a maximum; but for safety, allowing for unforeseen random fluctuations, the population level should be kept a bit above the point of fastest population growth.

This analysis was focussed wholly on the interests of man, the exploiter of nature. Much the same conclusion is reached if we focus entirely on the species being exploited. Whenever there are too many animals in a habitat the animals themselves show all the signs of misery, if our empathic projections are to be trusted at all. The animals become skinny and feeble; they succumb easily to diseases. The normal social instincts of the species become ineffectual as starving animals struggle with one another for individual survival.

In a state of nature the unsavory consequences of exceeding the carrying capacity are prevented by natural predation. Putting entirely to one side the exploitative goals of animal husbandry, whenever men maintain a population of animals free of predators they should, if they are humane, pursue a regular program of killing animals so as to keep the herd size below the carrying capacity of the habitat.

We see that the ethics of game management is not an absolutist ethics but a relativistic or situational ethics.[3] The foundation of situational ethics is this: *The morality of an act is determined by the state of the system at the time the act is performed.* Ecology, a system-based view of the world, demands situational ethics.

Unfortunately, situational (ecological) ethics creates difficult problems for the law. It is difficult to write statute law if we are deprived of the simplicity of flat, unqualified *dos* and *don'ts*. Qualifications can be written into law, but it is hard to foresee all the particularities of future situations. Our insufficiently informed efforts leave "loopholes" for rascals to crawl through. When found, loopholes can be plugged, of course; but that takes time. The legislative process is a slow one. Situational ethics seems almost to demand an administrative approach; by statute, administrators can be given the power to make instant, detailed decisions within a legally defined framework. Rules promulgated by an administrative agency are called administrative law.

On paper, the system may look fine, but the general public is understandably afraid of it. Administrative law gives power to administrators, who are human and hence fallible. Their decisions may be self serving. John Adams called for "a government of laws, and not of men." We rightly esteem this as a desirable ideal. The practical question we must face is how far can we safely depart from the ideal under the pressure of ecological necessity? This is the harrowing *Quis custodiet* problem;[4] it has no easy solutions.[5]

When a well-defined problem is virtually ignored as long as the commons problem was—more than a hundred years—we naturally suspect the interference of taboo. This plausible supposition is by its very nature, nearly unprovable. Taboo is a composite thing:[6] there is "the primary taboo, surrounding the thing that must not be discussed; around this is the secondary taboo, a taboo against even acknowledging the existence of the primary taboo."

A taboo may be sustained in part for good tactical reasons: breaking it may open up a nest of problems not yet ripe for productive discussion. We may speculate—we can hardly know—that the long avoidance of the commons problem was due to a subconscious awareness of the intractable *Quis custodiet* problem, which would have been activated by any attempt to depart from the system of the commons.

Moreover, the theory on which the commons problem is based rests on the concept of carrying capacity, which so far we have assumed is static. This is a justifiable assumption when we are speaking of a deer pasture in the wild, a habitat we propose to leave wild for esthetic reasons. But when we talk about cattle pastures, fish culture in fresh water ponds, and oyster culture in estuaries, we are talking about areas in which it is possible to increase the carrying capacity by technological intervention. Much of what we have called progress in the last two centuries has resulted from increasing the carrying capacity of the earth by technological means. Agricultural productivity, for instance, has increased by more than an order of magnitude since the time of Malthus, whose theory clearly assumed a static carrying capacity. Malthus' historical failure has understandably made many intelligent people very skeptical of any theory founded on the idea of a static carrying capacity.

Thus has it come about that many of the decisions made at the present time (insofar as they are explicitly rational) are based on balancing today's demand against tomorrow's supply, a type of bookkeeping that is frowned upon by certified public accountants. For the past two centuries we've gotten away with this practice because Science and Technology have generated miracles. But can such progress continue without end? The chorus of those who say it must come to an end grows ever larger.[7,8] Whom shall we believe: the Technological Optimists, or the Limits Lobby? If we are wrong, which way of being wrong is more dangerous? What is the proper policy for the true conservative?[9]

The concept of carrying capacity calls for the conservative, balanced-equation type of thinking that has led to the triumphs of thermodynamics[10] and modern chemistry. But applied to human problems connected with exploiting the environment the concept of carrying capacity has been perceived as a threatening one. As regards populations of non-human animals and plants, we are just now beginning to grapple with the implications of carrying capacity. When it comes to humanity itself, it is doubtful if we yet have the courage to systematically examine all possibilities, as the following report by Nicholas Wade, from *Science* (1974) makes clear.

The famine that struck the six Sahelian zone countries of West Africa last year is thought to have killed some 100,000 people and left 7 million others dependent on foreigners' food handouts. The same or worse may happen again this year. The essence of the tragedy is that the famine was caused not by dry weather or some putative climatic change but, primarily, by man himself. Could not Western skills, applied in time, have saved the primitive nomads and slash-and-burn farmers from destroying their own land? Western intervention in the Sahel, Western science and technology, and the best intentioned efforts of donor agencies and governments over the last several decades, have in fact made a principal contribution to the destruction.

"One of the basic factors in the situation is overpopulation, both human and bovine, brought about by the application of modern science," says a former Food and Agricultural Organization (FAO) sociologist. According to a recent in-house report on the Sahel prepared by the Agency for International Development (AID), "To a large extent the deterioration of the subsistence base is directly attributable to the fact that man's interventions in the delicately balanced ecological zones bordering desert areas have usually been narrowly conceived and poorly implemented." "Too many of our projects have been singularly unproductive and . . . we have tediously reintroduced projects which ought never to have been attempted in the first place," says Michael M. Horowitz, a State University of New York anthropologist who has studied the nomad peoples of Niger. And, to quote the AID report again, "It must be recognized that assistance agencies have ignored the principles [of effective resource management], and the consequence of indiscriminate support has produced negative results or, on occasion, disaster."

The symptoms of distress in the Sahel are easier to perceive than the underlying causes of the disaster. The six countries concerned—Senegal, Mauritania, Mali, Upper Volta, Niger, and Chad—are former French colonies that stretch along the southern edge of the Sahara desert. [See Figure 13.1.] The land is mostly semidesert that enjoys only 4 months of rainfall a year. But the grasses are sufficient to support the herds of cattle tended by the nomads, and in the southern regions millet and sorghum are grown, together with cash crops such as peanuts and cotton. By 1970, just before the collapse, the fragile steppe and savannah ecology of the six countries was supporting some 24 million people and about the same number of animals. This burden amounted to roughly a third more people and twice as many animals as the land was carrying 40 years ago.

The agent of collapse was a drought—the third of such severity this century—which began in 1968 and cannot yet be said to have ended. The grasslands started turning to desert, the rivers dwindled to a trickle, and by 1972, the fifth year of the drought, people, cattle, and crops began to die. "Our country is already half desert and our arable lands left are extremely reduced," the director of Chad's water and forestry resources told

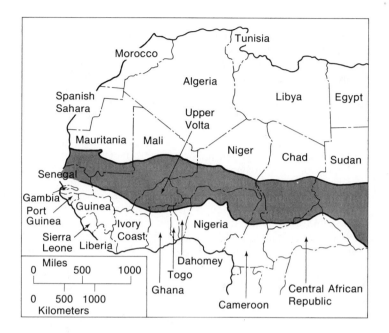

FIGURE 13.1

Sahelian zone countries. The Sahel also extends into Sudan and Ethiopia. (Map by Eleanor Warner.)

the FAO. By last year, Lake Chad had in places receded 15 miles from its former shorelines and split into three smaller lakes. The ancient cultural center of Timbuktu, a port fed by an inlet of the Niger river, was completely cut off and boats lay in the caked mud of its harbor. The nomads, forced to sell the surviving cattle that afforded their only means of subsistence, were reduced to the status of aimless refugees in camps around the major cities. Probably 5 million cattle perished, the staple grain crops produced low harvests, and nearly a third of the population faced a severe food shortage which, but for a massive infusion of relief supplies from the United States and other donors, would have ended in widespread famine.

Drought has clearly been the precipitating cause of the ecological breakdown in the Sahel, but attempts to blame the desiccation of the land wholly on the dry weather, or a supposed southward movement of the Sahara desert, do not quite hold water. A global weather change may indeed have squeezed the Sahel's usual rain belts southward, as climatologists such as H. H. Lamb argue, or, as others believe, the drought may be no more than an extreme expression of the Sahel's notoriously variable climate. The Sahara desert may indeed appear to be advancing downward into the Sahel—at the rate of 30 miles a year, according to a widely quoted estimate (which works out at 18 feet per hour). But the primary cause of the desertification is man, and the desert in the Sahel is not so much a natural expansion of the Sahara but is being formed *in situ* under the impact of human activity. "The desertification is man-caused, exacerbated by many years of lower rainfall," says Edward C. Fei, head of AID's Special Task Force on Sahelian Planning. According to the French hydrologist Marcel Roche, "The phenomenon of des-ertification, if it exists at all, is perhaps due to the process of human and animal occupation, certainly not to climatic changes."

Perhaps the most graphic proof of man's part in the desertification of the Sahel has come from a curiously shaped green pentagon discovered in a NASA satellite photograph by Norman H. MacLeod, an argonomist in American University, Washington, D.C. MacLeod found on a visit to the site of the pentagon that the difference between it and the sur-rounding desert was nothing more than a barbed wire fence. Within was a 250,000–acre ranch, divided into five sectors with the cattle allowed to graze one sector a year. Although the ranch was started only 5 years ago, at the same time as the drought began, the simple protection afforded the land was enough to make the difference between pasture and desert.

The physical destruction of the Sahel was not an overnight process. Its beginning can be traced to the French colonization of the late 19th century, when the Sahelian peoples lost with their political power the control over their range and wells which was vital to the proper manage-ment of their resources.

The Sahel—a term derived from the Arabic word for border—was once one of the most important areas of Africa. In the middle ages it was the home of the legendary trading empires of Ghana, Mali, and Songhai.

The key to the Sahelian way of life was a remarkably efficient adap-tation to the semidesert environment. Although the nomads' life-style may seem enviably free to those who dwell in cities, there is nothing random about their migrations. The dry season finds them as far south as they can go without venturing within the range of the tsetse fly. Be-tween the nomads and the sedentary farmers who also inhabit this area there is a symbiotic arrangement: The nomads' cattle graze the stubble of the crops and at the same time manure the fields. In exchange for manure the nomads receive millet from the farmers. With the first rains, the grass springs up and the herds move northward. The rains also move north and the cattle follow behind in search of new grass. According to Lloyd Clyburn of AID, "The migration continues as long as the grass ahead looks greener than that at hand, until the northern edge of the Sahelian rain belt is reached. When that grass is eaten off, the return to the south begins. This time the cattle are grazing a crop of grass that grew up behind them on their way north, and they are drinking standing water remaining from the rainy season." Back in their dry-season range the cattle find a crop of mature grass that will carry them for 8 or 9 months to the next growing season.

The traditional migration routes followed by the herds, and the amount of time a herd of given size might spend at a particular well, were governed by rules worked out by tribal chiefs. In this way overpasturage was avoided. The timing of the movement of animals was carefully cal-culated so as to provide feed and water with the least danger from disease and conflict with other tribal groups.

By virtue of what one writer has called "the essential ecological rationality of the nomadic pastoral regime," the herders made probably the best possible use of the land. The settled part of the population, the farmers, had an equally capable understanding of their environment. They knew to let the land lie fallow for long periods—up to 20 years—before recropping, and they developed an extraordinary number of varieties of their main staples, millet and sorghum, each adapted to different growing seasons and situations. Within the limits of their environment and technology, the peoples of the Sahel have, over the past centuries, demonstrated what University of London anthropologist Nicholas David calls "an impressive record of innovation . . . which is quite at variance with the common negative criticism of the African as unduly conservative." In fact, when the Sahelian peoples have been conservative and resisted changes advocated by Western experts, it has often been with reason.

It could be absurd to blame the collapse of this intricate social and ecological system solely on Western interference, and yet rather few Western interventions in the Sahel, when considered over the long term, have worked in the inhabitants' favor. Those who have studied the farmers' and herders' traditional methods, says an FAO report on the Sahel, believe that the destructive practices that are now frequent are due to the cumulative effects of "over-population, deterioration of the climatic conditions and, above all, the impact of the Western economic and social system."

Western intervention has made itself felt in many ways, some inadvertent, some deliberate. Introduction of a cash economy had profound effects on the traditional system. The French colonial division of the Sahel into separate states has faced the nomad tribes with national governments which have tried to settle them, tax them, and reduce their freedom of movement by preventing passage across state boundaries. Curiously, however, it has been the West's deliberate attempts to do good that seem to have caused the most harm. The West in this case means the French, up until 1960, when the Sahelian countries were granted independence, and the French, Americans, and others thereafter. The French should probably not be held particularly to blame; they were only following conventional wisdom, and there is little reason to believe that other donor countries would have handled the situation very differently.

The salient impact is of course the increase in human and animal population that followed the application of Western medicine. The people of the Sahel are increasing at a rate of 2.5 percent a year, one of the highest rates of population increase in the world. If the nomads could have been persuaded to kill more of their cattle for market, the animal population might have been kept within bounds. Not foreseen was the fact that cattle are the nomads' only means for saving, and it in fact makes good sense—on an individual basis—for a nomad to keep as many cattle on the hoof as he can.

As a result herd numbers increased hand over fist in the decade following independence, aided by 7 years of unusually heavy rains. According to the FAO, the number of cattle grew from about 18 to 25 million between 1960 and 1971. The optimum number, according to the World Bank, is 15 million.

While the herders were overtaxing the pastures, the farmers were doing the same to the arable land. Population increase led to more and more people trying to farm the land. An even sharper pressure was the introduction by the French of cash crops to earn foreign exchange. With the best lands given up to the cultivation of cotton and peanuts, people had to bring the more marginal lands into use to grow their own food crops. In many cases these ecologically fragile zones could not take the strain of intensive agriculture. The usual process is that the fallow periods of 15 to 20 years are reduced to five or even one. Fertility declines, slowly at first, and then in a vicious spiral. Poor crops leave the soil exposed to sun and wind. The soil starts to lose its structure. The rain, when it falls, is not absorbed but runs off uselessly in gulleys. Desertification has begun. "Let us be under no illusion," President Leopold Sedar Senghor of Senegal told a symposium on the African drought held in London last year, "the process of desertification had been precipitated since the conquest of Senegal [by the French], since the introduction of growing peanuts without either fallow or crop rotation."

What cash crops have done for the Sahelian farmland, deep borehole wells have done for the pasture. A thousand feet or more beneath the Sahel lie vast reservoirs of water that can be tapped by deep wells. Thousands of these boreholes, costing up to $200,000 apiece, have been drilled across the Sahel by well-intentioned donors. The effect of the boreholes was simply to make pasture instead of water the limiting factor on cattle numbers, so that the inevitable population collapse, when it came, was all the more ferocious. "Few sights were more appalling at the height of the drought last summer," according to environmental writer Claire Sterling in a recent article in *The Atlantic*, "than the thousands upon thousands of dead and dying cows clustered around Sahelian boreholes. Indescribably emaciated, the dying would stagger away from the water with bloated bellies and struggle to fight free of the churned mud at the water's edge until they keeled over. . . . Enormous herds, converging upon the new boreholes from hundreds of miles away, so ravaged the surrounding land by trampling and overgrazing that each borehole quickly became the center of its own little desert forty or fifty miles square."

Overgrazing of the Sahelian pasturelands was a consequence of too many cattle having too little place to go. As the farmers spreading out from the towns took more land under cultivation, they tended to squeeze the nomads and their herds into a smaller strip of space. Moreover, the nomads' ability to manage their own resources was slowly slipping away. Government interference reduced their freedom of movement, and the boreholes threw into chaos the traditional system of pasture use based on agreements among tribal chieftains. With all the old safeguards in abeyance, the cattle numbers began to chew up the ecology across the whole face of the Sahel. First the perennial grasses went. These usually grow up to 6 feet tall and put down roots as deep. If the plant is heavily grazed, its roots make a shallower penetration and, in dry periods, may fail to strike water. The perennial grasses are replaced by coarse annual grasses, but these, under heavy grazing and trampling, give way to leguminous plants that dry up quickly and cannot hold the soil together. Pulverized by the cattles' hooves, the earth is eroded by the wind, and the finer particles collect and are washed by rains to the bottom of slopes where they dry out into an impermeable cement.

Desertification has been hastened by the heavy cutting of trees for firewood. Trees recycle nutrients from deep in the soil and hold the soil together. Slash-and-burn techniques—the only practical method available to the poor farmer for clearing land—are the cause of numerous fires which, according to a World Bank estimate, kill off 50 percent of the range grass each year.

Under these abuses, the Sahel by the end of the 1960's was gripped by a massive land sickness which left it without the resilience to resist the drought. A whole vast area which might with appropriate management have become a breadbasket providing beef for half of Africa instead became a basket case needing more than $100 million worth of imported food just to survive.

The future prospects for the Sahel and its people are not very bright. Sahelian governments and the various donors have not reached any kind of agreement on long-term strategy for rehabilitation. Some donors—AID excepted—are still digging boreholes. Most of the development projects now under consideration were drawn up before the drought struck and are based on the unlikely assumption that when the rains return everything can go on as before. (A recent meeting of American climatologists concluded that planners should assume drought conditions in 2 years out of every 3.)

Much of the development money for the Sahel will have to come from the United States and France, but there seems to be little coordination or exchange of ideas between the two countries. Nor is there any general agreement on how the Sahel can be restored to self-sufficiency. Optimists, such as William W. Seifert of MIT, who heads a $1million long-term development study for AID, believe that the Sahel could support its present human population provided that cattle numbers were reduced by a half or more. Unfortunately, there is no way, short of a major social upheaval, that the nomads will consent to reduce their herds. Projects involving controlled grazing, such as in the Ekrafane ranch, are impractical because there is not enough land to go around. AID plans to open up the lands to the south of the Sahel by clearing them of tsetse fly, but this would benefit only 10 percent of the population. Others are not so hopeful. "I don't think there is much optimism that significant improvements can be expected in the short term. All you can do is to try to increase their margin for survival and hope that something turns up," says an agricultural specialist conversant with both the AID and MIT development plans.

"Neither the leverage of modern science and technology," concludes an in-house AID report on the Sahel, "nor the talents and resources of large numbers of individuals and institutions currently being applied to relevant problems has occasioned more than minor progress in combatting the natural resource problems and exploiting the undeveloped potential." Which is another way of saying that Western ideas for developing the Sahel have not proved to be a spectacular success. Its ecological fragility and the vagaries of its climate make the Sahel a special case. But there are many other areas in the world where unchecked populations are overloading environments of limited resilience. The Sahel may have come to grief so soon only because mistakes made there show up quickly. Other Western development strategies, such as the Green Revolution, are, one may hope, more soundly based in ecological and social realities. If not, the message of the Sahel is that the penalty for error is the same Malthusian check which it is the purpose of development to avoid, except that the crash is from a greater height.[11]

A curious feature of this excellent report is that nowhere does it specifically point out that the tragedy in the Sahel is precisely the tragedy of the commons, though the detailed account could hardly be improved upon as an illustrative example. The ommission is especially curious because the report was published in *Science,* the journal in which "The Tragedy of the Commons" was published six years earlier.

The significance of Wade's report did not escape bioethicist Van Rensselaer Potter, who wrote in a letter to the editor:[12]

> The report on the Sahelian drought by Nicholas Wade . . . is a dramatic illustration of "the tragedy of the commons" as described by Hardin.
> When I first read Hardin's article, I wondered if the users of the early English commons weren't prevented from committing the fatal error of overgrazing by a kind of "bioethics" enforced by the moral pressure of their neighbors. Indeed, the commons system operated successfully in England for several hundred years. Now we read that, before the colonial era in the Sahel, "overpasturage was avoided" by rules worked out by tribal chiefs. When deep wells were drilled to obtain water "the boreholes threw into chaos the traditional system of pasture use based on agreements among tribal chieftains." Thus, we see the tragedy of the commons not as a defect in the concept of a "commons" but as a result of the disastrous transition period between the loss of an effective bioethic and its replacement by a new bioethic that could once again bring biological realities and human values into a viable balance.[13]

The distinction between the old way of treating common property in the Sahel and the new way can be seen in terms of the political responsibility table given in Chapter 9 (Table 9.1). In the old days, the Sahelian environment was managed approximately according to the system of Case II, using informal sanctions ("an effective bioethic," in Potter's words). Then, as a result of intervention by well-meaning men of the European culture, part of the environment—the grazing land—was changed to Case III management, with the usual tragic results.

Mind-boggling photographs of the earth from space played an important role in bringing home this tragedy. There is no necessary logical connection between a mere photograph and the idea of conservation; but, as Marshall McLuhan has said, "The media is the message" and in our visually oriented society a striking photograph can become the symbol of an idea or a program.

In 1965, shortly before his death, while he was the U.S. Ambassador to the United Nations, Adlai Stevenson made a most memorable statement:

> We travel together, passengers on a little spaceship, dependent on its vulnerable reserves of air and soil; all committed for our safety to its security and peace; preserved from annihilation only by the care, the work and, I will say, the love we give our fragile craft.

The "we" of this statement is presumably all of the earth's inhabitants. It became a cliché of environmental activism to place Stevenson's statement alongside a blow-up of a NASA photograph of the earth as seen from space. The message implicit in this justification was evidently something of this sort: "This little blue ball, this unity, this Earth must surely be treated as a unity." What the activists did not realize was that they were calling for treating the earth as a commons—with all the perils that implies.

The atmosphere and the seas are certainly global commons, but (as we have seen) global methods for managing them have not yet been devised. As regards environmental problems generally, Raymond Dasmann has remarked that "Those of us in international organizations are likely to assume a globalist viewpoint." Dasmann, who is himself a member of such an organization, then goes on to point out that "only a few environmental problems are really global in nature." When one realizes this, one is apt to ask rather interesting questions about the motivation of people who insist on treating nonglobal questions globally.

Faint beginnings of a shift in public attitude could be detected following the reproduction of the NASA photograph that showed the green hexagon in west Africa referred to in Wade's article. The resolution of this photograph from space was not very good, but its meaning was clear. The green part was restricted to the area protected (as private property) from uncontrolled grazing, while the dead-looking area around it was an unmanaged commons. Follow-up ground surveys verified this interpretation and noted the effect of environmental degradation on the grazers, the cattle. As William Forster Lloyd had cogently asked in 1833: "Why are the cattle on a common so puny and stunted? Why is the common itself so bare-worn, and cropped so differently from the adjoining inclosures?"

For more than three centuries intellectual and emotional fashions have increasingly veered toward the global outlook. Our thoughts have been significantly molded by John Donne's "No man is an island . . ." and Karl Marx's ". . . to each according to his needs." The thoughts engendered by these banners are generous thoughts, whereas speaking of local responsibility for local environments seems to many to be a miserly and selfish way of looking at the world's problems. There are a thousand to praise generosity for every one who has a kind word to say for selfishness. Yet biology clearly tells us that survival requires a respect for carrying capacity, and points to the utility of territorial behavior in protecting the environment and insuring the survival of populations. Surely posterity matters. Surely there's something to be said for selfishness.

Altruism versus selfishness: It is all too easy to polarize the argument, to maintain the univalence of facts. But the facts are ambivalent, as wise men have recognized for millenia. A Talmudic saying puts the matter rather well:

> If I am not for myself, who will be for me?
> If I am for myself only, what am I?
> If not now—when?

Notes

1. Garrett Hardin, 1974. "The rational foundation of conservation." *North American Review,* **259** (4) :14–17.
2. David R. Klein, 1968. "The introduction, increase, and crash of reindeer on St. Matthew Island." *Journal of Wildlife Management,* **32**:350–367.
3. Joseph Fletcher, 1966. *Situation Ethics.* Philadelphia: Westminster Press.
4. Garrett Hardin, 1972. *Exploring New Ethics for Survival: The Voyage of the Spaceship Beagle.* New York: Viking. (Chap. 16)
5. P. MacAvoy, ed. 1970. *The Crisis of the Regulatory Commissions.* New York: Norton.
6. Garrett Hardin, 1973. *Stalking the Wild Taboo.* Los Altos, Calif.: Kaufmann. (p. xi)
7. Donella H. Meadows, Dennis L. Meadows, Jørgen Randers, and William W. Behrens III, 1972. *The Limits to Growth.* New York: Universe Books.
8. Mihajlo Mesarovic and Eduard Pestel, 1974. *Mankind at the Turning Point.* New York: Dutton. Unlike the "first report to the Club of Rome" (note 7 above), the "second report" does not aggregate the world's natural resources but seeks to deal with them on a regional basis. In going from facts to implications, however, this second report is not always consistent. See Garrett Hardin, 1975. "Will humanity learn from nature?" *Sierra Club Bulletin,* **60** (8):41–43.
9. It is one of the ironies of history that those who are generally labelled as economic "conservatives" at the present time are people who believe in limitless growth and hence see no need for what scientists regard as truly *conservative* thinking, that is, thinking in which the variables are conserved, and in which equations balance. For a particularly emotional defense of

the conventional wisdom see Melvin J. Grayson and Thomas R. Shepard, Jr., 1973. *The Disaster Lobby: Prophets of Ecological Doom and Other Absurdities.* Chicago: Follett.

A book with a similar message, by the editor of the English journal *Nature,* is more sophisticated but scarcely better: John Maddox, 1972. *The Doomsday Syndrome.* New York: McGraw-Hill. For the most intellectual criticism of the limits to growth thesis see H. S. D. Cole, Christopher Freeman, Marie Jahoda and K. L. R. Pavitt, 1973. *Models of Doom: A Critique of The Limits to Growth.* New York: Universe Books. This, the American edition of the "Sussex Report", has the merit of including a postscript by the Meadows, et al. that throws much light on the nature of the controversy.

10. Nicholas Georgescu-Roegen, 1971. *The Entropy Law and the Economic Process.* Cambridge, Mass.: Harvard University Press. This is the only book published to date that sets economic theory on a firm foundation of thermodynamics, thus bringing together economics and ecology. (Etymologically, this is as it should be, since both words use the Greek root *oikos,* home. Both are concerned with the management of the "home," which classical economics sees almost entirely as made up of men only, with other organisms and the physical environment playing the role of "givens"—to which little attention is *given.* In the perspective of ecology, however, all organisms, as well as nonliving elements of the environment, are viewed as coexisting and interacting variables in this earthly home of ours.)

11. Nicholas Wade, 1974. "Sahelian drought: no victory for Western aid." *Science,* **185**:234–237. Copyright 1974 by the American Association for the Advancement of Science.

12. Van Rensselaer Potter, 1974. "The tragedy of the Sahel commons." *Science,* **185**:183. Copyright 1974 by the American Association for the Advancement of Science.

13. Van Rennsselaer Potter, 1971. *Bioethics: Bridge to the Future.* Englewood Cliffs, N.J.: Prentice-Hall.

14

Rewards of Pejoristic Thinking

Garrett Hardin

The geneticist Theodosius Dobzhansky[1] tells a charming story of a Victorian lady's reaction to Darwin's evolution theory. Informed that the theory implied the descent of man from apelike creatures, the wife of the Canon of Worcester Cathedral cried out, "Descended from the apes! My dear, we hope it is not true. But if it is, let us pray that it may not become generally known!"

The reactions of many people at the present time to the tragedy of the commons is similar to this. There are a number of plausible explanations. For one thing, the legacy of Rousseau is not yet lost: there are still many people who think that man is essentially good and that we should be able to build the Good Society on this assumption. Their utopias avoid coercion. Then, too, there is the pessimism-optimism disjunction. In the popular mind pessimism is seen as an evil, optimism as a good. The tragedy of the commons is regarded as pessimistic and hence unacceptable.

There is certainly much to be said for optimism. Optimists are often pleasanter to be with than pessimists. Pessimism saps the vitality of a man of action. Optimism creates a climate of opinion favorable to finding venture capital and embarking on grand commercial projects. Optimism justifies individual liberty and the idea of *laissez faire*—letting each person "do his own thing," confident that all will turn out for the best in the end, both for the individual and for society as a whole. The most famous justification of *laissez faire* is that which Adam Smith gave in 1776:

> Every individual . . . indeed, neither intends to promote the public interest, nor knows how much he is promoting it. By preferring the support

of domestic to that of foreign industry, he intends only his own security; and by directing that industry in such a manner as its produce may be of the greatest value, he intends only his own gain, and he is in this, as in many other cases, led by an invisible hand to promote an end which was no part of his intention.[2]

This was said at the very peak of the Age of Reason. Intoxicated with rationality, the intellectual leaders of the day had pretty well thrown overboard all belief in a providential God, one who provides for and takes care of mankind. Many no longer used the word God in serious discourse. But it is easier to jettison the label of a belief than the belief itself. Under the guidance of Adam Smith, providential God was replaced by providential *laissez faire,* and mankind continued in much the same way as before, bumbling along without policy, each man doing his own thing, trusting in the providence of the "invisible hand" to convert private gain into public benefit.

The historical importance of Smith's invisible hand in delaying the development of public policy in the commercial realm is well known. It is astonishing how powerful an effective metaphor can be in suppressing recognition of contradictory facts.[3] We were well into the 20th century before there was significant legal recognition of the fact that unrestrained *laissez faire* did not always lead to social good. Anti-trust laws and the Pure Food and Drug Act were among the first such recognitions to be embodied in the law. An even more far-reaching limitation of *laissez faire* was the National Environmental Protection Act of 1970, which in effect said that all future interventions in the environment would be evaluated by the principle of "Guilty until proven innocent," a reversal of the assumption of English law.[4]

Belief in the efficacy of the invisible hand has persisted longer in the area of philanthropy. As explained in Chapter 9, philanthropy (no matter how meritorious) is in its essence irresponsible and not subject to "the discipline of the market place." There are more than a few philanthropists who act as if all that is necessary to help the poor is to anoint them with money and then leave them alone to work out their own salvation (guided, presumably, by some sort of invisible intelligence that seems not to have supervised their affairs hitherto). That such a belief is in fact held is shown by a statement made to the Democratic Party Platform Committee by Dr. George A. Wiley[5] in 1968: "The basic cure for poverty is money. We believe that the way to do something about poverty is to give people the money they need . . . without degrading investigations and harassments." There is no perception here of poverty as a *process,* only of poverty as a *state.* States are easily altered; processes are not. People in the grip of processes, as Kenneth Boulding has pointed out, all too often act as if they were propelled by an "invisible foot."

Our trust in the providence of *laissez faire* is greatest in the area of international philanthropy (where we are farthest from the objects of our attentions). Political intervention in the affairs of foreign nations is no longer fashionable; on the whole this is a good thing. In addition, anthropologists have convinced us of the complexity of all cultures, even the poorest, and the difficulty of bringing about cultural change that will produce the beneficent results desired. So we take the easy way out. Trusting in the invisible hand of philanthropy, we now shower billions of dollars onto poor nations, enabling them to build dams, sink wells, plant crops, generate electricity, build factories, spray with DDT, staff hospitals, inject penicillin, and install IUDs in the uteruses of women firmly entrapped in the mystique of pronatalism. Beyond the initial gift, *laissez faire* prevails. That is to say, we still believe in providence.

For a quarter of a century international philanthropy has been largely guided by optimistic *laissez faire* doctrines, and now there are a billion more poor people than there were when we started trying to save the world. Belief in providence dies hard. One is reminded of Bertrand Russell's cynical aphorism: "Men would rather die than think. Some do."

But it is not necessary to fail from inadvertence. The *laissez faire* of Adam Smith is not the only philosophy available as a guide. There is at hand another philosophy—using the word "philosophy" in an imprecise but popular sense—that is even older, though less often mentioned. I refer to the guiding spirit of Gresham's Law, enunciated in 1558 by Sir Thomas Gresham, but commonly stated in words used by H. D. Macleod in 1857: "Bad money drives out good." It will be worth our while to look deeply at the implications of this "law," to see how it differs in spirit from *laissez faire.*

The practical situation that leads to Gresham's Law is quite simple. Imagine a country in which two sorts of coins are circulating: real coins and counterfeit ones. In the course of time, what will happen? Whenever a person with two coins in his pocket, one genuine and one counterfeit, decides to use one to buy something from a vending machine, which one will he use? Most probably the counterfeit one, saving the genuine coin for some occasion when it is more difficult to pass a counterfeit. Not everyone need behave this way to produce the effect Gresham postulated; but many will. As a result, with the passage of time, bad money drives good out of circulation (as people store the good coins under the mattress). The process is devastating to commerce, of course, and the state intervenes. Invoking the naked power of coercive laws, rulers make it a criminal offense to manufacture or circulate counterfeit coins. States behaved in this way long before the explicit statement of Gresham's Law.

Let us imagine someone who was absolutely convinced that *laissez faire* is the only right approach to all problems. Were we to follow such advice in monetary matters, we would allow genuine and counterfeit coins to compete freely in the market place, confident that an invisible hand would protect us. Needless to say, disillusionment would soon follow.

Enthusiasts of individual freedom often acknowledge the existence of evil in the world, but they believe that the majority of mankind is basically good and that the majority is decisive in determining what happens. Sometimes this may be true; but there are many social processes that work in such a way that even the smallest minority spoils the results.

Suppose the great majority of men and women are paragons of virtue and refuse to pass on counterfeit coins: will their behavior negate Gresham's Law? Not at all; the process by which the law prevails takes place in two steps. First of all, a call for voluntary compliance would be counterproductive: it would reward noncooperators, who would prosper. Secondly, when the hypothesized majority who had complied observed the increasing prosperity of the minority who had not, the majority would be overcome by envy. Some would defect, and the ranks of the non-cooperators would swell. A vicious circle would thus be established and soon all but an unimportant residue of true believers in Rousseauan goodness would be living out Gresham's Law.

We often use the cliche, "overwhelming majority"; the process we have just described is obviously driven by an *overwhelming minority*. If humanity were not infected with the poison of envy, social processes might not work in this way and we could rely on individualistic voluntarism instead of laws. But we are descended from an unbroken line of envious ancestors, and it would be unwise to assume that we are any different. Those few of us who are are less likely to be the ancestors of posterity. As Leo Durocher said: "Nice guys finish last." Our ancestors did not finish last.

Note that when we are dealing with a monetary system a policy of voluntary compliance fails no matter how small the initial minority of noncooperators. *Only a minority of zero would permit a voluntary system to work.* Obviously we would be fools to adopt any political or economic system that functions successfully only if literally everyone is virtuous.

The problem of dealing with "error" (noncompliance, in the example given) is millennia old. The mathematician John von Neumann has called for a new attitude toward variation and error.[6] In working out the logic of computer construction, von Neumann saw that it was nonproductive to complain of the unreliability of the elements used in making them. Error, said he, is customarily viewed "as an extraneous and misdirected or misdirecting accident" to which we react by devising nongeneral, ad hoc solutions. It is far more fruitful, he said, to accept error and unreliability as essential characteristics of the components, and then devise systems that are reliable in spite of the unreliability of their parts. Paradoxical though it may sound, it is, said von Neumann, possible to synthesize reliable organisms from unreliable components. To do this one must *accept* component unreliability in much the same sense that a psychoanalyst accepts the vagaries of his patients. A political or economic system that works must similarly accept humanity as it is, "warts and all."

Once we adopt a systematic rather than an ad hoc view of error, the pessimism-optimism disjunction is less attractive. Is it pessimistic to hold that "Bad money drives out good"? Is it pessimistic to believe in the law of gravity which (in a simple form) says that "All that goes up must come down"? Calling either law pessimistic seems rather silly, and is certainly nonproductive. The law of gravity is not an *ad hoc* thing, but "of the essence" of the world. By accepting it we are enabled to devise flying machines that do what we want in spite of the apparent prohibition of the simple statement of the law. So also, by accepting Gresham's Law are we enabled to devise stable monetary systems. It is usually when we forget the inescapability of this law that we permit unwise tinkering with the monetary system that brings the economic system down in ruins. If it is pessimistic to believe in Gresham's Law, then we must admit that the survival of civilization is dependent on pessimists being in control.

Obviously we need a better disjunction than that based on optimism and pessimism. One is at hand, and this is the meliorism-pejorism disjunction.[7] The Latin root *meliorare* means to become or to make better; *pejorare* means to become or to make worse. Both refer to processes. Optimist and pessimist, by contrast, are derived from *optimum* and *pessimum*, which refer to states. Maintaining this distinction between process and state permits us to create two useful new words, meliorist and pejorist (which are not, therefore, synonyms of optimist and pessimist). In the light of what we know of the power of Freudian denial it is perhaps significant that meliorist is to be found in English dictionaries, but pejorist is not.

A melioristic process is one that continually tends to improve—something. In spite of the popularity of meliorism as an attitude, it is not easy to think of purely melioristic processes. One that comes to mind is the process of domestication of grains with respect to the property of "shattering." The heads of wild grasses naturally shatter early, scattering the seeds on the ground. It is in the interest of the propagation and dispersal of the species that shattering should occur. But when "man" (probably really *women*) began gathering seeds it was to his interest that shattering be delayed, preferably indefinitely. By planting only the seeds he gathered—he could hardly do otherwise!—man selected for nonshattering genes. Without any conscious program at all, the beginning of plant domestication started a melioristic process.

Pejoristic processes are easier to descry. Every pesticide, for example, selects for its own failure. (DDT, for instance, selects for DDT-resistant flies.) The rhythm method of birth control selects for arhythmic women.[8] Voluntary population control selects for philoprogenitive instincts that mock at the system.[9] Free competition among currencies selects for bad money.

The distinction between pessimist and pejorist can be seen as rooted in motivation. A pessimist settles for describing the evil of the world without being motivated to do anything about it. It is no wonder that the generality of mankind represses the pessimist's descriptions. A pejorist, by contrast, looking for the providential workings of things, is likely to look also for ways of improving the system. In the realm of money, a pessimist may be satisfied to observe that everybody is so damned selfish, and to settle for the minimum policy of "Let every man look out for himself, and the devil take the hindmost."

A good pejorist would refuse to regard this as acceptable policy; he would look for some way whereby men might collectively band together to create a more acceptable system. Laws that specify penalties for counterfeiting are the pejorist's response to the wishful thinking of the optimists and the cynicism of the pessimists. The pessimist is unhappy because he is cynical, the optimist because he is soon disillusioned; only a pejorist can be truly happy. He is busy trying to remake the world nearer to the heart's desire—and with occasional success.

Perhaps this all seems terribly obvious, but I think it needs to be said. Though men have long assumed the general applicability of *laissez faire,* they have not hitherto generalized from Gresham's Law to policy. In effect, they have treated this law as a special case. Had its generality been recognized earlier, we might sooner have recognized that in an unmanaged commons, greedy herdsmen drive out considerate ones, grasping hunters drive out moderate ones, polluting industries drive out clean, and rapidly reproducing parents displace those who accept the limits to growth.

That such statements have not been encouraged is understandable. They sound like the sort of thing pessimists say, and the common man distrusts pessimists because they all too often prefer to nourish insoluble problems rather than to look honestly for solutions. The pejorist differs from the pessimist in taking the negative statement as the beginning of action, not the end of it. As Francis Bacon said, "Nature to be commanded must be obeyed." Both pejorists and pessimists begin by obeying; the pejorist then takes the next step and seeks a way to command nature (at least in part).

A serious charge to be laid against the optimist is that he is unwilling to obey nature even at the outset. Let me illustrate this point with some examples taken from the theory of population control.

Kingsley Davis[10] has identified as the "Population Establishment" a group of men and women who are united in believing that population control can be achieved under the guidance of *laissez faire*. Society need supply only the means of birth control and population control will follow automatically, without pain, without policy, without coercion. Being composed of kindly people, the Population Establishment wants to give poor people both contraceptives and food, under *laissez faire* conditions. On a priori grounds this is a risky course to follow. In all other species of animals, better nutrition produces higher fertility. Why should man be an exception? The Establishment hopes, and apparently believes, that man *is* an exception, but the best that can be mustered in the way of evidence is always ambiguous and often contradictory. The burden of proof surely lies on anyone who asserts that better nutrition will cause a lowering of fertility. Feeling the weight of this burden the proponents of that view should present their evidence in the clearest and most rigorous terms. Alas! they do not. Language is tailored to fit a belief in providence. Two examples from Establishment publications will serve:

> Alleviation of childhood and maternal malnutrition could encourage smaller families.

> Possibilities for successful contraceptive programs may be enhanced if women's nutrition improves.

The key words in these sentences are *could* and *may*. Where the pessimist avoids acting by clinging to presumed insolubilities, the optimist avoids decision by saying nothing definite. . . . Almost anything *could* be true; almost anything *may* happen.

The grand tradition of all serious investigation is to *risk* saying something, to risk one's reputation in order that the work of understanding the world may go forward. For an example, consider the following passage from Chapter VI of Darwin's *Origin of Species:*

> Natural selection cannot possibly produce any modification in a species exclusively for the good of another species, though throughout nature one species incessantly takes advantage of and profits by the structures of others. But natural selection can and does often produce structures for the direct injury of other animals, as we see in the fang of the adder, and in the ovipositor of the ichneumon, by which its eggs are deposited in the living bodies of other insects. If it could be proved that any part of the structure of any species had been formed for the exclusive good of another species, it would annihilate my theory, for such could not have been produced through natural selection.

"Natural selection *cannot possibly* . . ."—What a contrast with the mushy *could* and *may* of the optimists! With this unqualified, unambiguous statement of the implications of his theory, Darwin cuts himself off from all possibility of a strategic retreat. Even a single instance of exclusive "do-goodism" on the part of a single species serving the needs of another would (Darwin acknowledges) annihilate his theory. No finer example of intellectual courage is imaginable; nothing less will do for the gaining of secure knowledge.

Bad money drives out good. Perpetual motion machines are impossible. There is no such thing as a free lunch. Pure altruism has no survival value. The end result of an unmanaged commons in a crowded world is tragedy. . . . It is with blunt statements like these that we uncover the mystery of the world—and learn to cope with it.

* * *

To those who have research ambitions in the social and political field, one bit of advice can be given with confidence: the payoff is in pejorisms. For two related reasons.

First, there is the concentrating effect resulting from previous investigations that had a melioristic bias. In the beginning, all the unknown principles of the world constituted a certain mixture of melioristic and pejoristic principles. Since people prefer to think pleasant thoughts, thoughts that do not imperil the status quo, they discover the melioristic ones first. Adam Smith's "invisible hand" is a good example. Selective blindness also leads observers to overlook the limitations of meliorism, as they stretch the evidence. They search avidly for more melioristic applications, with some success. The result of all this selection is to leave the collection of principles-yet-to-be-discovered relatively richer in pejorisms. Consequently the pejoristically-minded investigator finds the research mine increasingly rich in his kind of ore.

The second reason focuses on the minds instead of the mine. Since Freudian denial is a normal resting point of human minds the minority who are fortunate enough to escape the clutches of denial have few to compete with. Fewer competitors and richer pay-dirt—what more could one ask? We should not complain too bitterly if most people, by one rhetorical device or another, justify their avoidance of pejoristic thinking.

Notes

1. Theodosius Dobzhansky, 1956. *The Biological Basis of Human Freedom.* New York: Columbia University Press. (p. 3)
2. Adam Smith, 1776. *The Wealth of Nations.* (Book IV, Chap. II)

3. For a pejoristic discussion of the limits of *laissez faire* see Chap. 21, "The cybernetics of competition: a biologist's view of society," in Garrett Hardin, 1973. *Stalking the Wild Taboo.* Los Altos, Calif.: Kaufmann.

4. See Chap. 7, "Guilty until proven innocent," in Garrett Hardin, 1972. *Exploring New Ethics for Survival: The Voyage of the Spaceship Beagle.* New York: Viking.

5. Quoted in *I. F. Stone's Weekly,* **16**(18):2, 9 September 1968.

6. John von Neumann, 1956. "Probabilistic logics and the synthesis of reliable organisms from unreliable components." In *Collected Works,* **5**:329–78. New York: Macmillan. (p. 329)

7. First proposed in 1974 by Garrett Hardin in an essay reprinted as Chapter 25 in this volume. There are some differences between the use of the word pejorism in that chapter and the present one. Describing the differences is "an exercise left to the reader."

8. Garrett Hardin, 1963. "A second sermon on the mount." *Perspectives in Biology and Medicine,* **6**:266–71. (Reprinted in the book cited in note 3 above.)

9. Charles Galton Darwin, 1960. "Can man control his numbers?" In *Evolution After Darwin,* Sol Tax, ed. Chicago: University of Chicago Press.

10. Kingsley Davis, 1973. "Zero population growth: the goal and the means." In *The No-Growth Society,* Mancur Olson and Hans H. Landsberg, eds. New York: Norton.

PART III

Grappling with the Commons

15

A Primer for the Management of Common Pool Resources

John Baden

The fundamental truth that people in a commons have an incentive to ignore the social impact of private behavior provides the key to developing plans for managing the commons. Their behavior adversely affects social welfare, generating a demand for governmental intervention. The following essays analyze various types of intervention and their expected outcome. In each case, some constraint on individual freedom is imposed in order to preclude a greater loss. Questions of equity, freedom, and morality are quite near the surface. It is not surprising that discussions involving the management of common pool resources often resemble religious arguments conducted by nontheologians. The primary goal of this and the following essays is to offer an orderly perspective on issues that have in the past been muddled and confused.

Why Recourse to Political Organization?

There is a danger inherent in reliance upon political organization: government involves coercion rather than willing consent to coordinate behavior. Even the few surviving classical anarchists acknowledge the necessity for occasionally relaxing the rule of willing consent.

We generally find that the market tends to be an under-appreciated and misunderstood mechanism for generating cooperative behavior.

Among the compelling advantages of market-coordinated behavior are that it moves people voluntarily to participate and that prices serve as effective and efficient coordinating, rationing, and incentive-generating devices. It is generally agreed that a government is needed for at least the following purposes: to serve as an arbiter among parties when disagreements arise; to protect the weak from the strong; and to prevent market forces from being disrupted and distorted by monopolists and other factors. Government is needed also to enforce property rights and to maintain a context of law and order in which productive social relations can be undertaken. I believe that among the sane we could obtain perfect agreement that all of the above functions must be carried out in a modern society if social welfare is to be served. The key question then becomes, to what extent should the scope of government be expanded beyond those tasks?

The Expansion of Action: Public Goods and Common Pool Resources

A public good is one which, if available for anyone, is available for everyone. (A similar definition applies to public bads.) This suggests that the good is not easily packageable and hence people cannot be excluded from its consumption; in other words, property rights cannot be readily established for public goods. Standard examples of public goods have included the benefits derived from national defense, lighthouses, or mosquito control programs. If people cannot be excluded from the benefits of these programs, they do not ordinarily have an incentive to contribute to the provision of such goods. In the market context, where willing consent is required for action, these goods will be undersupplied. To correct this, governmental action, in the form of tax collecting, is instituted.

There are exceptions to these generalizations. First, in small groups (as in some communal situations) social pressure can induce contributions for public goods. Second, if there is a situation in which the private benefit from providing a public good is greater than its private costs, the public good will be supplied privately. An example of this situation occurs when a logging company maintains a road to a public area used by hunters, snowmobilers, and other recreationists. This, of course, is done to provide access for the company. The provision of the public good is a positive externality generated by the company's selfish action.

The second area where governmental action is required is the management of common pool resources. Briefly, a common pool resource is a resource for which there are multiple owners (or a number of people who have rights to use the resource) and where one or a set of users can have adverse effects upon the interests of other users. In the situation where there is no agency with the power to coordinate or to ration use, action which is individually rational can be collectively disastrous. This is the central point of the "tragedy of the commons."

As a simple example, assume a valley airshed that has air-breathing citizens and two copper smelters owned by different companies. In this situation, the air is the common pool resource and the breathing citizens and the copper smelters are the resource users. If it is costly to reduce the air pollution caused by the smelters, and the damage done by the smelters is greater than the cost of cleaning the air, there is a net advantage to be gained by controlling pollution. Yet the copper companies cannot be expected voluntarily to reduce their despoliation. A relaxation of the rule of willing consent is necessary, therefore, to reduce pollution and increase social welfare.

An alternative example involves the overexploitation of a common pool resource. If we consider whales or salmon a common pool resource with independent harvesters, each harvester has an incentive to maximize his catch. In the absence of collective management and rationing of the resource, we can expect the catch to go beyond sustained yield. Further, after it is understood that the resource is being depleted, we often find overinvestment in harvesting technology as each resource user tries to sustain his catch in the face of a diminishing resource.

Thus, in the absence of clear property rights to the resource and of a coordinating arrangement based on some rule other than that of willing consent, the resource will be unnecessarily depleted. Furthermore, a socially inefficient capital investment will be made in the equipment required to harvest the resource. Imagine, if you can, the dynamics we would find in the national forests if all the timber were suddenly put up for grabs on a cut out and get out basis with no provision for owner-ship and storage of the stumpage. In addition to a speedy mining of the forests, there would be great overinvestment in logging machinery. This example is directly analogous to the behavior found in the exploitation of common pool resources in the absence of institutions geared to manage and ration the resource and to adjudicate conflicts among the competing users.

Private Solutions

There are situations in which significant social advantages may be gained by establishing agencies and bureaucracies and assigning them respon-sibilities and power. In principle, it would be possible to accomplish the same ends through voluntary agreements among the interested parties. In practice, however, we always encounter a number of factors that preclude this solution except by groups small enough to coordinate and enforce behavior on a face-to-face basis. A common pool resource is managed or a public good provided because these actions are projected to increase social welfare. If this can be demonstrated to the satisfaction of all parties involved, why must one resort to governmental action? Why will this action not be undertaken voluntarily?

The Free-Rider Problem

The first reason is the free-rider problem. Assume we know from energy cycling studies that by investing 200 units in nutrient enrichment, fish production will be increased by 1000 units in a fishery resource harvested by 400 commercial fishermen. Also assume that there are no relevant externalities involved in the nutrient enrichment program. Clearly, there are great advantages to such a program. In this situation, however, each fisherman has an incentive to avoid contributing his share of the 200 units. If he doesn't contribute and others do, he will be far ahead, having withheld his contributions from the enrichment program to invest his half unit in more effective harvesting tools. (This is true if we assume, within the range given here, a linear relationship between enrichment and production. Obviously, if we were dealing with a step function whose first threshold was encountered between the 199.5 unit and the 200 unit in investment, then the marginal contribution of the last fisherman would be enhanced. Such possibilities should not detract from the thrust of the example.) The marginal improvement of any one contribution would be spread over the 400 fishermen. So unless each fisherman knows that he can collect a share of the marginal improvement generated by the contribution of each of the other 399 fishermen, it is to his advantage not to invest in the program and to be a free rider on the backs of those who do contribute. Under such assumptions, no fisherman would contribute his share.

It is thus necessary to relax the rule of willing consent and rely upon the potential for coercion (governmental action) if the resource is to be rationally managed. A similar logic is involved in efforts to protect or improve the quality of an airshed or a body of water. In each case, reliance upon voluntary agreement yields a less than optimal resource base. To what degree is freedom to be sacrificed through the replacement of willing consent by coercion in order to protect or enhance an environmental resource? One of the most substantial costs of an increasing population is precisely the sacrifice in freedom necessitated by the need for maximizing production in a context of increasing interdependence and increasing demands on the resource base. In general, the world is taking on an ever-greater resemblance to a common pool.

Decision-Making or Bargaining Costs

In the absence of enforceable property rights to a resource or service, it is extremely difficult for those involved to reach voluntary agreements. Clearly, two neighbors may be able to agree to construct and maintain a lane serving their contiguous holdings. Because the marginal costs of additional usage tend to be quite low, each has an incentive to come to an agreement with the other. In principle this could be extended to *n* parties.

However, it is obvious that there are at least two sets of costs involved in building the road. First, there is the actual cost of construction and maintenance. Second, there are the opportunity costs associated with the time spent in agreeing how to finance and administer the road. The number of possible roads is quite large and there is a finite probability of my wanting to use any road physically accessible to me, though this probability increases as the proximity of the road to my holdings increases. I have a potential interest in a very large number of roads. If I attended negotiations for each road in which I have an interest, I would not have time for anything else. Hence, the opportunity costs of voluntary agreement become grossly unreasonable.

We can now develop a general statement describing the role of governmental action. As Gordon Tullock has remarked, government is nothing more than a prosaic instrument designed to coordinate human behavior through potential resort to coercion when the costs associated with reliance upon voluntary agreement are considered to be excessively high by a group of people possessing sufficient power to set and enforce the rules under which rules are made. That sentence contains the rationale for instituting a government; it is the definitive rejection of anarchy.

Dangers Inherent in Bureaucracies

In the previous sections, I have tried to explain why there are situations in which net welfare can be enhanced by relaxing the rule of willing consent and permitting coercion for the coordination of human affairs. This, however, was not to suggest that the assignment of decision-making capabilities on other than a voluntary basis and the establishment of bureaus and agencies to provide goods and services will necessarily result in welfare gains. Unless careful attention is given to the information and incentives with which bureaucrats are provided, the order the bureau was established to provide will occur only rarely. Following are some examples to aid in understanding this problem, with the hope that improvements in bureaucratic performance will result.

The Potential for Bureaucratic Performance
in a Common Pool Situation

Consider an airshed with a capacity for assimilating X_1 industrial stack emissions, X_2 metric tons of auto pollutants, and X_3 metric tons of natural pollutants (aerosols from conifer forests, etc.) with a very low environmental cost. Assume that dispersion rates are fixed and that X_n is accepted as optimal. Assume no interactions among the pollutants. Accepting natural pollution as optimal, our concern is with the impact of $X_1 + X_2$, and with the costs of controlling each variable. Current pollution production, however, is running at $4X_1$ and $2X_2$ with an environment cost, reckoned as $16. Not all environmental costs can be satisfactorily converted to dollars, but this is the best tool we have in our kit. For an expenditure of $2 the cost of the pollution damage could be reduced to $4. There is a net gain of $10 (minus administrative costs). Thus, instituting an agency to compel rather modest investments in pollution control produces substantial gains in environmental quality. (For social efficiency, we would want to stop control when the marginal benefit of the improvement equalled the marginal cost of additional control. This point is discussed later.)

Assume a game herd with a sustained yield potential of y if in an unmanaged habitat (A), and y_{ma} if in a managed habitat (D), as illustrated in Figure 15.1.

Note that with no rationing (via pricing, lottery, etc.) and no management, at zero price the demand for the game animal will be greater than the sustained yield. Hence, after a short period of time, the herd may

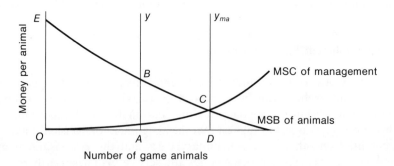

FIGURE 15.1

Social benefit of wildlife management. Relation of marginal social cost to marginal social benefit.

be hunted beyond the level necessary for replacement and may vanish from the habitat in question. Under assumptions of no habitat management, this will result in a net social loss of $OEBA$ each year into the indefinite future. If the habitat were to be managed at level y_{ma} but not rationed, the net loss each year would be $(EOCD) - (OCD)$ for the indefinite future. It is this amount, $(EOCD) - (OCD)$, that is the potential to be gained by establishing an agency to regulate and manage this resource. The cost of not doing so is the value of the lost resource less administrative costs discounted into the indefinite future. Again, there is a compelling argument for establishing a bureaucracy to manage this resource if the resource is to remain public.

The Potential for Bureaucratic Performance
in Providing Public Goods and Services

Within a prescribed territory, the provision of law and order has important aspects of a public good. Assume, for example, that during the evening hour when a man walks his brace of German shepherds around and around a block in New York City, crime on that block is reduced to 10 percent of its normal nighttime level. By the strictly private action of exercising his dogs, this man is providing a public good. But public goods, when provided privately, tend to be undersupplied. The man does not walk his dogs when it is raining, and he does not walk them all night. The provision of this public good is of no importance to the man. It is merely a positive externality generated by a strictly private action. If plotted on a graph, the values take the form illustrated in Figure 15.2.

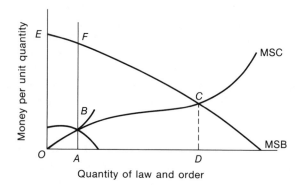

FIGURE 15.2

Costs and benefits of providing law and order. Relation of marginal social cost to marginal social benefit.

In this case there is OA quantity of law and order provided privately with a value of $OAFE$. The optimum amount of law and order to be provided is $O - D$ with a net value of $(OECD) - (ABCD)$. Again, there is a compelling reason to establish an agency with the power to tax and to use this revenue to provide a public good.

There is an important distinction between the common pool and the public good situation. The cost of failing to manage a common pool is the loss, perhaps irretrievable, of a valued resource. A failure to supply a public good merely results in an undersupply of some good or service, which presumably could be provided at some later time. In sharp contrast, were we to "blow it" now, we may never again have a chance with the polar bears, leopards, or great whales.

Actual Bureaucratic Performance

Any common pool or public good problem can be substantially ameliorated if we assume the conjunction of well-intended, intelligent, and informed bureaucrats and the appropriate technology. The bureaucracy will then perform up to the level where the marginal social benefit curve intersects the marginal social cost curve. At this level of production, social welfare will be maximized for the resource or good in question. Unfortunately, however, this is rarely the case.

Several of the factors that keep this from happening are obvious. First, we have very poor estimates of the value of the social benefits that flow from various actions. Because these benefits are not packaged and sold, we simply do not know what they are worth to people. It is especially difficult to determine the optimal demand for some resources. In addition, various competing parties are strongly motivated to give highly distorted estimates of the values.

Second, we lack adequate scientific information about most of the processes with which we are concerned. We simply do not know what impact submicroscopic air pollution has on human health or upon natural systems. Hence, we cannot estimate costs (or perhaps even benefits) of this type of pollution.

Given these considerations, even the best-intended and most intelligent agency would not know at what level to produce.

The Political Economy of Bureaucracies

Quite apart from the above considerations, there is a subtle and more pervasive problem inherent in reliance upon bureaucratic order to provide public goods and manage common pool resources. Every bureau has a bias toward growth beyond the point where marginal cost equals marginal benefits. Nearly every bureaucracy is more comfortable and rewarding when it is expanding at a moderately rapid rate than when it is stationary or declining in size. With a 6 to 10 percent rate of growth, promotions are relatively frequent and can come from inside the agency, and incompetent or marginally competent personnel can be hidden or their efforts ignored. People are secure, their futures are relatively bright, and morale tends to be high. This was the picture of the universities in the late 1950's and 1960's. The contrast between those times and the wailings of doom that one now hears is very striking. Growth and lack of growth are both costly, but the implications of the two are quite different.

Assume that line AB in Figure 15.3 is the marginal social benefit function generated by an agency's actions, and that line CD is the marginal social cost, that is, what society has to give up in taxes for producing that benefit. Under these circumstances, social welfare will be maximized if the bureaucracy produces F quantity of its good or service. Beyond F, society has to give up more to expand the bureaucratic output than it gets in return for the additional expenditure. Hence, production and budgeting should stop at F, leaving society with a net gain of $(OAEF)$ − $(OCEF)$ or the area in CAE.

When producing items that are consumed publicly, it is very difficult to determine when "enough" has been reached. Firms can judge with fairly tight tolerances when they have produced enough Edsels, golf balls or cotter pins. Determining when we have "enough" national defense is a problem of higher magnitude. Compounding the problem is the fact that preferences for varying amounts of national defense must be summed and in some way averaged. Obviously some people would wish to buy more national defense than they now obtain while others believe that they are already buying too much and would prefer lower

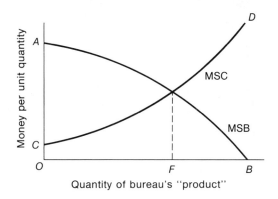

FIGURE 15.3

Optimum level of bureaucratic production.

taxes or greater medical coverage. It is, then, incumbent upon the military bureaucrats to identify those segments of the public who want more national defense expenditures and provide them with information useful for lobbying on behalf of increased military appropriations.

Weather forecasting and environmental monitoring are also extremely complex. Hence, it takes moderately sophisticated mathematics in the form of sensitivity analysis to even roughly determine the socially efficient investment in obtaining information. Nearly all high level bureaucrats seem to believe that their program is indeed vital, critical, imperative, necessary, and essential to the national well being, and that legislators would be well advised to increase the agency's budget. It just happens that what is best for the country (or district, or whatever unit) also makes the particular agency a more comfortable place. Bureaucrats carry on a continuous struggle to increase their budgets, and the most "successful" bureaucrat is the one who can claim responsibility for obtaining the largest budget increase.

Referring again to Figure 15.3, the tendency is for bureaucracies to push beyond the F level toward B. William Niskanan, a former RAND scientist now teaching in Berkeley, has a fairly involved mathematical argument that shows that a bureaucracy will expand its performance beyond F to the point where the entire net social benefit (ACE, if stopped at F) is consumed by the deviation of the increasing marginal social cost curve CD from the marginal social benefit curve AB. In a mature bureaucracy, the area in DEB has increased as production moved to the right (toward B) until it is equal to area in ACE. At that point, of course, society is not better off with the bureaucracy than it would have been without it. An analogous example is the purchase of a hunting dog and the resultant discovery that not only is he a nuisance, but he also eats enough to outweigh the extra game he brings in.

16

The Social Costs of Reducing Social Cost

Gordon Tullock

During much of my career as a sort-of economist I have been a specialist on social cost. During the first part of this career, I continuously told people (and muttered to myself) that there were vast profits to be made in our society by reducing a number of obvious social costs. In recent years I find myself warning people (and muttering to myself) that, quite commonly, action taken to reduce these social costs turns out to be worse than doing nothing. It is my personal experience, in changing from an advocate of expanded government to an opponent of specific government action, that prompted this discussion.

If the government engages in an unwise action, it does not indicate that without government action the situation would have been ideal. Indeed, it seems undeniable that very large profits are available to our society from carefully calculated government action in a wide variety of areas where there are large social costs. I perceive the problem to be simply that the government is apt to impose social costs rather than to eliminate them.

Since it is not possible to talk about everything at once, I propose to omit from this discussion certain serious problems which democratic action can raise. The first of these is the Arrow problem, which is the prospect that democracy actually produces random results due to problems of aggregating preferences. I shall assume throughout this discussion that the voting process produces an outcome which is, on the whole, in accord with majority preferences and that terrible mathematical problems associated with democracy do not exist.

Secondly, I shall assume that the bureaucratic problems discussed in Niskanen's *Bureaucracy and Representative Government* have somehow been solved or, perhaps, are not real.[1] Using a simple maximizing model of the bureaucrat and looking at the type of institutional structure we have in our federal government, Niskanen argues that the profits from establishing a government activity are apt to be entirely consumed in the expansion of the bureaucracy itself. Thus, in equilibrium, in the Niskanen model, the society would be indifferent to maintaining the bureaucracy at the size it reaches or abolishing it. The entire profit of eliminating some social costs would be eaten up in the cost of supporting additional bureaucrats. Niskanen's arguments for the frequency of this phenomenon are fairly powerful, but here I simply assume that it does not occur.

In 1949, I was in North China. The country was backward, as it had been for a long time, and as it is today; furthermore, it was also disturbed by civil war. Nevertheless, the doctors there maintained that their medical practice was better than that currently in use in the United States. Their argument was that various new drugs were not permitted for general use in the United States because these drugs had not yet been approved by the appropriate federal authorities, but they were widely available in China.

Let us temporarily assume that these Chinese physicians were completely correct in their evaluation of the situation. Here was a case in which the federal government of the United States was attempting to reduce certain private costs—the prospect that in purchasing a product for my own use, I might find that I had been misinformed about its effects. But this action was generating what we must concede was a social cost, specifically, a government rule that reduced the availability of certain medicines in the United States. The government was taking action which, in this case, created a social cost where none existed before.

Obviously, this particular effect has been greatly magnified by the recent expansion of government control in medicine. It is clear that people who live outside the United States have certain advantages over us. They are able to purchase newly developed drugs immediately, rather than waiting the nine months or more that it takes to get government approval for sale in the United States. Furthermore, the cost of obtaining approval for sale has surely led to a reduction in total research for new medicines.

Note that my discussion so far does not indicate that these provisions prohibiting the sale of new drugs until they have been tested to the satisfaction of the federal government are, on balance, causing additional deaths. New drugs are, indeed, dangerous, although it should be noted that we have better technical advice in the purchase of drugs than in the purchase of any other single commodity. Restricting general use of such drugs reduces unexpected patient reactions, and this may be more important than the rise in death rate and the retarding of medical research that come from wide usage of such drugs. My point here is simply that the individual cost that is reduced through this particular bit of government action is clearly offset by a social cost.

An even better example of this phenomenon is the development of automobiles so designed that passengers are less likely to be killed in accidents. Clearly, this reduces the private danger to the driver and his passengers while it increases the social danger, as the driver of such a car presumably uses fewer resources in attempting to avoid accidents. If we were interested in actually reducing the social cost of automobile accidents—their externality component—we would go exactly opposite to the direction being taken by Ralph Nader. We would require that every car be equipped with a dagger mounted in the hub of a steering wheel pointing toward the chest of the driver; this would surely be a good device for reducing the likelihood that the driver would be killed through someone else's fault in an automobile accident. In a less radical vein, lowering the speed limits and enforcing them very vigorously sharply reduces the social cost of accidents but at the cost of imposing private inconvenience on individuals. Thus, we inflict a private cost in the sense that we compel the individual to purchase safety devices which he would rather not purchase in order to reduce the possibility that he will be killed and, thereby, increase the likelihood that other people will be killed.

Note that I have not argued that either of these policies is, in and of itself, undesirable. It may be that probable death rates would be higher under a system in which any type of medicine could be freely prescribed by a physician than under a system in which most new medicines are not generally available before very thorough testing. Similarly, the laws which make it impossible to buy a new car without a number of life-protecting devices built into it may, indeed, reduce the overall death rate from automobile accidents. In each case, however, the result is to generate a social cost in a fairly pure form. No social cost is eliminated.

Let me, however, return to my basic subject, namely, the effects that may be expected from efforts to reduce cost in a democracy. A recent problem in the generation of atomic energy is a simple example. There have been a number of sensational public claims that the Atomic Energy Commission has set its limits for radiation emission much too high. As a result, the AEC, although denying a response to pressures, has sharply lowered these limits. The result is, by any criteria including simple minimization of radiation with no other cost considered, highly uneconomical. If the cost of meeting these new standards were put simply as a tax on the atomic energy generation industry, with the returns used to reduce exposures to medical X-rays, then radiation exposure for the average

American would decrease greatly. Furthermore, although the data are meager, it appears likely that replacement of a fossil fuel generating plant by an atomic energy plant, under present technology, would reduce the effective national death rate because the current atomic plants produce fewer dangerous contaminants in the air than do the fossil plants.

In fact, of course, the data on which all of these decisions are made are extremely incomplete. It seems likely that the best use of funds in this area would be to finance a search for better data and to defer further decisions based on present data. Nevertheless, on the basis of the data now available, it appears that the Atomic Energy Commission was not only wrong, it was pathologically wrong; and it is clear that the decision was the result of what we may call democratic factors.

These examples are by no means unusual. Indeed, something like this is the norm in government attempts to reduce social costs. Why may such behavior be expected in a democracy? Let us begin by taking Pigou's well-known example of the smoking chimney, which has become traditional in discussions of social costs. Suppose we have a factory chimney that smokes, and living around it are a number of people who dry their washing on an outside line. These householders suffer loss from the soot that accumulates on their clothing, but they cannot, individually, enter into an agreement with the factory owner because of the free-rider problem. Each individual could reasonably suppose that any payment which he might make to the factory owner to reduce smoke emission would have only a trivial effect on the total amount of smoke which fell on his laundry. Thus, even though the damage suffered by the householders may be much greater than the benefit obtained by the factory owner, no private bargains will be made. This is, of course, a motive for the householders to organize and form a uniform bargaining coalition; but, obviously it is less costly and certainly easier for the individual householder to stay outside of this bargaining coalition and enjoy its profits without making any payment. Under the circumstances, nothing is done, and we turn, following the traditional line of reasoning, to governmental control.

Given the possibility of governmental intervention each individual votes on the issue of smoke emission, and since the government will use coercion to require all people to carry out whatever decision is made by its democratic processes, no individual has any motive to conceal his preferences in this voting procedure. Therefore, according to this traditional line of reasoning, one should anticipate that this problem would be handled better by a democracy than by free-market activity.

This line of reasoning is unexceptionable as far as it goes, but the problem of information is not considered. The decision as to how much the factory smoke should be restricted, or what particular method should be used to restrict it—for example, by a tax on smoke emission—is a technical problem, but not a terribly difficult one. Should the individual voter take the trouble to become informed on these matters? Traditional reasoning indicates clearly that the voters should not bother. Just as each householder would find that his individual benefits from a payment to the factory owner are very small, so any time spent on gathering information would mainly benefit other people.

Indeed, the case is much stronger. I have not specified any particular voting model for the government of this community, but if the number of citizens exceeds about one hundred, in almost any voting scheme several propositions would be true. If the individual improves his information and hence changes the criterion by which he would vote, the odds are great that this change would have no effect whatsoever on the outcome; or if it does, the effect would be extremely small. Under the circumstances, the benefits of improved information are practically nil, and the individual would probably not bother to seek it. Hence, the free-rider problem returns. In the market with externalities, the individual can be a free rider in the sense that he does not make payments. In governmental dealing with externalities, the individual can be a free rider in the sense that he acquires no information, and therefore, his decisions are uninformed.

I began this discussion with examples of restrictions on the purchase of medicine and automobiles without certain safety devices. These examples were selected with malice aforethought. In each case, the advocates of these plans have argued that individuals are not well enough informed to make sensible decisions. In the case of medicine, the individual characteristically first selects an expert advisor and then purchases the medicine on the advice of this expert. The only argument for restrictions is that the individual may injure himself because he is inadequately informed. Note, however, that it is the individual himself who bears the full cost of any such injury. Surely he would be motivated to acquire information for making this decision more strongly than he is motivated to acquire adequate information whether or not to have a seat belt in his car. It must be assumed that he is not motivated to acquire information as to how he should cast his vote or to write his congressman on a particular issue.

Now it might be thought that all of this is a matter of little importance. The individual presumably has some preferences about smoke, which he can simply express by voting, leaving to others the problem of how those decisions shall be implemented. However, this attributes to the government apparatus some intellectual capabilities which it does not have, but let us defer that matter for the moment. The present question is simply whether the individual knows his own preferences well enough to cast an informed vote.

I presume that most people object to industrial smoke. The issue confronting the voters in this small hypothetical community, however, is not whether they object to the smoke, but how strongly they feel this preference. How much are they willing to sacrifice to reduce smoke emission? Thus, the individual voter, if he were to cast an informed vote, would have to go through an elaborate mental process in which he determined how much he would be willing to pay for various reductions in smoke level. Most people are not accustomed to this kind of thinking, and, moreover, the gain to each voter from undertaking it is virtually nil. Once again, we suspect that voters would prefer not to engage in this type of thinking.

If the voter does undertake any such an analysis, however, he is likely to look upon the problem as one of obtaining not an optimum allocation of resources, but a transfer of wealth from the factory owner to himself. Hence, he is not particularly motivated to reach the correct conclusion. The situation is one in which the voter has substantially no motive to examine his preferences with any care, but if he does, he is likely to ask the wrong question.

In practice, of course, there may be offsetting public goods. The reduction in the factory smoke by legislation may reduce the likelihood of new factories settling in the area, and lead to lower average wages. Here again, the individual is offsetting two different considerations, both of which are fairly complicated; there is no reason why he should devote any energy to reaching the correct conclusion.

Before going further with my analysis of democracy, I should like to deal briefly with an alternative theory of social cost elimination which I think is quite widely held, although it is not usually articulated. According to this theory, the people do not actually make basic decisions, either by direct voting or by voting for politicians who make the decisions in terms of their expected benefits. Instead, civil servants make the basic decisions. Further, these civil servants are not deeply influenced by political factors. Indeed, they are a quite unusual group of people. Instead of being primarily concerned with their own careers and only secondarily interested in such matters as the public interest, they are a wise and objective group of people. These paragons, then, reach the correct conclusions because they are wise and devoted to the public interest.

Such decisions are, of course, superior to market decisions. It will be noted, however, that there is no evidence that civil servants are one whit different from the rest of us. One can always "solve" any government problem by assuming a person or group both devoted to the public interest and intelligent. For example, we could assume that all business-men are devoted to the public interest, and hence would never generate externalities except when it is in the national interest to do so. In the real world, however, the central problem is to design institutions that produce general benefits, even though each person is primarily interested in his personal well being rather than the public interest. If we do, indeed, find exceptional individuals like those described above, it would be sensible to discontinue democracy and simply put them in complete charge of the government. I doubt that we are going to find such paragons in the near future.

To return to my main theme, I believe I have demonstrated that the voters are characteristically ill-informed when voting on reducing social costs. Furthermore, their primary concern is with wealth transferred to themselves, rather than with social cost efficiency. Logically, this would mean that a democratic government would be inefficient in reducing social costs. What type of behavior could we expect in such a government?

First, individuals would make their decisions not through careful thought or study, but as a result of information which came to them casually. Fad and fashion would be of tremendous importance. No one can look at the real world without realizing that this prediction has been fulfilled.

Subsequently, we would anticipate that media personalities and other people in a position to influence the current intellectual fashions would be of great importance in determining action taken in any given area. This would mean that individuals in television broadcasting, journalism, and so on could find their personal power and position in society improved by the expansion of government activity. Hence, these people might well be in favor of greater government activity in this area.

It is also conceivable that private corporations would develop fairly elaborate procedures set up for the sole purpose of influencing the media and, consequently, public opinion. Thus we could predict the modern phenomenon of the corporate president selected because he is thought to be able to present a good image for the company rather than because he is efficient. Other factors also contribute to the selection of such men, so the existence of corporate presidents of this sort cannot be used as evidence for our hypothesis.

A government official, whether a civil servant or a politician, would also favor further government programs for purely selfish reasons. Washington, D.C. has recently blossomed forth with a number of very expensive restaurants, in which a single meal may cost $50. It is clear that these restaurants are not supported by the native rich of Washington, because there are none, nor are they supported by civil servants and congressmen, few of whom can afford such a bill. Who, then, does support them? A vice president of General Dynamics—who happens to live in Washington and who has been named to his position not because he is an engineer, but because he knows 8 congressmen and 27 civil servants—is the charactteristic customer. Further, these specialists on government manipulation do not, in general, take each other to lunch at these restaurants. The people they take to lunch are newspapermen, TV reporters, civil servants, etc.

Although I believe most American high-ranking civil servants are still unbribable in cash, they do find their living standards increased somewhat owing to their positions. Under the circumstances, it is easy to see why civil servants should be interested in expanding the power of the government to regulate (although they also have other good reasons for this particular bias). Also, it is fairly certain that major corporations are not wasting money when they establish Washington offices; they do indeed influence government policy in their own interests.

Thus, we could expect that the voters' lack of information and thought would lead both to an increased importance of fashion and other fluctuating influences, and to the manipulation of the system by various interest groups. Probably civil servants and the media are the most powerful special interest groups.

In order to discuss another charactteristic resulting from lack of voter information, let me go back to one of the problems which was fashionable among intellectuals before ecology became the all-encompassing rage: fluoridation of water. Normally, if the question of whether water should be fluoridated was put to the voters, anti-fluoridation organizations staged a campaign and won. After a good deal of name-calling, some serious research was undertaken and an explanation for the vote was discovered. The pro-fluoridation people argued that a child who drinks fluoridated water throughout his childhood will have fewer cavities in his teeth than one who does not. In general, the reduction of cavities was proportional to the length of time the child drank the water; hence, delaying introduction of fluoridation by two or three years would result in only a fairly small change in what is, after all, a fairly small health problem for most children. The anti-fluoridation people, on the other hand, had much more spectacular charges, alleging, for example, that fluoridation caused cancer. Both sides produced technical specialists to argue their points, and the average voter was not able to choose between the competing technical experts.

The cost of delaying fluoridation was, even by the claims of its advocates, not very great. The cost of introducing fluoridation, on the other hand, according to the claims of its opponents, could be very great indeed. Under these circumstances, the voter chose to play safe.

We have observed the same behavior in a number of social cost problems in the United States. On one side is the utility president who argues that unless he is permitted to begin construction of a new generating plant within three years there will be power shortages at certain times of the year. On the other side are people who maintain that construction of the utility plant will cause fairly spectacular and serious damage. The voter is unable to determine the relative expertise of the specialists on each side and, hence, chooses to play safe by voting against the construction. We can hardly blame the voter for this conclusion, assuming that he has no motive to become informed and that (particularly in this case) becoming well informed would be quite difficult. Decisions of this sort lead to optimum allocation of resources only by accident. However, a large number of such decisions are being made today, and it is likely that the cost to our society will be quite great.

I must say, in this case, I do not have very much to offer as a solution. It is certainly true that social costs exist and are important and that the market in general will not deal with them adequately. The problem is that the government also deals with them badly. In essence, the market has a systematic bias toward producing certain kinds of "bads," and while the government has no such calculable bias, it does have a systematic tendency to take ill-judged action.

Under the circumstances, there is one very obvious recommendation. Government action should be resorted to only when the social cost emanating from the market is quite great. The level of efficiency of government action is apt to be low, and the possibility of damage through erratic, ill-informed decisions is great. The situation is like that of a person who was ill in 1700 and considering whether or not to call the doctor. The best rule was to call the doctor only if the person was *very* ill. The doctor, using the medical technology of the day, clearly brought with him a real chance of death from his treatment. Unless the possibility of death from the disease itself was greater, one was best advised not to call the doctor.

I have another recommendation which should occur almost immediately to any scholar, but, so far as I know, has not been proposed by anyone else. We should try to invent a new form of government. Democracy is at least 2500 years old and probably older. It was developed by a group of very primitive people and was not the result of a great deal of careful thought. In general, with the advance of science we anticipate that we will be able to replace old devices and institutions with new inventions. One would therefore assume that a great many people are searching for a better form of government than democracy. This assumption is directly contrary to fact.

As far as I know, the strongest argument for democracy is Winston Churchill's statement "democracy is the worst of all possible forms of government, except those others that have been tried out from time to time." No one really regards democracy as highly efficient; the fact that it is better than despotism or consulting the augurs is surely extremely modest praise. I think we should begin an effort to invent something better. I myself have been trying to think of a better form of government for some time, and I must confess that I have failed totally. This does not mean that it is impossible. Democracy is not a holy institution, but a mechanism for achieving some fairly prosaic goals. It does not appear to be a very efficient mechanism. Under the circumstances, I can think of few more important fields for research than looking for something better.

Note

1. William A. Niskanen, *Bureaucracy and Representative Government* (Chicago: Aldine-Atherton, 1971).

17

A Theory for Institutional Analysis of Common Pool Problems

Vincent Ostrom and Elinor Ostrom

Common Pool Resources

Wildlife, fish, oil, groundwater, lakes, streams, and the atmosphere are all examples of common pool resources. Particular problems occur in the utilization and management of these kinds of resources whenever the following conditions are present:

1. Ownership of the resource is held in common.
2. A large number of users have independent rights to the use of the resource.
3. No one user can control the activities of other users or, conversely, voluntary agreement or willing consent of every user is required in joint action involving the community of users.
4. Total use or demand upon the resource exceeds the supply.

As soon as these conditions prevail, efforts of any one user to increase his supply of the resource from a limited common pool leads to an adverse effect on others. Any one user, following an economic calculus, will attempt to increase his utilization of the resource until his marginal costs equal his marginal benefits without taking into account the spillover costs he creates for other users. Some spillover costs will be felt by

This essay was originally prepared for the Great Lakes Research Program planned by the Battelle Memorial Institute, 1969.

others who wish to utilize the common supply for the same purpose and must now pay higher costs to do so. Other spillover costs will be felt by users who wish to utilize the common supply for different purposes and may now be excluded from doing so or may have to pay higher individual costs to do so.

Since spillovers may be extensive, each user may be led to adopt strategies which produce high costs for others while acting only in relation to his own private costs and private benefits. In addition, each user may be led to overinvest in developments concerned with his own individual use. Intense competition for the limited supply will result unless institutional arrangements require all users to take spillover costs, as well as their own individual costs, into account when making decisions regarding the utilization of the common resource. Such competition may force users out of existence and produce extraordinarily high costs in the continued utilization of the resource.

A consequence of utilizing the rule of willing consent in the development of a common pool resource will be the relative lack of attention to investment in projects which would provide a common benefit. Even though total benefits exceed total costs, the specific benefit to any single user will rarely exceed the total costs. Thus, the single user is not apt to invest in projects of common benefit without some arrangement requiring other benefited individuals to contribute their share. Consequently, many potential spillover benefits will not be realized. Spillover costs or spillover benefits may, when they have a reciprocal effect among a community of users, be viewed as joint costs or joint benefits. The essential problem in managing a common pool resource is how to reduce the joint costs and increase the joint benefits so as to improve the net welfare of the community of users.

Therefore, reliance only upon the rule of willing consent in the development of a common pool resource may lead to overinvestment in facilities for private use and benefit, and, simultaneously, underinvestment in facilities for joint benefits. Investment in facilities to utilize a lake system as a fishery is an example of this paradoxical problem. Unless institutional facilities are established to change the structure of incentives and deterrents, individual fishermen will be led to overinvest in fishing gear and boats for their private use while underinvesting in the development of the common fishing stock.

Not all uses of a common pool resource need be competitive. An increase in water quality of benefit to a municipal water supply may also be of benefit to those who use the same resource for such purposes as fishing and recreation. The construction of a flood control dam on a river system may create joint benefits in the production of hydroelectric power and in recreational use of the reservoir. However, the building of that dam may create costs for using the water system as a navigation and fishlife resource.

Once a competitive common pool situation develops, users relying upon a basic decision rule of willing consent, and following an economic calculus, will be led to accelerate their competitive race with one another for the limited supply. Individual users may be led to adopt any or all of the following patterns of conduct:

1. To conceal or to minimize recourse to essential information.
2. To ignore adverse effects on the resource in the conduct of his own enterprise.
3. To follow a "holdout" strategy in relation to other parties drawing upon the same resource pool.

Since information about how much of the resource any one individual is using may lead others to try to limit his activities, an individual may attempt to conceal information about his own use pattern. Further, an individual may ignore the general consequence of his personal actions. A single user, changing only his own actions so as to take into account the social costs he creates, will seldom have much effect on the whole system unless all other users also change their behavior similarly. Thus, any effort to force one individual in a competitive common pool situation to take into account the social costs he creates, leaves that person at a disadvantage in competition with others without fundamentally altering the excess demand being made upon the common pool resource. It is only when efforts can be made to change the cost calculus of all similar actors that a real social benefit can be achieved without undue harm to any single individual. If efforts are made to gain voluntary agreement by all users to change their production patterns so as to reflect the total costs of their activity, some individuals will be led to adopt "hold out" strategies. If all users except a few reduce their demands upon a limited common pool resource, this increases the supply available to those who hold out and refuse to go along with a voluntary arrangement. If any user is free to terminate a voluntary agreement regarding the utilization of a resource, most users will be unwilling to enter into such an agreement. Few individuals are willing to make considerable personal sacrifices if the primary benefit, or the lion's share, will go to the least cooperative joint user.

It is therefore necessary to forego willing consent as the sole decision rule in order to enforce joint decisions on all parties. Solutions to common pool problems inevitably involve some form of public organization to assure collective decisions that can be enforced against all users. This requires recourse to the coercive capabilities inherent in governmental authority.[1]

Evolution of a Monopolist

One "solution" of the common pool problem is to allow intensive competition to run its course until one individual or group forces out others and acquires a monopoly position over the resource. A monopolist in such circumstances would become the exclusive owner of the common pool resource and would be able to develop the resource potential to maximize his own net return. This would be an "efficient" solution in the sense that a level of development would occur where private benefits exceeded private costs. The monopolists, however, would be the exclusive supplier for others who would depend upon the common pool resource. He would be able to charge a price that extracts the economic rent as a producer profit from resource development. Others would forego an opportunity to derive economic rent. The consequences would be extreme inequalities in economic opportunities. If the resource is as essential as water in a desert region, the dominant position of a private monopolist may be unacceptable to other people. Range wars in the early American West illustrate the consequences that can follow.

Appeal to Existing Public Agencies

The existence of intensive competition does provide an incentive for a community of affected users to seek some common solution to their problem. The reduction of spillover costs through the adoption of policies which take each other's interests into account represents a potential benefit. This benefit can be captured only if a community can have recourse to appropriate institutional arrangements normally found in the public sector. The potential benefit in the form of reduced spillover costs and increased spillover benefits can be conceptualized as a potential political (or community) surplus available for capture by those who develop institutional arrangements to undertake joint management and development of the common pool resource.

A public jurisdiction may already exist with an appropriate boundary and range of capabilities for dealing with some common pool problems. Articulation of demand for new services from such an agency would probably involve less time, money, and energy than development of a new arrangement. Often, however, the boundaries of existing public agencies are either too small or too large.[2]

Jurisdictions which are too small can encompass only a portion of the individuals affected by the development of a common pool resource, and can only effect changes in relationship to the citizens included within its boundaries. The citizens of that jurisdiction may pay to reduce their own spillover costs only to be forced to bear the spillover costs created by others.

Jurisdictions which are too large may include persons who have no direct interest, and are thus extraneous to solving the common pool problem. If extraneous populations become involved in the management of a common pool resource (such as paying a general tax to support some activity of local benefit only) they may require some benefits or side payments from those directly benefited as the price of participation. The presence of extraneous interests creates incentives to make side payments in the form of log rolling or vote trading in order to sustain necessary voting coalitions. Side payments for sustaining voting coalitions represent a cost in political decision making, and in its most aggravated form may raid the public treasury as a common pool resource. Therefore, wherever a governmental jurisdiction represents constituencies of a significantly different magnitude from those affected by its actions, an increasing bias toward inefficient solutions can be expected.

Even where an existing public jurisdiction has boundaries that include the relevant public, it may not possess the necessary decision-making capabilities. Management of a common pool resource normally requires extensive investment in information-gathering facilities concerning the nature and extent of the resource, the demand or patterns of use, and an assessment of the likely consequences of alternative management programs. In addition, a jurisdiction may need a complex mix of taxing and pricing powers to distribute the costs of the enterprise in a way that will lead toward an optimal pattern of use. It may also need police powers to enforce various regulations designed to achieve the desired result.

Formation of New Collective or Public Enterprises

If individuals adversely affected by spillover costs in their utilization of a common pool resource, or desiring to invest in projects producing spillover benefits, cannot find an appropriate solution available among existing public jurisdictions, they may then contemplate forming a new collective or public enterprise. Establishment of new institutional arrange-

ments in the public sector involves costs of two types: potential deprivation costs, and potential decision-making costs.[3]

Potential Deprivation Costs

Whenever authority for making decisions about joint activities is
moved into the public sector, someone may be forced to abide by a
decision to which he does not agree. The creation of such a public jurisdiction means that an individual can be deprived of his free choice when
a collective decision is made. Deprivations may be relatively low if the
enterprise adopts a policy only slightly at variance with the preference
of those who do not agree. However, deprivations may at times be
relatively great if severe sanctions are necessary to insure conformance
to a collective decision.

At the time of instituting a new enterprise, individuals cannot predict
all the decisions that will be made in the future. However, for given voting
rules, individuals can predict the likelihood of their concurrence or disagreement with decisions. For example, if only one person, or a small
group, will make all important and binding decisions, disagreement with
many decisions is predictable. In such a case, affected individuals may
expect to suffer high deprivation costs. In contrast, if majority votes
will be taken on all issues. participants can predict that they have a
chance of agreeing with at least half of the decisions. Therefore, potential
deprivation costs would be lower under majority rule than under a rule
allowing only one person to decide for all. Potential deprivation costs
continue to decrease as the proportion of individuals that must agree
prior to a decision increases. If unanimous agreement is necessary before
actions can be taken, potential deprivation costs would be zero, although
the cost in time and effort to reach such agreement could be extremely
high.

Figure 17.1 illustrates the relationship between voting rules and potential deprivation costs as discussed above. The vertical axis measures
total costs or benefits from collective action. The horizontal axis represents
the proportion of individuals required to agree to a decision before action
can be taken.

Potential Decision-Making Costs

When people must agree to a decision before action can be taken,
time, money, and effort which could be used for other purposes must
be devoted to gaining agreement. The opportunity to take other actions
may pass by and other opportunities to invest for joint benefit may be
lost. Therefore, time, money, and effort devoted to collective decision
making, and the opportunities foregone while deliberations are in process,
can all be conceptualized as potential decision-making costs.

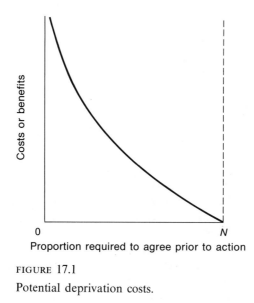

FIGURE 17.1

Potential deprivation costs.

Figure 17.2 illustrates the relationship between potential decision-making costs and different voting rules. If only one person were required to make legitimate decisions for a public enterprise, decision-making costs would be minimal. As the number of persons required to agree

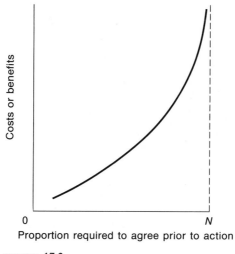

FIGURE 17.2

Potential decision-making costs.

increases, so does the time, money, and effort that must be invested to reach a collective decision, thus increasing the decision-making costs. As unanimous consent is approached, decision-making costs become very high.

Total Costs of Collective Choice

If it were not for the very high decision-making costs associated with unanimous consent, profit maximizing entrepreneurs would attempt to organize private enterprises to deal with common pool problems. On the other hand, if potential deprivation costs were not so high when decision-making authority is given to one or a few individuals, public enterprises might be managed by a small oligarchy or a dictator. It is evident, then, that the most economic and acceptable method for dealing with common pool resource problems lies somewhere between the extremes of unanimous consent and dictatorship.

The effects of both cost functions are illustrated in the combined, U-shaped cost curves of Figures 17.3, 17.4, and 17.5. If the deprivations that can be imposed by a prospective public enterprise are limited, while the decision-making costs are relatively high, the low point of the total cost curve will occur towards the low side of the proportion of persons required to agree in making an authoritative decision (Figure 17.3). If

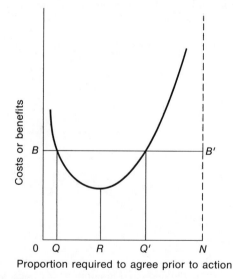

FIGURE 17.3

Total costs of collective choice, when decision-making costs are high.

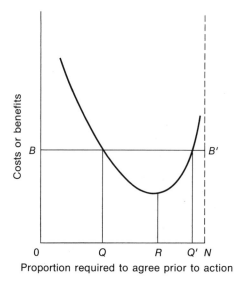

FIGURE 17.4

Total costs of collective choice, when decision-making costs are low.

the deprivations are very high and the decision-making costs relatively
low, the low point will occur where a relatively large proportion must
agree in making a decision (Figure 17.4). If the potential deprivations
and potential decision-making costs are relatively balanced, the low
point will fall approximately in the middle range of potential voting rules
(Figure 17.5).

Whatever the shape of the total collective choice cost curve, if a portion
of that curve lies below the benefit level, a net benefit can be achieved
through some form of collective action. The line *BB'* in Figures 17.3,
17.4, and 17.5 represents the potential net benefit which could be derived
by reducing spillover costs to a community of joint users, by investing
in projects producing joint benefits, or by a combination of both. This
line represents the present value of the flow of future benefits derived
from collective action, less the flow of future production costs involved
in undertaking such a program. These benefit levels indicate that a
political surplus is available, the amount that can be realized being
dependent upon which decision rules are adopted.

Consequently, if full information were available concerning the shape
of these curves, most affected individuals would be willing to agree to the
formation of a new public enterprise when the proposed decision rules
involve less cost than the benefits to be derived. In Figures 17.3, 17.4,

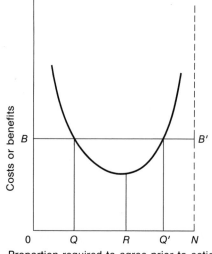

FIGURE 17.5

Total costs of collective choice, when decision-making costs and potential deprivation
are reasonably balanced.

and 17.5 any rules requiring decision prior to action would result in an
increase in net benefits to the community. Social benefits would be maximized if the decision rule represented by the low point on the total costs
curve was adopted. In each case, the rule producing the maximum benefit
has been labeled R. If the optimal rule were proposed, individuals affected
by the organization of a new enterprise would maximize their net benefits
through its establishment even though they would be forced to abide
by some future decision to which they did not agree, and they would
also have to pay some opportunity costs.

However, the optimal decision rule (R) varies in each of the three
cases illustrated. Individuals faced with differently shaped total cost
curves might attempt to devise separate enterprises to prevent each type
of social cost or to gain each type of social benefit from individual action.
Alternately, individuals might constitute themselves into one enterprise
for dealing with all issues but utilize different decision rules for each
set of issues.

Lack of a Permanent, Long-Run Solution

The dynamics of our society dictate that decisions and constraints be
viable. What is established as an optimal solution to a common pool

resource problem at one point can never be considered as a *permanent* solution. Some of the factors that mitigate against the permanence of a solution include:

1. The boundary of those affected by spillover costs may change.
2. Individuals may obtain better or new information that shows a need for changes in arrangements.
3. New technologies may be developed that create or prevent spillovers.

The Boundary Problem

Some natural resources subject to common pooling may be very large, such as the Great Lakes. The system itself may also be composed of a large number of subsystems. Human utilization of the resource will lead to the establishment of many common pools within common pools where individuals at one location may not be affected by actions taken at another location. Establishing a new public agency to deal with a particular common pool problem may create new spillover costs for others outside its boundary who were previously unaffected. One way for a public agency to reduce spillover costs within its own boundaries is to dispose of some spillover costs beyond its boundaries. The city of Chicago, for example, was able to reduce pollution in Lake Michigan by diverting the flow of its sanitary system into the Mississippi River system, but at the cost of increased diversion of water from the Great Lakes which could have an adverse effect on that system.

If a public agency is physically located in relationship to a natural resource system so that it can dispose of spillover costs beyond its boundaries without adversely affecting the utility of the resource for its own citizens, it can be expected to do so. Reduction of spillover costs created by public agencies may become particularly difficult when resource systems are larger than the general units of government, such as states, provinces, or nations. Regulation of rivers which pass through a number of different states frequently generates prolonged conflicts among the states and sometimes requires recourse to the U.S. Supreme Court, to Congress, and to federal executive agencies. The problem of finding long-run solutions to common pool problems is complicated still further in the case of any resource system which extends beyond the boundaries of a single nation.

As a population affected by the development of a vast common pool resource increases, the boundaries of public decision-making arrangements capable of dealing with common pool problems may become inadequate. New jurisdictions may be needed, but not necessarily just the creation of larger and larger districts. Gigantic jurisdictions responsible for comprehensive planning for a common pool resource may be unable to envision and realize many of the particular benefits desired by small groups of affected individuals utilizing various aspects of a complex system. Consequently, it may be desirable to create a structure of incentives and deterrents among numerous agencies functioning in a public enterprise system so the spillover costs created by each public agency will be taken into account in its relationships with other agencies.

When each set of interests is articulated through some agency, a variety of mutual interests can be handled by negotiations so long as some known judicial or political remedy is also available should negotiations fail. Through negotiated contractual relationships, agencies may be able to reduce the total level of spillover costs in the larger resource system, or to enter into joint investment which could produce a greater joint benefit from the resource pool. Such negotiation of contractual relationships among special and general governmental agencies may be facilitated by the threat of eventual takeover of certain functions by a larger political jurisdiction if existing agencies cannot reach a satisfactory arrangement. Court actions have also goaded public agencies into reaching agreements. However, the process of negotiating mutually agreeable arrangements may involve relatively high decision costs in time, effort, and opportunities foregone.

The Uncertainty Problem

If individuals solving problems through the political process possessed perfect information, they would be capable of reaching optimal solutions. However, individuals attempting to solve common pool problems face a number of uncertainties, many related to the complexity of the natural resource system itself, or the way information is presented to those concerned with constituting new institutional arrangements.

As noted, there is a general tendency for a party involved in a common pool problem to conceal information about his own utilization patterns for fear that this information may be used against him. This tendency to conceal may be exaggerated by underestimation of future demands for joint benefits. If it appears that the common benefit will be provided in any case, an individual may understate his own demand in hopes of reducing his share of the cost. If the common benefit is provided as a public service, each individual will benefit no matter what share of the costs he bears. The absence of a quid pro quo in the provision of many common pool benefits leads to a systematic downward estimation demand by users of collective services who do not control production decisions.

On the other hand, there are those who envision the possibilities of joint gain through collective action, and assume the initiative in putting together a public enterprise. Individuals who function as public entrepreneurs will expect: to have access to better-than-average information about the nature of the common pool resource; to be more than proportionately harmed if joint action does not occur, or more than proportionately benefited if it does; and to likely function as an official decision maker in any new institutional arrangement.

A portion of the expected deprivation costs perceived by most individuals involved in a constitutional process may be considered as potential income by public entrepreneurs. Taxes, fines, and assessments enable entrepreneurs to undertake the activities they think are important. Deprivation costs may also provide a source of personal income to a public entrepreneur. Since those who function as public entrepreneurs are more assured of a significant voice in most decisions, they are less concerned about future adverse decisions. Thus, public entrepreneurs will have an expected deprivation costs curve which is lower than that of others involved in a constitutional process, the difference being potential income to the public entrepreneur.

On the other hand, public entrepreneurs perceive decision-making costs more directly than many others involved in a constitutional process. They are the ones who spend large amounts of time and effort trying to reach agreements, have greater access to information, and are more aware of the opportunities foregone while individuals argue about what should be done. The expected decision-making cost curve of public entrepreneurs will usually lie above that of others involved in the constitutional process, the difference being potential costs impinging more directly on public entreprenuers than on others.

As a result of the difference in perception between public entrepreneurs and others involved in a constitutional process, the public entrepreneur's expected total collective choice cost curve would resemble in shape line 1 in Figure 17.6, while the expected total collective choice cost curve of others might look like line 2. The optimal decision-making rules from the perspective of the public entrepreneur would be G, while the optimal decision rules from the perspective of others affected would be U. At G, those affected by the provision of a collective benefit will realize a net return from collective action equal to EF. At U, the net return from collective action would be equal to RT, while public entrepreneurs will pay higher costs than others equal to ST.

This divergence between the expected costs to affected individuals and those to public entrepreneurs will lead public entrepreneurs to stress decision-making costs and to discount deprivation costs in any discussion of a common pool problem. They will tend to exaggerate the crisis nature of problems, thus shifting the estimated total collective choice cost curve of most individuals upward to the right. This has the effect of moving the estimated optimal decision rule to the left or toward a less inclusive

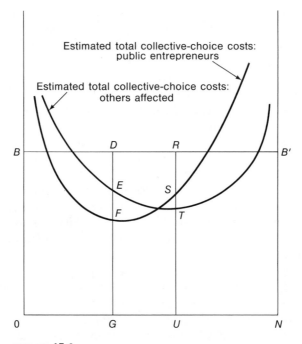

FIGURE 17.6

Divergence between expected total collective-choice costs of public entrepreneurs and other affected individuals.

rule. If public entrepreneurs are successful in leading individuals to believe that important opportunities will be foregone unless authority is given to a few to make decisions rapidly, a decision rule delegating responsibility to a limited proportion of affected individuals may be adopted. Affected individuals may later feel that the deprivation costs of such a decision are too high and attempt to change the basic rules.

Development of New Technology

Uncertainty created by lack of knowledge about a complex physical system, plus systematic biasing of information, may be complicated still further by technological innovations that create new opportunities and constraints requiring alteration of existing institutional arrangements. The introduction of new industrial processes (such as the production of thermonuclear power) may produce new spillover costs which previous institutional arrangements did not anticipate. On the other hand, technological advances may make possible projects previously considered infeasible, as the introduction of Coho salmon into the Great Lakes fisheries created an important new resource potential. Realizing the economic potential of this new development may, however, require institutional arrangements to control chemical residues from hard pesticides such as DDT.

Some Special Problems of Institutional Change

Since an optimal solution to the common pool problem at one point cannot be considered a permanent solution, there is need for generalized institutional arrangements to facilitate a continuing process of learning and readjustment.[4] Individuals affected by common pool problems can benefit from reliable and accurate information provided by disinterested third parties. In addition, such third parties may be able to formulate alternative actions which take into account mutual interests as well as individual interests involved in a common pool problem. Individuals dealing with a high degree of uncertainty can make more optimal decisions if there is an independent source of information without systematic biases. To avoid such bias, an independent source should not have responsibility as either a producer or user of services related to the common pool resource beyond providing reliable information.

Government institutions are formalized ways of arranging third-party offices when individuals are not able to reach a satisfactory resolution of a conflict among themselves. Courts have frequently appointed impartial, disinterested third parties to supply information on utilization of the common resource. For example, the Conservator of the Thames, established approximately a century ago, was charged with the responsibility to provide information concerning the effect on the river of diverse proposed uses. In the absence of formalized governmental institutions, parties to conflicts may act jointly to employ the services of a third-party intermediary. Lawyers have traditionally performed such services. In collective bargaining situations, the services of labor mediators are often procured jointly by labor and management. Similar services have been provided by private engineers to agencies concerned with the development of groundwater management programs.

Individuals trying to achieve optimal development of a common pool resource will also be aided by some form of pricing or taxing. While not as easy to establish as with packageable private goods, the price (or tax) reflects social costs (foregone opportunities for others), and so encourages the individual user to take the social costs of his actions into account. Pricing mechanisms add a form of cost calculus to the multitude of individual decisions made concerning the use of a common pool resource. The use of a pricing or taxing mechanism also provides needed revenue for joint projects, preventing costly spillovers and creating joint benefits.

In addition, pricing mechanisms increase the amount of information available concerning the demand for certain types of services. A form of a quid pro quo relationship insures that those who want to utilize a resource have a definite way of articulating that demand. It also insures that those who want to play the role of the holdout are discouraged from that strategy. If the price is right, the potential holdout has nothing to gain by such a strategy.

Thus, while there cannot be a permanent solution to the institutional problems associated with the management of common pool flow resources, a mix of institutional facilities may enable individuals affected by these problems to learn from past experience and to continue changing institutional patterns toward more optimal management systems. Such management systems will contain a large variety of public agencies of differing boundaries and powers. They will include provision for reliable, unbiased information, and will most likely use diverse forms of pricing or user charges where applicable.[5]

Notes

1. Mancur Olson, *The Logic of Collective Action* (Cambridge, Mass.: Harvard University Press, 1965).
2. Vincent Ostrom, Charles M. Tiebout, and Robert Warren, "The Organization of Government in Metropolitan Areas: A Theoretical Inquiry," *American Political Science Review,* **55** (December 1961), 831–842.
3. James M. Buchanan and Gordon Tullock, *The Calculus of Consent: Logical Foundations of Constitutional Democracy* (Ann Arbor: University of Michigan Press, 1962).
4. Elinor Ostrom, "Some Postulated Effects of Learning on Constitutional Behavior," *Public Choice,* **5** (Fall 1968), 87–104.
5. These management systems that rely upon multiple agencies, independent information systems, adjudicatory arrangements, and user charges imply a different theory of public administration than is used in most analysis of management problems. The differences are emphasized in Vincent Ostrom's *The Intellectual Crisis in American Public Administration,* rev. ed. (University: University of Alabama Press, 1974).

18

Collective Action and the Tragedy of the Commons

Elinor Ostrom

Garrett Hardin discusses in "The Tragedy of the Commons" a class of human problems lacking technological solutions.[1] That class includes resources which remain in common ownership even though the patterns of individual use have reduced the usefulness of the resources for all potential users. The lack of a solution is tragic in the sense that "the remorseless working of things" leads individuals, acting in their own best interest, to produce joint consequences not in their long-term interest.

Since natural science cannot provide sufficient technical solutions to deal with these problems, Hardin feels the search for solutions will require the development of social or institutional arrangements involving *mutual coercion mutually agreed upon*. Hardin does *not* imply that solutions exist for all problems of the commons. However, he is optimistic about solving these problems once their nature is recognized and social arrangements to break up or to manage the commons are developed.

In a response to the Hardin article, Beryl L. Crowe challenges Hardin's confidence.[2] Crowe argues that "no current political solutions" exist for such problems as "population, atomic war, environmental corruption, and the recovery of a livable urban environment." To Crowe, Hardin is professionally foolhardy to assume his social science colleagues have anything to offer toward solving common pool problems.

This paper was originally written for the Workshop in Political Theory and Policy Analysis, Indiana University, Bloomington, 1969.

Two factors suggest that Crowe is excessively pessimistic. First, the tragedy of the commons has at times been avoided by collective solutions to common pool problems. Individuals have developed a variety of institutional arrangements for allocating common pool resources efficiently. Social scientists may not know as well as the individuals directly involved how to solve these problems. Water producers using groundwater basins threatened by salt water intrusion along the Southern California coast, for example, have developed a number of ingenious arrangements to avoid the tragedy of the commons.[3] As Hardin points out, many little-noticed institutional devices, such as parking meters, are designed to avoid the tragedy of the commons.

Secondly, social scientists working at the borders of political science and economics are developing an analytical theory which begins to provide an explanation of the problem of the commons itself and the type of decision making engaged in by individuals who face such problems. A brief discussion of some recent developments was presented in the previous chapter. A further analysis here should enable us to evaluate whether potential political solutions are available for resolving some of the most critical common pool problems.

The Tragedy of the Commons Revisited Again

Several basic assumptions underlie this type of analytical theory. To begin, we assume that individuals affected by common pool problems are self-interested, rational, and maximizing actors. Second, we assume that individuals do not necessarily share the same preferences. Let us assume further that complete information is available concerning the state of the environment and the preferences of affected individuals. Let us also assume the existence of a basic constitutional order which assigns certain rights, duties, privileges, and responsibilities through and among different governmental structures. Finally, let us assume that individuals have considerable freedom to organize or enter into a variety of public or collective enterprises.

As defined in the previous chapter, common pool situations occur in most resource systems. Problems occur in the utilization and management of common pool resources whenever the following conditions are present: (1) ownership of the resource is held in common; (2) a large number of users have independent rights to the use of the resource; (3) no one user can control the activities of other users or, conversely, voluntary agreement or willing consent of every user is required in joint action involving the community of users; (4) total use or demand upon the resource exceeds the supply.

When these conditions exist, use of the resource by one individual leads to an adverse effect on others. Since both Hardin and Crowe discuss the problem facing each herdsman in an overgrazed pasture, let us return briefly to the same illustration. Other illustrations, including the calculations facing the individual slum landloard, the individual commercial fisherman, and the individual water producer utilizing a ground-water basin, could as easily be utilized. As shown in Figure 18.1, marginal private costs (MPC) felt by an individual herdsman when adding animals to a herd rise slightly as animals are added. This cost (or negative utility) is felt *directly* by the specific herdsman. While his private costs rise slightly, marginal social costs (MSC) rise more rapidly as the addition of one more animal by one herdsman adversely affects all other herdsmen. However, the individual herdsman does not take marginal social costs (spillover costs) into account when deciding upon how many animals to graze. The maximizing herdsman continues to add animals until his marginal private costs are equal to the value of the marginal product (VMP) derived from one more animal. The maximizing herdsman, taking his own costs into account, is led to add animals equal to *OB* where MPC are equal to VMP. However, as both Hardin and Crowe point out, these private calculations lead to a net loss for the community.

The community of herdsmen would be better off if the individual herdsman reduced the number of animals in his herd to *OA* and compensated his neighbors for the difference between individual and social

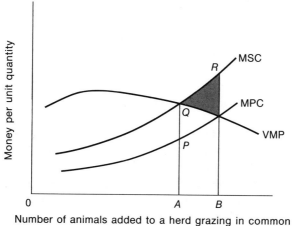

FIGURE 18.1

Costs of adding animals to a herd grazing in common.

costs. At *OA,* the individual herdsman could compensate his neighbors up to the equivalent of full social cost and still break even. If social arrangements were adopted to enable the individual herdsman to reduce his herd and compensate his neighbors (possibly by buying a portion of the land from the commons and grazing his animals only on that land) then a *net decrease* in the social costs of individual actions could be derived. The amount of net decrease is equivalent to the shaded area in Figure 18.1. The prevention of spillover costs can be conceptualized as a *potential net social benefit* achievable through some form of social arrangement.

A similar problem can occur when individuals contemplate investments in improving the commons. Unless the private return from an investment exceeds the private cost, no individual will be motivated to invest in the commons even though the full social return exceeds the full cost of such an investment. Potential spillover benefits will not be produced until some form of social arrangement is devised to enable all benefited individuals to pay a share of the costs.

In the short run, all herdsmen are motivated to allow the relentless working of things that evoke tragic consequences. A different dynamic may occur in the long run. The presence of a potential net benefit achievable through an appropriate social arrangement provides an opportunity and incentive for capturing potential benefits to those who devise a form of collective or joint action. By changing the legal structure of incentives and deterrents, or by constituting a collective enterprise, or both, the community of individuals using a common pool resource may be able to avoid the social costs of individual actions or obtain the social benefits of collective action. The previous chapter in this book provides a theoretical framework for constituting new social arrangements or a social technology that is capable of managing the commons and of halting the "remorseless working of things."

Is This Theory Empirically Relevant?

If this analytical theory of common pool problems has empirical relevance, we would expect individuals affected by common pool problems who have recourse to institutional facilities that allow decisions to be taken under rules of less than unanimity to develop arrangements to solve these problems in the long run. The only common pool problems left unsolved would be those for which the benefits of collective action did not exceed the costs of collective action for any decision rule.

Solutions would involve a wide variety of institutional arrangements. The boundaries of public enterprises developed to solve common pool problems would vary from problem to problem. Some would be nation-wide, others, international in scope. Some would include only small areas. Decision rules utilized by agencies would vary from less than a majority to unanimity. Types of coercive measures developed would also vary substantially from the use of small fees to more extreme sanctions.

What meaning should be given to these contradictory observations? One interpretation is that the conditions necessary for the theoretical long-run dynamics are not uniformly present in all common pool situations and in all general governmental jurisdictions.

We posited above that complete information is available concerning the state of the environment and the preferences of affected individuals. This condition is rarely met in real common pool situations. Rather, the level of information possessed by affected individuals varies widely from one situation to another. A small group of water producers utilizing a ground-water basin may be able to gain a high level of information concerning the threat of salt water intrusion to their joint supply. All potential parents in the world may find it much more difficult to gain information about the total number of births and the threat of over-population to the well being of future generations. Consequently, one can hypothesize that if all other factors are similar, increased information concerning the problem should increase the likelihood that individuals will solve common pool problems.

The degree of freedom that individuals possess to enter into a variety of public or collective enterprises also varies substantially among different governmental jurisdictions as well as in different common pool problems. Some states, such as California, have a home-rule tradition built into the state constitution which facilitates a wide variety of public solutions to a diverse range of common pool problems. Other general political jurisdictions have basic constitutional ground rules that discourage the creation of such enterprises. It is especially difficult under the American political system to create institutional arrangements dealing with common pool problems that affect more than a single state, but that do not come within federal jurisdiction.

Not only would it appear that the capacity of individuals to enter freely into a variety of public or collective enterprises varies significantly within the American political system, it would also appear that the reforms recommended by many social scientists for the last 75 years have consistently attempted to reduce this degree of freedom. Social scientists have frequently urged urban reforms that would substantially reduce the number of locally constituted general and special purpose governments.[4] This reduction affects the capacities of individuals to find a unit with approximately the right boundaries and set of decision rules to cope with common pool problems. Consequently, social scientists may have attempted to reform our political system in a manner that inhibits the development of the very solutions needed. If all other factors are equal, individuals will be more likely to accomplish long-run solutions to common pool problems where a wide variety of institutional arrangements are available and considerable freedom to establish new public or collective enterprises exist.

Is Bureaucracy the Only Regulation?

Social arrangements for dealing with common pool problems frequently involve the creation of "watchers" who are responsible for administering the commons. Hardin pointed out that this has led to the time-worn question: "Who shall watch the watchers themselves?" The question is not answered easily. When social benefits are created by changing social arrangements, opportunities may also exist for individuals to obtain considerable private gain at others' expense. There is, as Crowe asserts, considerable evidence that when national regulatory agencies are utilized as the only administrative arrangements for dealing with common pool problems, small, highly organized groups have subverted the regulatory process to their own advantage. Large but unorganized groups of affected individuals have blocked effective representation in such proceedings. Crowe is handicapped in attempting to answer this question by focusing on the nation-state as the only effective political unit and one which must have a monopoly of coercive force. He, like many others, assumes that bureaucratic control is the only form of public regulation.

Other forms of public regulation are possible. For example, in Southern California, water producers cannot perfect legal title to the continued use of ground-water unless they record with a state agency the amount of water put to beneficial use, and establish a pattern of use for at least a five-year period. If the recording of use were the only administrative device for regulating ground-water withdrawals, producers would be led to withdraw as much as they could and to bias their reporting of use upward. However, water producers are also required by a local special district to pay a pump tax on all water withdrawn. The amount of the pump tax is determined by the amount of money needed to support a ground-water basin replenishment program intended to keep the basins in approximate long-run balance. If the pump tax were the only form of regulation, water producers would be led to bias their reporting of use downward. The combined efforts of two different agencies pursuing related but different programs lead to a system of regulation that is reasonably honest and effective, achieve the objectives of ground-water basin management, and protect the interests of affected but unorganized individuals in the area. The existence of special taxing arrangements developed by some special-purpose districts enables them to provide the corrective feedback that Hardin argues is necessary "to keep the custodians honest." By focusing on the nation-state and on the need for a monopoly of coercive force, social scientists may have blinded themselves to the relevance for social analysis of the inventiveness of those who directly face common pool problems.

The Problem of Sequential Decision Making

Crowe argues that recent developments have undermined the conditions necessary for solving common pool problems, but he shifts ground in his concluding section to assert that these conditions may never have existed in the United States. He cites the important work by Wildavsky describing the national budgetary process as proceeding by a sequential and incremental calculus rather than by a comprehensive plan. Crowe feels that sequential decision making is incapable of adapting to the range of disturbances occurring in the United States. He longs for some form of generalized adaptability which will produce comprehensive solutions reflecting a singleness of purpose. Such visions are impossibilities for fallible creatures. W. Ross Ashby has demonstrated that adaptation to a complex environment is most efficient when subsystems have considerable independence and can proceed to adapt serially. Totally integrated systems may not be able to adapt to complex environments in sufficient time to enable them to survive over the long run.[5]

Crowe cites Vietnam as an example of the type of error produced by sequential decision making typically found in the United States. Serious errors were made concerning our involvement in Vietnam. However, Crowe seems unaware that, in the area of national defense, the U.S. political system most closely approaches his ideal model of a single center of authority able to arrange values hierarchically and impose its decisions on others through considerable aggregation of coercive capabilities. The multiplicity of decision centers which have to be taken into account in most domestic issues do not exist to the same extent in the management of the defense establishment. Decision making about Vietnam was sequential to the extent that information about the future is never fully available, even to the chief executive. If such gross errors as Vietnam could result from the operation of the most hierarchically organized decision making unit in the United States, why does Crowe insist that there can be no solutions to other common pool problems unless a similar political unit can be found to arrange values hierarchically, utilize a monopoly of coercive force, and impose decision on those who disagree?

Are Critical Problems Unsolvable?

Toward the end of his article, Crowe charges Hardin and other natural scientists with absolving themselves of responsibility for meeting the environmental challenges of the contemporary world by relegating the problems for which there are no technical solutions to the political or social realm. Are these problems really unsolvable?

If by the term "solution" we mean a cost-free process for dealing with diverse common pool problems, then one must agree that there are no solutions. Unfortunately, too much of our social theory involves wishful thinking about cost-free solutions to problems. Such utopian "solutions" can never exist. On the other hand, if we have in mind the development of social arrangements to deal with common pool problems that will cost less than the benefits to be derived from such arrangements, solutions do and can exist for many common pool problems. However, a single social arrangement will not necessarily solve more than one type of common pool problem. Consequently, fixing our attention on one type of social arrangement may inhibit our ability to discover solutions to diverse types of common pool problems.

There are some critical tasks ahead for social scientists if we are to do our share in solving these problems. First, there is the further development and extension of a theory that is appropriate to the solution of common pool problems, and the testing of this theory in empirical research. A preliminary sketch of such a theory presented in the previous chapter appears to have considerable surface validity and seems to explain phenomenon which have previously been considered inexplicable. If this theory has empirical relevance, solutions to common pool problems will be more likely to occur when: (1) a high level of accurate information is provided to all affected individuals; (2) considerable freedom to enter into a wide variety of social arrangements exists; and (3) individuals can devise social arrangements (user charges, prices, taxing arrangements or other forms of regulation) that will induce individuals to take into account the social costs of their individual action in regard to any particular common pool when making their own individual decisions.

Second, the development of alternative conceptions of order is needed in the social sciences. For many social scientists, order exists only when there is a single hierarchy of formal organization. Ordered states of affairs resulting from a multiplicity of agencies making relatively autonomous decisions are frequently treated as disorderly or chaotic. Economics has long focused on the nature of order produced by a multiplicity of independent decision makers functioning in a market. The other social sciences can also benefit from the conception of dynamic ordering in nonhierarchical arrangements. Social systems may be subject to polycentric orderings as well as hierarchical orderings.[6]

Third, there must be further development of methods of analysis for dealing with incommensurables. Consequences which cannot be measured directly in dollar terms have often been ignored. While we may not be able to attach money value directly to some consequences, all events can be evaluated in terms of the alternatives foregone. Tradeoffs among alternative sets of events can be more fully examined in relation to the consequences which can be measured in dollar terms.

Finally, there must be further development of indicators of performance in the public sector. We have relied on a number of indicators in the past which may not have given us an adequate representation of the performance of many public agencies charged with managing common pools of different kinds. We may need to develop independent surveys which will begin to obtain information about social costs which are never reported in official statistics.

Notes

1. Originally published in *Science*, **162** (1968), 1243–1248; reprinted as Chapter 3 of this volume.
2. Beryl Crowe, "The Tragedy of the Commons Revisited," *Science*, **166** (1969), 1103–1107; reprinted as Chapter 8 of this volume.
3. These arrangements are described in considerable detail in Elinor Ostrom, "Public Entrepreneurship: A Case Study in Ground Water Basin Management" (Ph.D. dissertation, U.C.L.A., 1965). See also Vincent Ostrom and Elinor Ostrom, "Legal and Political Conditions of Water Resource Development," *Land Economics*, **48** (February 1972), 1–14; Vincent Ostrom, *Institutional Arrangements for Water Resource Development—With Special Reference to the California Water Industry* PB 207 314 (Springfield, Va.: National Technical Information Service, 1971).
4. For a description of this reform literature see Elinor Ostrom, "Metropolitan Reform: Propositions Derived from Two Traditions," *Social Science Quarterly*, **53** (December 1972), 474–493.
5. W. Ross Ashby, *Design for a Brain*, 2nd ed. (New York: Wiley, 1960).
6. Michael Polanyi develops the concept of polycentric orderings in *The Logic of Liberty* (Chicago: University of Chicago Press, 1951). Vincent Ostrom suggests the applicability of such a concept to political organization in *The Political Theory of a Compound Republic* (Blacksburg, Va.: Center for Study of Public Choice, Virginia Polytechnic Institute and State University, 1971); and *The Intellectual Crisis in American Public Administration* (University: University of Alabama Press, 1973).

19

Communes and the Logic of the Commons

Kari Bullock and John Baden

Among the sources of tension in American society is a substantial ambivalence toward competition. American children, like those in most modernized societies are given a dual behavioral standard. For most social interactions, competition is an accepted and even a favored mode of behavior. In the family, however, unselfish and altruistic behavior is upheld as the ideal. The child is expected to learn to adjust his behavior to differing situations. Careful discrimination, then, becomes very important in determining appropriate action in any given situation.

No society is perfectly successful in its acculturation of its children. Further, no individual is capable of perfect discrimination. He cannot apply one standard with perfection outside the family context, and concurrently apply another within. These weaknesses invariably create problems and tensions.

One effort to resolve the problem involves the establishment of a communally organized society. Such a society is noted for its relative absence of individual property rights. Material wealth is dispersed equally among the members of the group and property is held in common. Since all share equally in group assets, the opportunity for discrimination among individuals on the basis of wealth is reduced, if not entirely absent.

It has been assumed that in the absence of private property and wealth, individuals have little incentive to be competitive and that, therefore, greed, selfishness, and other negative characteristics associated with competition would be greatly ameliorated in a communal setting. Hence, the cooperative behavior held to be the ideal within the familial order is expanded and applied to the communal order, giving greater consistency to society's ideal patterns for behavior.

Experiments with such social arrangements are essentially experiments with institutional design. The underlying assumption is that with institutional change, behavioral change will follow. The United States witnessed dozens of these experiments during the first half of the 1800s. Among the more famous are the communities of the Shakers, the Rappites, and the Zoarites.

In none of these cases were the institutional arrangements sustained. Either the attractions offered by communal life were not as great as the perceived opportunities in the larger society, or the organization was incapable of operating as a viable economic unit. In order to understand the causes of this type of institutional failure, a close examination of one unsuccessful and one successful experiment may be useful.

Communal Organization of the Mormons

One of the most successful institutions in the world today is the Mormon church. This organization, officially known as The Church of Jesus Christ of Latter-Day Saints, has experimented with various institutional designs. Through a gradual process of testing, modification, abandonment, and change, the church has evolved to its present form. One of the earliest Mormon efforts was the development of a communal organization in Jackson County, Missouri, during the years 1831 to 1834. This effort, like many others throughout America at that time, was destined to fail. The logic of common pool resources will be useful in understanding the reasons for this failure.

Logic of the Commons

A common pool resource has certain defining characteristics.[1] First, ownership of the resource is held in common by the community of users. Second, each user has independent rights of access to that resource. And third, voluntary agreement for cooperation is necessary for any project requiring joint action or community participation.[2]

Each individual drawing upon the common pool resource is expected to attempt to maximize private benefits. The benefits of resource utilization are directly realized by the individual, but, because ownership of the resource is dispersed among the community of users, the costs suffered in resource depletion are also dispersed. In adopting maximizing strategies, then, the individual user need not take into account the entire costs of his actions, but only that small fraction of the costs which he must bear directly. If the private benefits of an action exceed the costs, he will logically engage in that action, maximizing his take and ignoring any spillover costs to the community.

When demand upon the resource begins to exceed the supply, the situation begins to generate tragedy. Every individual seeking to maximize his gain follows the same logic. Competition for the resource results and spillover costs are largely ignored. Detrimental impacts upon the resource are overlooked and depletion accelerates. When the commons becomes overloaded, eventual ruin is likely to be the outcome.

In the tragedy of the commons, predictions of individual behavior expose the inherent problems. Problems arise, for example, whenever voluntary cooperation for joint action is the only means of generating possible collective benefits. Only if the entire community of users participates and follows the rule of willing consent will each user share equally in the costs of the endeavor. If individuals are able to withdraw cooperation, some will surely do so. Such strategies would enable an individual to reap the benefits of the collective action without paying any of the costs.

The Law of Consecration and Stewardships

Joseph Smith established the Mormon church in 1830. Immediately after its conception, the church began to flourish and attract new converts at a rapid rate. The expanding membership quickly created a potentially independent society. A cohesive socializing force was needed, which would aid in assimilating new members and perpetuate a discrete identity; the ministry of the church required a source of support; and funds had to be provided for church projects. This gave Joseph Smith the opportunity and incentive to combine the church's practical needs with utopian idealism in synthesizing a new Christian society.

It is likely that the variety of experiments in communal living prevalent at the time influenced Smith's idealism. Initial stimulus for his plan seems to have derived from a visit he made to Mentor, Ohio where he preached to and converted some members of the Morley Family, including its leader Jacob Morley.

This communal group was attempting to live by a rule that required the complete sharing of all goods and possessions. According to an account given by a contemporary church member, the family was "going to destruction very fast as to temporal things [because] they would take each other's clothes and other property and use it without leave, which brought on confusion and disappointment."[3] Seeing this state of confusion which plagued the Morley Family, Smith instructed them to abandon their attempt, and instead endeavor to live by the more perfect law of the Lord. These instructions necessitated an explication of this higher law, which Smith provided on February 9, 1831 in, as he termed it, a revelation from God. The body of the revelation outlined what became known as the Law of Consecration and Stewardships.

The fundamental premise of this law was that everything belongs to the Lord and that men are merely stewards over their earthly possessions.[4] Dissolution of private property, and management of stewardships in harmony with religious imperatives follow from the premise. When applied to social organization, the result was an initial establishment of relative equality, and ideally, a perpetuation of that equality. The Mormons who attempted to organize themselves in compliance with the law called their society The Order of Stewardships.[5]

Upon entering the Order of Stewardships, members of the Mormon church were required to consecrate to the Lord, via the bishop, all their properties and possessions, both in kind and liquid, both real and personal. The bishop then reciprocated by alloting each family head a stewardship, which included many of the initially consecreated items such as clothing, furniture, a building lot within the community, and some form of an inheritance. The "inheritance" was a means by which a family could make a living. It might be a farm, a workshop, a store, or a factory. The size of the stewardship varied from family to family. Apportionment of material goods and the allocation of inheritances was based upon relative rather than absolute equality. The law defined equality according to the size of a family, its circumstances, and its "just wants and needs." It therefore allowed for inequalities in individual responsibilities and individual control in management of enterprises.

After the initial allocation of a stewardship, the church ceased to exercise control over its operation. Inheritances were deeded to the individual steward, and he was accountable only to God. Even if the individual was excommunicated or voluntarily withdrew from the Order, his ownership of the inheritance was absolute. (However, all other properties that were initially or subsequently consecrated remained in church ownership.) Competition was therefore not entirely absent; however, it was potentially diminished by a further provision of the Law of Consecration and Stewardship.

By requiring an annual socialization of surpluses, the order hoped to provide a mechanism by which the initial equalization of material wealth could be maintained. Each year, the family heads or stewards were required to make an account of the year's production to the bishop. Surplus incomes, above that which constituted a family's "just wants and needs," were to be consecrated to the Order, and held in the Bishop's Storehouse for further distribution. These surpluses were to be used in the support of widows, orphans, the poor, and any who failed to produce enough for themselves. The support of the public ministry, as well as payments on church expenditures such as publications, buildings, and land acquisitions, were to be supplied by the surpluses. Any additional surpluses could be used by stewards who wished to expand or improve upon their expenditures.

Individual participation in the Order and cooperation with the mandates of the law were essentially voluntary. In fact, the entire outline of the Law of Consecration and Stewardship lacked coercive control. Any member of the Mormon Church was free to join the Order of Stewardships, each new member was free to determine the extent of his initial consecration, and each steward was free to consecrate annually as much or as little as he desired. These freedoms rendered the Order susceptible to the economic problems associated with common pool resources.

The town of Independence in Jackson County, Missouri became the focal point for the gathering of the church membership. In another revelation, Joseph Smith identified it as Zion, the centerplace of God's people and their church. Various other revelations instructed the people to gather in Zion, to prosper and flourish, and to build the kingdom of God. Here they were to establish the Order of Stewardships. The Mormons responded enthusiastically to these commandments and quickly began to immigrate to Zion.

Tapping the Common Pool

From its beginning, the Mormon church has been actively involved in proselytizing and converting new members. Each new convert was a potential, and eager, immigrant to Zion. This precipitated a flux of immigration larger and more rapid than was anticipated by church leaders.

Immigration to Zion was open and no one was refused admittance to the Order upon arrival in Jackson County. For the potential immigrants, the benefits of close association with other Mormons, and especially the benefits of receiving a stewardship, outweighed costs of moving to Zion. Obviously, the poorer members could improve their economic situation by joining the Order. Soon, demand for a place in the Order of Stewardships began to exceed supply.

Each new family was supplied with an inheritance and a building lot within the community. Lands had to be bought, houses built, and mercantile goods provided. These required time and money to obtain and neither were in sufficient supply. The problem was compounded by the arrival of increasing numbers of families without possessions. Some were utterly destitute.

The church leadership made an attempt to regulate the over-rapid immigration. Through another revelation, and again in the church newspaper, church members abroad were instructed to gather "not in haste, nor by flight."[6] They were to make advance preparations by notifying church officials of their desire to move to Jackson County, and by sending money ahead to buy land. They were then to move to Kirtland, Ohio to await permission to join the Order in Zion. Compliance with these regulations, however, was essentially voluntary as those who arrived without having made advance preparations were not turned away. One Mormon later reflected upon the problem and said that "the church got crazy to go up to Zion, as it was then called. The rich were afraid to send their money to purchase lands, and the poor crowded up in numbers, without having any places provided, contrary to the advice of the Bishop and others."[7]

As the poor crowded up in numbers they became the dominant exploiters of the commons. In attempting to provide stewardships for the influx of poor families, the bishop was forced to draw heavily on the Order's limited resources. The prospect of forfeiting material well-being to accommodate such a large proportion of poor deterred migration of the wealthier Mormon converts.

The benefits of receiving a stewardship so greatly outweighed the personal costs incurred by migration, that the poor had little incentive to comply with the regulations for advance preparation. Each immigrant could also ignore the high costs his arrival inflicted upon the Order, because those costs were paid by the entire group out of consecrated funds. Because of the large percentage of poor, the size of stewardships diminished, as did opportunities for economic growth and expansion. Attempts to curb the influx of the poor and to encourage immigration of the well-to-do were many but ineffective; the poor continued to come.

Consecrations and Stewardships

"Every man must be his own judge, how much he should receive and how much he should suffer to remain in the hands of the bishop."[8] These are the words of Joseph Smith spoken in reference to the consecrations made by each new member of the Order of Stewardships. When a family desired to enter the Order, they consecrated their possessions to Bishop Partridge, overseer of the Order, and subsequently received from him a stewardship. Most consecrated items were loaned back to the family as part of their stewardship. Surplus from consecrations was kept for redistribution. The Church leadership expected that in many cases the consecrations would substantially exceed the allotted stewardship, to compensate other cases where the consecrations were expected to be less.

With every man as his own judge, Bishop Partridge had little, if any, control over the size of consecrations he received. The existing members of the Order had little control over incoming members, the goods they supplied, or the demands they made, other than by appeals for voluntary cooperation in consecrations.

There is only one surviving legal document recording an individual consecration and stewardship, that of a man named Titus Billings.[9] Upon entering the Order of Stewardships, Billings consecrated $316.52 in personal belongings. All these items were subsequently loaned back to him as part of his stewardship as sufficient only for himself and his family. There was nothing left over to buy lands for Zion, to help in the support of the ministry, or to help in the support of the poor. Billings himself was poor. His consecrations weren't even enough to pay for the $27\frac{1}{2}$ acres of farm land he was given.

Surpluses and the Bishop's Storehouse

The maxim "from each according to his ability; to each according to his need" summarizes the ideal underlying the annual consecration of surpluses to the Bishop's Storehouse. Each year, members of the Order of Stewardships were required by their initial covenant to render up an accounting of their year's production, and to consecrate all goods and profits above what was required for their own just wants and needs. These annual surpluses were turned over to Bishop Partridge and kept in the Bishop's Storehouse for future distribution.

The Law of Consecration and Stewardship as applied in Jackson County overestimated the extent of human altruism. The amount of the yearly consecrations was left completely to individual discretion. The only guidelines consisted of loose terms such as "just wants and needs," "frugality," and "simplicity." Voluntary cooperation was the only means of perpetuating the commons of the Storehouse. If an individual decided to keep his surplus, it was entirely within his rights to do so, and "in the final analysis, the Order [was] powerless to enforce its basic stipulations."[10]

Years later, Brigham Young, who "never knew a man yet who had a dollar of surplus property,"[11] commented on the success of voluntary cooperation in annual consecrations.

> Some were disposed to do right with their surplus property, and once in a while you would find a man who had a cow which he considered surplus, but generally she was of the class that would kick a person's hat off, or eyes out, or wolves had eaten off her teats. You would once in a while find a man who had a horse that he considered surplus, but at the same time he had the ringbone, was broken-winded, spavined in both legs, had the pole evil at one end of the neck and a fistula at the other, and both knees sprung.[12]

The problems encountered by the Order of Stewardships led Leonard J. Arrington, presently the Church Historian, to make the following observation.

> Since the plan provided that each steward voluntarily consecrate his annual surplus, the faithful gave much, and the unfaithful little. A pre-

mium was placed on liberality and honesty. In the distribution of charity out of surplus, some demanded much, others little, and there was not always correspondence between need and participation in the consecrated surpluses.[13]

The key sentence here is "A premium was placed on liberality and honesty." It was to any single participant's advantage to underestimate his surpluses and to overestimate his just wants and needs. Liberality and honesty were expensive, and those who joined in the practice of these virtues were penalized by being placed at a competitive disadvantage. By maximizing private benefits and minimizing private costs, many stewards were led to underinvest in the maintenance of the common surplus and to overinvest in its depletion.

Management Policies and Institutional Design

The problems associated with managing the communal Order of Stewardships focused attention on the need for a management agency. And so, on April 26, 1832 Joseph Smith organized the United Firm as the governing agency of the Order of Stewardships. Not only was the Firm charged with the management of several of the community's vital business concerns, but it possessed ultimate control over the community lands and the community wealth that was held in the Bishop's Storehouse.

This newly formed institution was organized as a joint stewardship for its members. That is, initial financing came from church funds. The United Firm drew upon the Bishop's Storehouse and consecrated surpluses to pay operation expenses and to provide for the needs of the member's families. It was hoped that the Firm would quickly become at least partially self-sufficient, presumably through the profits from the mill, tannery, printing press, and real estate. At this point further grants from the Storehouse would diminish and the Firm would operate largely on its own profits with any surplus profits consecrated to the Storehouse.

The five members of the United Firm were primarily religious leaders, mainly concerned with the establishment and viability of their new religion. With the possible exception of two members, the Firm could boast no outstanding business talents capable of solid management.

Had the United Firm been engaged in a purely market situation in which the personal incomes of its members directly reflected the successes or failures in policy, fluctuations in these incomes would have provided a strong incentive for efficiency. However, since the support of the Firm was guaranteed by the Order, this incentive was removed. In fact, success in this situation may have proved a negative incentive; if the Firm had indeed become self-supporting, the security of a guaranteed income coming from the church would have been absent.

In the absence of a strong economic incentive, the United Firm had its motivation in the religious nature of its mandates. The duties of the

Firm were God-given and thus prudence was best served by obedience to the command. It is always wise for believers to obey the directives of someone as powerful as God, just as it is foolish to question His judgment. In addition to this incentive, the members of the Firm had a large measure of credibility to maintain with their followers. As God's instruments they were expected to function efficiently. Failure to do so would generate doubt and skepticism.

But again, the incentive tended to operate perversely. As the leaders were primarily concerned with religion, economic concerns were secondary. Perhaps the assumed divine guidance and inspiration tended to shift the burden of responsibility from the Firm to God. After all, He had promised them prosperity. Success was regarded as inevitable as long as the people remained faithful to their religion. Problems and internal strife were treated as signs of unfaithfulness and spiritual faltering. Rather than adjusting management policies to increase efficiency, the church's leaders called upon the members of the Order of Stewardships to repent of their selfishness and trust in the Lord.

The Order was a victim of the tragedy of the commons. It attempted to implement a level of human altruism that proved unattainable. The motivations to substantially contribute to the success of the Order through consecrations were in direct opposition to the motivations for maximizing personal success.

The Mormons suffered continual and ever-increasing opposition and persecution by their non-Mormon neighbors in Jackson County. In early 1834, hardly three years after its birth, the Order of Stewardship was abruptly ended by the expulsion of the Mormons from the county.[14] The United Firm was dissolved and its properties were divided among its members. The Law of Consecration and Stewardship was suspended by revelation on June 22, 1834. To provide an alternate source of church funds, Joseph Smith instituted the Law of Tithing, and later forbade any further attempts at establishing the Order of Stewardships.[15]

We hope to have explained how the best of intentions may go awry due to a failure of institutional design. The following section demonstrates how the goals of a communal order may be achieved through appropriate institutional design.

The Hutterite Communes

In marked contrast to the Mormons' failure at communal organization is the success of the Hutterite communes.[16] These groups, also based on revelation and theological dictates, comprise a highly successful and fast-growing set of agricultural enterprises. Although the Hutterites faced the problems inherent to the logic of the commons, they evolved a set of institutions adequate to the test.

The two hundred agricultural colonies of the Hutterites are spread throughout the northern Great Plains of the United States and Canada. From their initial three small settlements established in the Dakota Territories in the 1870's, they have, without benefit of converts, expanded to over 20,000 members, their population and per capita holdings nearly doubling each sixteen years. Their life style is marked by extreme simplicity and frugality but not exceptionally hard work by North American agricultural standards. While the life expectancy of communal orders is brief indeed, the Hutterite communes of North America have persisted and prospered for nearly a century. Within a collectively run, viable economic system, political conflict has been managed without the cost of collective paralysis.

Individuals are born into a Hutterite colony; the Hutterites thus need not decide who will share the public goods. The Hutterites freely acknowledge that "all wheat has chaff" and they provide each individual with the option of leaving. Should this decision be made, however, he has no claim on the benefits provided by the colony, nor may he take any resources with him.[17]

The organization of the Hutterites reflects an especially good understanding of social behavior. For example, they acknowledge that the efficiency of their enterprise decreases if the size of a colony is much below 60 or above 150 people. Underpopulation creates problems in lack of specialization and economies of scale. Problems of overpopulation, however, may be less obvious.

The relation between the size of a group and its productivity is discussed in Mancur Olson's *The Logic of Collective Action*.[18] With reference to a committee meeting, Olson has stated that "When the number of participants is large, the typical participant will know that his own efforts will probably not make much difference to the outcome, and that he will be affected by the meeting's decision in much the same way no matter how much or how little effort he puts into studying the issues."[19] This implies that, "The decisions of the meeting are thus public goods to the participants (and perhaps to others), and the contribution that each participant will make toward achieving or improving these public goods will become smaller as the meeting becomes larger."[20]

There is a common saying among Hutterites: "All colonies [especially other colonies] have their drones." Further, it is recognized that the number of drones increases more than proportionately with an increase in colony size. Given that all goods are in the common pool, individual economic incentives are minimal, material differentials are outlawed, and everyone has equal rights to the resources but the allocation of resources is not individually defined, then a rational, maximizing person would operate to maximize his pleasure, including leisure. He might engage in such self-seeking activities as trips into town or to a neighboring ranch to "check on" or "pick up" something allegedly relevant to his assigned task. In such circumstances, a necessary tool is more likely to "need" immediate replacement when the boss or preacher is absent or otherwise engaged.

In a relatively small colony, the proportional contribution of each member is greater. Likewise, surveillance by each of the others is more complete and an informal accounting of contributions is feasible. In a Hutterite colony, there are no elaborate formal controls over a person's contribution. Thus, in general, the incentive and surveillance structures of a small or medium-size colony are more effective than those of a large colony, and shirking is lessened.

In the following section, we describe the way the traditional Hutterite political structure operates. The basic argument is that colony life is so structured that the best strategy for the individual colony member coincides rather closely with the interests of the whole.

Scarcity virtually guarantees the existence of conflicts of interest among people with differing tastes and abilities. In a society without private property, where so many decisions are collective and thus politically made, these conflicts do not disappear. Instead, the increased interdependence expands the scope and intensity of the political problem as it decreases the need for, and importance of, private decisions. In a commune, with minimum privacy and maximum interaction, questions of how things should be run must be made to generate as little animosity as possible. This requirement is not easy to meet. Under any decision rule, some choices contrary to any particular individual's interests will be made.

To survive and prosper, the Hutterites must select decision rules that handle conflict with minimum rancor, but which yield rational, reasonably prompt decisions.

Using external costs to mean labor, drudgery, or deprivation resulting from the action of others, when the decision rule requires unanimity for action the expected external costs for any individual approach zero. As a corollary, any individual has the capacity to preclude the enactment of a decision. We assume that the individual engages in a calculus that includes himself as a beneficiary.[21]

In addition to the external costs, every individual undergoes some costs in the form of effort in arriving at a decision. When more than one person is required to make any given decision, time and effort are involved, and the time and effort required appear to be rapidly increasing functions of the size of the group. When the consent of the entire group is required for agreement, these costs may be very high indeed. Any given member, in an attempt to maximize his advantage, may attempt to extract an exorbitant price (up to the sum of joint-action benefits) for his agreement. Clearly, forms of decision making requiring less than unanimity have significant advantages.

Levy has stated that "In general the recruitment, ideally and actually, of the leadership roles of the government on the basis of predominantly universalistic criteria is quite modern and quite rare."[22] Yet if the Hutterite system is to remain viable in a modern and highly competitive setting, it is increasingly important that the positions of leadership be rationally allocated. The Hutterites have demonstrated ability to make consistently rational decisions in two crucial areas, the selection of the colony head, and the distribution of persons at the time of branching. Each of these situations is dangerous, for the stakes are high and the decisions are binding and inclusive. Not only must the decisions be rational in a technical sense, but also they must not split the colony into warring factions.

The dominant position in the colony hierarchy is that of preacher. He is charged with general responsibility including the settlement of personal disputes, the conducting of rites of passage, and political contacts with the world outside the colony.

Next in authority is the householder, or manager. The individual in this position manages the accounts and advises regarding the prudence of suggested purchases. It is either he or the preacher who negotiates with banks, implement dealers, feed mills, cattle buyers, insurance salesmen, realtors, tax assessors, and the buyers of produce. In the past, when relations with the outside could be restricted primarily to commercial transactions, the householder was commonly the only representative to the outside. He also received the local and regional newspapers reporting grain and livestock prices.

The major political question faced by the Hutterites becomes: How do we give God a rational way of making decisions? Every political system must identify those who are assigned primary decision-making roles. There are, of course, methods which deny those subject to the decision the responsibility for selection of decision makers. Given a relatively simple system with little coordination of roles necessary, selection may be based upon ascriptive characteristics, commonly sanctified by God.

As an alternative, the decision may be left up to God by enabling Him to render an opinion via a random generating device. Given the existence of varying competence and ambition among individuals, it is helpful to place a mechanism of constraint on such a selection process. Purely ascriptive or purely random criteria for leaders seem unlikely components of any viable political system in a highly modernized context.

With the very important exception of the preacher, positions are filled entirely by election. The council, which is also elected, initiates changes in appointments to lesser positions, executes justice, and determines who can go into town.

Due to the rapid growth in population and the upper limit of 130 to 175 persons who may live in a single compound, each colony must branch every 14 to 18 years. Upon splitting, a parallel structure is established and a new preacher selected. It would be difficult to overemphasize the importance of the preacher's position, especially as the preacher commonly fills the householder's position during the first few years of a colony's existence.

Although there is some variation in the means of choosing a preacher among the three endogamous groups of colonies, the following is representative. As the time for selection approaches, a group of preachers from nearby colonies assembles at the colony where the selection is to be made. Nominations of the baptized males of the colony are offered. If deemed satisfactory by the visitors, these individuals are entered as candidates. After all nominations are in, votes are cast by the local males and visiting preachers. The persons receiving five votes or more are entered in the runoff where, from the perspective of the Hutterites, God casts the deciding ballot.

For each individual in the final round there is a piece of paper put into a hat. On one piece is inscribed the word "Preacher"; the remainder are blank. Each candidate then draws a slip. After all have been drawn, the papers are unfolded and the preacher is known.

Given their traditional mean completed family size of 10+, it is essential that provision be made to accommodate population increase. Among the Hutterites the technique is called "branching out." In addition to providing additional resources, the split permits a solution to factionally aligned conflict. Given that a very large capital outlay (about $1,000,000) is required for a fully equipped colony, fragmentation by other than carefully planned bifurcation is prevented. Further, departure by the malcontented is severely inhibited by the fact that an individual has no claim to the corporate assets after leaving.

Political matters may be at least as important as economic necessity in reaching a decision to branch. There are only a limited number of managerial roles available within any colony and election based on good behavior. Thus, when the population of baptized males exceeds the number of leadership roles by an unknown but potentially predictable margin, problems involving the coordination and allocation of responsibility increase. Eventually severe strain is generated. Hutterites realize that branching should occur before the organization becomes unwieldy.

It is common for the mother and daughter colonies to divide the debt incurred in the establishment of the daughter colony. The mother colony, however, is a proven and productive ongoing enterprise. Although the labor pool of the mother colony will be reduced substantially by branching, there is relatively little danger of overwork—especially since one of the primary factors precipitating division was an excessive number of individuals for the number of productive roles available. Even after division, the man–work ratio will be much higher in the mother colony than on surrounding farms and ranches.

In the daughter colony, however, the situation is less favorable. A portion of the land at the time of purchase is likely to be of marginal or submarginal quality. Often land must be hacked out of the bush. Although the nucleus farm buildings will have been constructed prior to the actual division, facilities for both livestock and humans will be spartan. Fences must be built, stock ponds and corrals constructed, and the entire complex of largely unplanned but essential sheds, poles, trenches, and lanes must receive attention. Thus, there are clear and present advantages for those individuals who remain at the mother colony. Therefore, the selection of migrating individuals could be filled with tension, conflict, and charges of favoritism. Each of these factors could seriously disrupt the highly interdependent network of relationships that are requisite to the successful functioning of their social order.

Two matters must be settled in the process of division. First, there is the question of division into two groups with a preacher at the head of each. The rules for division prescribe that nuclear families are not to be split and that the two groups are to be nearly parallel regarding demographic and skill characteristics. In addition to spreading responsibility for the maintenance of nonproductive persons, the rule also guarantees a basis for cultural continuity keeping at least three generations in constant contact. In creating the two groups, informal measures are employed. This is possible since everyone knows the rules, and most adults claim to have an intuitive appreciation for the need for demographic balance.

The second matter involves determining which group goes to the new site. The Hutterites, in accordance with their pragmatic orientation, act on an awareness of rules for institutional design. As mentioned above, the basic facilities of the new colony are erected prior to permanent habitation, but to preclude anyone's neglecting his work on the assumption that he will move, no one knows if he will live in the old or new colony until the date of departure.

Prior to departure the members divide into two parallel groups. On the day before departure everyone in both groups packs all personal belongings. The following morning, the junior and senior preachers heading each group meet in the schoolhouse church, pray for divine attention, and draw a slip of paper from a hat. One slip says "go," the other "stay." The group destined to stay helps those leaving to load the trucks. With prayers and tears, the division is completed, each group professing confidence that the will of God has indeed been expressed and that His people will continue to enact this bidding while transient participants in His earthly sector.

The charter of the Hutterites provides a suitable guide for the two extremely important decisions to be made by each colony during each cycle. The first is the selection of the new minister prior to division. The second involves the allocation of individuals upon division of the colony. Each of these decisions is made in such a way as to preserve the cohesiveness of the colony. The absence of overt, disruptive conflict is paramount in the decision-making process. The Hutterites cannot allow the situation to reach the point of binary opposition. This is accomplished by structuring the situation in such a manner as to have decisions made by chance with the accompanying assumption of God's active intervention. The intervention by God guarantees the legitimacy of the decision.

In selecting which group migrates, there is little problem when there are only two alternatives. The selection of a minister is more complex. The Hutterites are fully aware that all who are ascriptively eligible are not equally competent for governing roles. Therefore, the field is narrowed so as to make the task easier for God. In this way, the decision God makes will be relatively rational and the cost in terms of deliberation and bargaining will be kept to a minimum. In this manner, consensus can prevail, legitimacy will be attained, and traditional communal arrangements maintain viability.

Conclusion

Any society devoted to permanence and continuity must be economically viable. Optimally, the perceived opportunities and benefits flowing from membership in that society will be attractive to the individual participants, and individual maximizing strategies will harmonize with social goals. Under these conditions individually rational behavior will be collectively rational.

Competition has substantial social benefits. General equilibrium models demonstrate that under restrictive assumptions private exchanges in a competitive economy lead to Pareto optimum solutions. The assumption yielding this result is the independence of producers and consumers. Obviously then, the common property feature that distinguishes communally organized societies creates special problems. The benefits of competition come from the fact that the fruits of individual labor and management can be captured by that individual. Hence he faces pervasive incentives to improve the efficiency of his operation. In marked contrast, the individual in a communal situation finds that both the rewards of beneficial innovations and the costs of mistakes are diffused throughout the community. Communes amplify the problem of harmonizing private with collective rationality.

Neither of the two societies here examined succeeded, through the forces of religion and culture, in eradicating self-interest, competition, and their results. Although there are strong evolutionary pressures against pure altruism, we do not argue that humans are genetically competitive and selfish.[23] In principle, institutions could be created that substantially reduce the dysfunctions of competition.

The Mormon's Order of Stewardship and the Hutterian brotherhood provide a sharp contrast in the success of their institutional designs. While the Mormons seem to have assumed that changes in individual behavior would follow from changes in expectations for behavior, the Hutterites developed an intuitive appreciation for man's carnal or selfish nature. They evolved a set of institutional arrangements which tend to align individual maximizing strategies with the collective welfare.

When the Order of Stewardships failed to effectively limit its memberships, it invited and actually encouraged the congregation of the poor. These people drew excessively upon the limited resources of the Order without making commensurate contributions to its maintenance and perpetuation. The Hutterities, in contrast, established an upper limit to the population of any single community. By adhering to this limit, and branching out whenever it is exceeded, the Hutterites have developed a system of informal surveillance of individual work habits and contributions. Although it is accepted that "all colonies have their drones," the number of drones is held to a minimum, and those that exist are subject to informal pressures to produce.

Because the Mormons relied so heavily upon a system of voluntary cooperation in the production and allocation of goods and services, it became possible and profitable for any individual to withdraw cooperation and exploit the system. Such strategies, though individually beneficial in the short run, were collectively disastrous. To keep individual economic incentives to a minimum, and thus avoid damaging exploitation, the Hutterites have rendered all goods and properties public and have disallowed significant differentials in material accumulation. One can realize only those benefits that are available to all other members of the colony.

Of eminent importance in any communal setting are management policies and decision-making capacities. The Mormons made two major errors in the management of the Order of Stewardships. First, membership in the governing body was determined solely through appointment by the revelator, and those appointed to positions of responsibility had no incentives to function efficiently in the economic interests of the Order. Second, although costs in terms of deliberation and bargaining were minimized by the small size of the governing body, costs in terms of disproportionate deprivations to particular individuals (the wealthy) were high.

The Hutterite system for allocating the position of head preacher employs a balance between rationality and revelation. Achievement records of candidates narrow the field of possibilities, fostering rational selections. To avoid conflict and rancor, God makes the final decision and manifests His will through the drawing of lots. Other positions of responsibility are filled by election. Since all baptized males have a vote, all enjoy a degree of participation in management. This acts to minimize deprivation costs to individuals. Bargaining costs are minimized as well by employing the elected council in most decisions, and by incorporating a measure of chance defined as divine intervention.

Notes

1. Garrett Hardin, "The Tragedy of the Commons," *Science*, **162** (1968), 1243–1248; reprinted as Chapter 3 of this volume.
2. Vincent Ostrom and Elinor Ostrom, "A Political Theory for Institutional Analysis," Chapter 17 of this volume.
3. John Whitmer, "John Whitmer's History," unpublished manuscript (Modern Microfilm Co., Salt Lake City, Utah), chap. 2.
4. Joseph Smith, *The Doctrine and Covenants of the Church of Jesus Christ of Latter-Day Saints*, Vol. 40 (Salt Lake City, Utah: The Church of Jesus Christ of Latter-day Saints, 1948), pp. 30–32. All subsequent references to Mormon doctrine in this article are taken from this source.
5. The Order of Stewardships is variously known by other names such as the United Order, the First United Order, the Order of Consecration and Stewardships, and the Order of Enoch.
6. *The Evening and Morning Star* (Nauvoo, Ill.), I (July 1832), 6.
7. John Corrill, *A Brief History of the Church of Christ of Latter-Day Saints* (printed for the author, St. Louis, 1839), pp. 18–19.
8. Joseph Smith, *History of the Church of Jesus Christ of Latter Day Saints*, Per. I, Vol. I, 2nd rev. ed. (Salt Lake City, Utah: Deseret Book Company, 1963), pp. 364–365.
9. Ibid., p. 365.

10. Joseph A. Geddes, *The United Order Among the Mormons*, (Salt Lake City, Utah: Deseret News Press, 1924), p. 149.
11. Brigham Young, Sermon of April 17, 1873, cited in *Journal of Discourses*, vol. 16, p. 11.
12. Brigham Young, Sermon of April 1854, cited in A. L. Neff, *History of Utah 1847 to 1869*, edited and annotated by L. H. Greer (Salt Lake City, Utah: Deseret News Press, 1940), p. 541.
13. Leonard J. Arrington, *Mormon Economic Policies and Their Implementation on the Western Frontier, 1847–1900* (Chapel Hill: University of North Carolina Press, 1952), p. 365.
14. It is not our intention to underestimate the importance of outside persecutions in the termination of Mormon settlements in Jackson County or elsewhere. However, this factor is extraneous to our discussion, as our focus is on the behavior of individuals *within* the Order and their effects upon its operation.
15. Joseph Smith, *History of the Church of Jesus Christ of Latter Day Saints*, Per. I, Vol. IV, 2nd rev. ed. (Salt Lake City, Utah: Deseret Book Company, 1963), p. 43.
16. This section draws upon John Baden and Richard Stroup, "Choice, Faith and Politics: The Political Economy of Hutterite Communes," *Public Choice*, Spring 1972, 1–11.
17. Net attrition has been roughly 5 percent.
18. Mancur Olson, *The Logic of Collective Action* (Cambridge, Mass.: Harvard University Press, 1965), pp. 53–65.
19. Ibid., p. 53.
20. Ibid., p. 53.
21. This section draws heavily upon the conceptualization presented in James M. Buchanan and Gordon Tullock, *The Calculus of Consent* (Ann Arbor: University of Michigan Press), esp. pp. 63–116.
22. Marion Levy, *Modernization and the Structure of Societies*, vol. 2 (Princeton, N.J.: Princeton University Press, 1966), p. 453.
23. E. O. Wilson, "Human Decency Is Animal," *New York Times Magazine*, October 12, 1975.

20

From Free Grass to Fences: Transforming the Commons of the American West

Terry L. Anderson and P. J. Hill

In his oft-quoted article describing "The Tragedy of the Commons," Garrett Hardin stated that "the commons, if justifiable at all, is justifiable only under conditions of low-population density. As the human population has increased, the commons has had to be abandoned in one aspect after another."[1] The reasons for such changes are clear: as utility-maximizing individuals make decisions, the costs and benefits of those decisions must be internalized if society is to obtain the optimal results. In other words, the way in which property rights are assigned, enforced, and transferred affects the allocation of resources and, hence, the amount and distribution of output. Who controls what resources? Who receives the benefits and bears the costs of various actions? How clearly are the property rights specified? How are they exchanged and how are these exchanges enforced? The answers to these questions clearly influence the consequences of human activity at any given time.

But Professor Hardin's statement raises another very important question: At what point is it advisable to transfer rights from common to

This article is a revision by the same authors of "The Evolution of Property Rights: A Study of the American West," *Journal of Law and Economics*, **12** (1975), 163–179. The new title was inspired by Robert Fletcher's *Free Grass to Fences* (New York: New York University Press, 1960).

private holdings? It is clear from the history of property rights in the United States that the structure of rights is continually changing. For example, as early as the second half of the seventeenth century, the commonly held forest lands of the New England colonies had been exploited to the point where regulation of their use was necessary. "By a law passed by the town in 1669, refusing permission to transport wood or timber by land or sea from the town commons, without leave of the selectmen, we can judge that a free use has been made of the native forest of Salem for lumber, staves, and ship building, as well as wood for the fishermen, and the common use of the town, and that the scarcity was beginning to be felt."[2] The settlement of the Great Plains followed a similar pattern. Cattlemen were initially willing and able to share the vast grasslands, but as pressure on the resource increased, an alternative structure of rights became necessary. It is also possible for rights to be converted back to a communal status, as in the case of horses in the 1920s in some western states.

What triggers these changes? Is population density the sole cause? Believing the cases to be more complex, we present below a perspective of the dynamic process of property right development which enumerates the variables responsible for changing definition and enforcement activity. Our theory is then tested in the case of property rights as they evolved on the American Great Plains. We shall concentrate on the economic and social relations which define the position of individuals with respect to the utilization of land, water, and cattle on the Plains. However, our analysis applies more generally to the mutually coercive, mutually agreed-upon, contractual arrangements between individuals.

Many historians have examined the relationship between ownership institutions and the economic and social institutions of the Great Plains.[3] Our interpretation, however, formulates the variables in terms of economic theory. Furthermore, it provides a general explanation of how and why existing institutions change in response to changes in variables such as demand, factor endowments, and technology. Consequently, the theory is extremely useful for explaining contemporary problems involving property rights.

A Theory of Property Rights Evolution

Works by Davis and North, and North and Thomas emphasize the role of primary and secondary institutions but provide only a broad framework for analysis in terms of benefits and costs.[4] Other works by economists such as Cheung, Demsetz, North, and Pejovich have posited theories of property rights change.[5] Demsetz, for example, suggests "that property rights arise when it becomes economic for those affected by externalities to internalize benefits and costs."[6] Pejovich states: "The creation and specification of property rights over scarce resources is endogenously determined" and that "some important factors which govern changes in the content of property rights are asserted to be: technological innovations and the opening of new markets, changes in relative factor scarcities, and the behavior of the state."[7] All of these works suggest that property rights decisions basically depend upon the marginal benefits and costs of such activities. None, however, explicitly specifies what is meant by "more private property" or what variables determine the benefits and costs. If the relevant economic variables are to be used for more than ad hoc theorizing, they must be developed into functional relationships which predict and are capable of being tested.

To narrow this analysis and overcome these deficiences we have chosen to focus specifically on property rights definition and enforcement activities expressed in terms of the traditional marginal decision model of neoclassical economics. Establishing and protecting property rights is very much a productive activity to which resources can be devoted. But like any other activity, the amount of investment will depend upon the marginal benefits and costs to investors of allocating resources to these endeavors. By expressing the amount of property rights definition and enforcement activity as a function of marginal benefits and marginal costs, and by specifying the shift parameter for each function, it is possible to explain the existing structure of property rights in a society and provide a vehicle with which we can analyze changes in property rights over time.

Figure 20.1 illustrates a hypothetical marginal benefit (MB) and marginal cost (MC) curve for property rights definition and enforcement activity. The vertical axis measures dollar values of private benefits or costs perceived by initiators of activities. On the horizontal axis we measure the amount of activities aimed at defining and enforcing property rights. In other words, a rightward movement along the abscissa implies an increase of inputs into the production of property rights and not necessarily an increase in the degree of private property.[8] This distinction is crucial, because the same amount of activity may yield different levels of private property under different circumstances. For example, where capital punishment exists, locking one's house may effectively deter burglars and insure a high degree of private property; where the penalty for burglary is a $5 fine, the same activity may deter no one. In the final analysis, however, it is the degree of private property rights that determines efficient resource allocation. As the level of property rights is not directly observable, and as there is some question about what constitutes more or less private property, we have confined our analysis to definition and enforcement activities, which are observable variables.

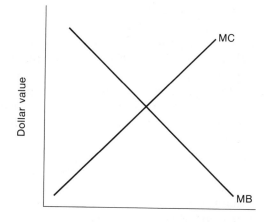

FIGURE 20.1

Hypothetical marginal benefit and marginal cost.

The slopes for the marginal gain and marginal cost curves in Figure 20.1 can be defended on theoretical grounds. The benefit from increasing levels of definition and enforcement activity accrues because of the increased probability of appropriating the worth of the asset. The rate of increase in total benefits, however, occurs at a decreasing rate for much the same reasons that the marginal physical product of any input declines. The marginal cost increases because of the increased opportunity cost of resources used in property rights activities.[9]

The equilibrium level of definition and enforcement activity occurs at the point where the curves intersect, but why does this level of activity vary over time and between areas? The benefits depend upon the value of the asset and the degree to which the activity insures that the value will be captured by the owner. Any change in the price of a well-defined and enforced bundle of rights changes the return on resources devoted to property rights questions. "The higher market value attaching to goods with strong ownership rights spurs individuals to seek laws that would strengthen private property rights."[10] For example, as our air, water, and scenery have become increasingly scarce, individuals or groups have attempted to better define their rights to these resources through legal action. Furthermore, any increase in the productivity of a definition and enforcement activity will shift the marginal benefit curve outward. An increase in the probability of loss of an asset will usually result in an increase in the productivity of property rights activity and thus will result in such a shift.[11] An increase in the neighborhood crime rate means that locks, burglar alarms, and watch dogs all will have higher benefits than previously because each does more to insure appropriation of an asset's value. The probability of loss is also affected by variables such as population density, cultural and ethical attitudes, and the existing "rules of the game" or institutional structure. These in turn will be directly influenced by the political structure, historical precedent, the decision-making rule (majority, plurality, etc.), the nature of the court system, and the penalty for infringements upon another person's property rights.[12]

The marginal cost of property rights reorganization is a function of the quantity and opportunity cost of resources necessary for a given amount of activity. Hence anything that reduces the quantity of resources or lowers the opportunity cost will shift the marginal cost curve. Changes in technology, resource endowments, and scale of operation all could cause such a shift.

The above discussion offers a starting point for explaining varying degrees of definition and enforcement activity and, concomitantly, arrangements covering the spectrum from completely common to completely private property rights. Furthermore, it provides a basis for assessing the importance of parametric shifts which influence the evolution of property rights.

It should be noted that this formulation of decision making has been solely in terms of private benefits and private costs while many activities involve economies of scale, and hence may lead to group action. Though the benefits from economies of scale through collective action are evident, the free rider problem and the burden of costs often preclude such action. Because of this divergence between private and social costs and benefits associated with definition and enforcement activities, property rights will not always be redefined in accordance with social welfare. Indeed, the gainers from reorganization may be able to make others bear the costs through such coercive devices as the government.[13] Institutionally organized externalities play an important part in what actually happens to the property rights structure.

Application of the Model

By extending the above model to include the costs and benefits of defining and enforcing, the existence and change of institutions can be explained. The following is a test of the model, based on historical data from the Great Plains.[14]

Property rights are at the heart of most issues discussed in the historical literature of the region. The Great Plains was one of the last regions of the United States to be settled, and climate and topography were considerably different from other regions. Webb captures the impact of these forces on the institutions of the region:

> The Easterner, with his background of forest and farm, could not always understand the man of the cattle kingdom. One went on foot, the other went on horseback; one carried his law in books, the other carried it strapped round his waist. One represented tradition, the other represented innovation; one responded to convention, the other responded to necessity and evolved his own conventions. Yet the man of the timber and the town made the law for the man of the plain; the plainsman, finding this law unsuited to his needs, broke it and was called lawless.[15]

In terms of our theory, the intersection of the marginal benefits and cost functions dictated different levels of property rights activity in the West than in the East. Therefore, opportunities for gain existed from the reorganization of institutions which were aimed at defining and enforcing property rights. Since much of the formal (legal) decision-making apparatus that controlled these institutions was centered in the East, it was often very costly to use the normal channels of change. As a result, various alternatives developed, including voluntary local agreements and extralegal institutions. These alternative activities are consistent with and predicted by our theory of property rights change.

Our theory will be tested by focusing on the property rights governing the three important productive factors on the Great Plains: land, livestock, and water.[16] Since some combination of these three resources was used in nearly every economic endeavor on the Plains, how they were controlled was crucial to the amount and distribution of output. The model suggests that the changing scarcity of these factors over time changed the benefits from establishing and enforcing exclusive rights to each factor's share of total output. Furthermore, these changing benefits in combination with the changing costs of establishing and enforcing ownership determined the system of property rights governing land, livestock, and water in the American West.

Land

Land in the Great Plains had several characteristics that affected its productive use. First, the mean average rainfall over much of the area does not exceed 15 inches annually, precluding the use of land for farming as practiced in the East.[17] Second, the forage was mainly short grass, implying a land-intensive output. And finally, the lack of trees over much of the Plains meant that it was difficult to fence with natural materials.

There was little precedent for the type of agriculture appropriate to the Great Plains. It has often been noted that the resource endowments of the arid, treeless West forced the farmer to alter the productive process drastically. These same characteristics also provided the impetus for a change in methods of defining and enforcing property rights. Initially, land on the Great Plains was not a scarce resource and little attention was paid to the property rights questions. "There was room enough for all, and when a cattleman rode up some likely valley or across some well-grazed divide and found cattle thereon, he looked elsewhere for range."[18] For much of the 1860s and 1870s "squatter sovereignty" was sufficient for settling land ownership questions. But the growing demand for land by cattlemen, sheepherders, and grangers eventually caused the value of land to increase and hence increased the benefits from definition and enforcement activity.[19] To remedy this situation, attempts were made to establish some extra-legal claims to property. "As yet, no ranchman owned land or grass; he merely owned cattle and the camps. He did possess what was recognized by his neighbors (but not by law) as range rights."[20] These rights provided some exclusivity over use of land, but as population increased, settlement became more dense and land values rose even more (see Table 20.1). Individuals and groups began devoting more resources toward the definition and enforcement of private property rights. Early laws provided punishment for those who drove their stock from the accustomed range. This idea of accustomed right on the basis of priority rights is also reflected in the claim advertisements run in local newspapers. Such activities certainly cost very little, but their benefits were also quite low because such advertisements were unenforceable in any court of law. For instance, they did not preclude sheepherders from also claiming some right to the land.

The inelastic supply of land meant that as demand increased, the rental value of the asset rose rapidly and hence made the rate of return

TABLE 20.1

Population of the Great Plains, 1850–1900[a]

1850	274,139
1860	872,892
1870	1,481,603
1880	3,549,264
1890	6,044,884
1900	7,377,091

[a]This series includes the states and territories of North Dakota, South Dakota, Kansas, Nebraska, Texas, Montana, Wyoming, Colorado, and New Mexico.

SOURCE: U.S. Bureau of the Census, *Historical Statistics of the United States, Colonial Times to 1957* (Washington, D.C.: GPO, 1960), pp. 12–13.

on definition and enforcement activity even more attractive. To capture these returns, cattlemen organized in groups and used the coercive authority of the government. By banding together in stock growers' associations, cowmen attempted to restrict entry onto the range through control of access to the limited water supplies. Furthermore, groups were able to put pressure on state and territorial governments to pass laws providing punishment for those who drove stock from their "accustomed range." In 1866, the Montana Territorial Legislature passed a law attempting to control grazing on public land, and in 1884 a group of cattlemen meeting in St. Louis suggested that the federal government allow leasing of unclaimed land.[21] To the extent that they were successful, such actions moved the West toward private property by restricting entry onto commonly-owned land.

The influence of these associations remained strong until the winter of 1886–1887. This winter was "the severest one the new businesses of the northern plains had yet encountered, with snow, ice, wind and below-zero temperatures gripping the area from November to April, in a succession of storms that sent the herds drifting helplessly, unable to find food or water."[22] Cattle numbers decreased dramatically because of the storm, and many ranchers went broke and left the area. The temporary decline in land values which accompanied the reduction in herds shifted back the marginal benefit curve for enforcement activity.[23] As the theory predicts, activity decreased. Associations established to enforce property rights declined. From 1886 to 1889 membership in the Wyoming Stock Growers Association dropped from 416 to 183.[24] Similar results of the winter were evident in the Montana Stock Growers Association. In his 1887 presidential address to only one-third of the members, Joseph Scott stated that "Had the winter continued twenty days longer, we would not have had much necessity of an Association; we would not have had much left to try to do."[25]

While all of the laws and restrictions on land use did provide a step toward exclusive ownership, they still did not stop livestock from crossing range boundaries. Only physical barriers could accomplish this, but in the grasslands of the West where wood and rock were scarce, the cost of fencing was high. Fences of smooth wire did not hold stock well and hedges were difficult to plant, grow, and maintain.

In the 1870s the introduction of barbed wire greatly reduced the cost of enclosing one's land. To the homesteader whose land was invaded by cowboys and their herds which trampled down crops, barbed wire "defined the prairie farmer's private property."[26] Some stockmen ridiculed the new fencing material, but others saw the advantage of controlling their own pastures. In Texas, for example, "they began buying land with good grass and water and fencing it. In 1882, the Frying Pan Ranch, in the Panhandle, spent $39,000 erecting a four-wire fence around a pasture of 250,000 acres."[27] Other cattlemen turned to enclosing their "accustomed range" with cheap and easily erected barbed wire. Such actions, however, were forbidden by a federal law of 1885 which provided for the "prosecution of those who stretched fences out upon the public domain."[28] The ensuing ownership conflicts were settled through range wars as well as legal institutions.

Between 1860 and 1900, changing land values and costs caused individuals and groups to devote more resources to definition and enforcement activity in order to capture potential rents to land. As a result of these activities, the institutions governing land ownership on the Great Plains moved successively toward exclusivity. Measures were enacted which attempted to control grazing on the public domain and efforts were made to lease from the government unclaimed communal property. During the 1870s and 1880s many acres were privately claimed under the homestead, preemption, and desert land laws. And finally, land was granted outright to the transcontinental railroads, who in turn transferred much of it into private hands.

Livestock

While the lack of rainfall made tillage impractical over the majority of the Great Plains, native grasses of the area could support livestock. By combining sheep, cattle, and horses with large amounts of arid land, settlers produced a marketable commodity. However, before the value of these assets could be captured, property rights definition and enforcement was again necessary. Although the livestock were similar in many ways to those used in other areas of the United States, the way they were combined with other factors of production in the West—the form of the production function—meant that previous methods of defining property rights were no longer appropriate.

In eastern regions where farms were much smaller, it was easy to watch one's animals and to know when they strayed from one's property. Positive identification by natural marking was also feasible on farms with only a few head of livestock. Furthermore, the lack of common property and the availability of rails for fencing made enforcement of property rights less costly. The western livestock producer, however, not only had to run his cattle over a large acreage, but also had to pasture them on lands over which he did not have exclusive control. These factors, combined with the difficulty of fencing the large areas where wood was scarce, made eastern methods of enforcement of livestock property rights costly on the Plains.

Since eastern methods produced a low, if not negative, rate of return, settlers on the Plains searched for alternatives. During the 1860s sheepmen turned to herding while "property rights in unbranded cattle were established by the fact that they ran on a certain range. . . ."[29] As long as individuals agreed upon the ownership of animals there was little need to devote valuable resources to the definition and enforcement questions. However, increasing human and cattle populations in the region did shift the marginal benefit curve and thus changed the equilibrium level of definition and enforcement activity (see Table 20.1). "The questions arising over the ownership of cattle and the rights of grazing, difficulties that have bothered the pastoral industry from the beginning of time, were intensified as the number and value of the herds increased."[30] This in turn raised the marginal physical product of enforcement activity and shifted the marginal benefit curve to the right.

The predicted response to this shift is increased property rights activities. Although branding had existed from the beginning of the settlement of the region, the laws governing branding activity changed.

> There was a time when brands were relatively few and a man could easily remember who owned the different ones, but as they grew more numerous it became necessary to record them in books that the ranchers could carry in their pockets. Among the first laws enacted by territorial legislatures were those requiring the registration of brands, first in counties and later with state livestock boards.[31]

The laws enacted by the early territorial legislatures of Wyoming and Montana provided for the central registration of distinctive brands,[32] but as the population increased, the benefit curve continued to shift to the right. Osgood captures the effect of this shift on enforcement activity in cattle raising:

> In a country of limited ranges and small herds, the legal protection would have been sufficient. Wherever and whenever the range-cattle industry developed, such laws were found to be wholly inadequate. In Wyoming, the arrival of the Texas herds in the seventies resulted in each legislature passing laws to adjust the grand system to the changing character of the business. The drover who brought cattle to or through the Territory must see to it that every head in his herd was branded. He must frequently examine his herd and drive away any cattle not his own. Because whole brands of cattle were changing hands, provision was made for the lawful purchase of a brand. Penalties were provided for those who failed to brand any animal over a year old, who used a "running brand," who failed to obtain a bill of sale with a full list of the brands of the animals purchased, who killed an unbranded calf, or who skinned an animal carrying another's brand, unless he could produce evidence of purchase. Conflicts over brands, which had been left to the county clerk for decision, were, in 1877, turned over to a committee composed of the clerk and two resident stock growers of the county; for with the increase of herds, the brand system became so intricate that it required the knowledge of the community to administer it. All owners bringing cattle into the

Territory were required to lay the brands of these cattle before the committee, which was instructed to reject all brands that were duplicates of
existing brands. The addition of a circle or a half circle, a bar or a box,
did not create a new brand and must be rejected. In 1879, all drovers
were required to brand with a road-brand before driving over any portion
of the Territory. Such a brand would distinctly set off trail cattle from
all others. At the same time, the law on illegal branding was strengthened
by making such an offense a felony with a penitentiary term attached.
Similar legislation in Montana as to the recording of brands, the changing
of brands, and the driving off of stock was passed at about the same time.
Not until 1881, when the arrival of thousands of Texas stock in eastern
Montana made it imperative, did the Montana legislature pass a road-
brand law.[33]

A cross-sectional comparison provides further evidence of differences
in the benefits and costs of branding between the West and other regions.
As early as 1864, laws were enacted in western territories which specified
brands as legal proof of ownership. However, in many midwestern states,
central brand registration is still absent and brands are not a requirement
for proof of ownership.

Although many efforts to define and enforce property rights in livestock were undertaken by individual ranchers, group activity was not
absent. Voluntary collective action afforded cattlemen the opportunity
to capture gains from economies of scale in certain activities. The roundup
is a case in point. Originally each rancher conducted his own gathering
and branding of cattle. On the open range, this meant that herds were
gathered as many times as there were individual operators in an area.
However, as the number of operators increased, the costs of handling
the cattle in this fashion increased proportionately and cooperation became profitable. The returns from these joint roundups were so high
that cattlemen's associations found it worthwile to elicit statutes such as a
Wyoming law of 1883 which provided for a legal roundup.

By the law of that year, no stock could be branded between February 15
and the commencement of the general spring roundup of the Association.
In practice, this meant that the calf roundup was wholly in the hands of
the Association. Since the chief reasons for rounding up in the spring
was to brand the calves, and since any roundup before February 15 was
dangerous to the cattle, the stock grower was practically prohibited from
an independent roundup.[34]

Technological change also decreased the cost of definition and enforcement activity in livestock. As noted above, in the 1870s homesteaders
and ranchers alike began using newly invented barbed wire to define
and enforce their rights to land. Cattlemen saw the value of barbed wire
for enforcing one's rights to livestock. By confining cattle to a certain

range, the losses from strays and the costs of roundup could be reduced. Furthermore, once cattle were separated, controlled management and breeding of herds could be practiced. Use of the wire started in 1874 when 10,000 pounds were sold. By 1880, just six years later, over 80,500,000 pounds had been sold and fencing was being used all across the West.[35] The rightward shift in the cost curve for fencing greatly increased definition and enforcement activity in both land and livestock.

All of the changes in livestock raising have been in one direction, i.e., the shifts in the benefit and cost curves have been such that increased definitions and enforcement activities have been forthcoming. The theory predicts decreases in activity if the shifts were in the other direction. An example of this occurred in the 1920s in Eastern Montana. From 1918 until 1926, horse prices in Montana dropped dramatically, from 98 dollars to 29 dollars per head (see Table 20.2). This occurred because mechanization on farms was replacing horses and, particularly in the West, because the U.S. Cavalry was no longer buying horses after World War I. The sharp decline in the price of horses shifted the marginal benefit curve to the left and significantly lowered the optimum level of definition and enforcement activity. Finding it unprofitable to define and enforce these rights, many horse owners allowed their animals to run the open range. The wild horse herds increased so rapidly during this period that community roundups were held in an attempt to clear the range of the unclaimed property.

TABLE 20.2

Value of Horses in Montana, 1918–1926

	Price per Head
1918	$98
1919	94
1920	61
1921	50
1922	42
1923	39
1924	33
1925	32
1926	29

SOURCE: *Livestock on Farms, January 1, 1867–1935.* U.S. Department of Agriculture, Bureau of Agricultural Economics (Washington, D.C., January 1938), p. 117.

Water

Water presented special ownership problems. Unlike land and live-stock, it moves freely across many different pieces of real estate and can change its course over time. Furthermore, the quantity of water can vary from season to season and even from day to day. This is especially true in the Great Plains states where average rainfall ranges between 15 and 20 inches annually. The ever-changing physical nature of the resource makes definition and enforcement of rights most difficult, and, as such, led the classic eighteenth-century jurist Blackstone to say: "For water is a moving, wandering thing, and must of necessity continue common by the law of nature; so that I can only have a temporary, transient, usufructuary property therein."[36]

To the frontiersman entering the Plains, it was clear from the start that access to water was a prime consideration when locating. Hence, initial settlement patterns can be traced to the river and stream bottoms.[37] As in the case of land, if an individual found a stream location taken, he simply moved on to another water supply. Under these circumstances the right to use the water accrued to the one who owned the bank of the stream and who had access to it by virture of position. These rights found historical precedent in Eastern laws which were, in turn, developed from English common law. Early judges and lawyers were familiar with nothing but Eastern law and thus transferred it to the legal system of the West.[38] Secondly, riparian rights were appropriate to the factor en-dowments of the region at the time. Initially, land with adjacent water was abundant. As long as these conditions continued, rights which granted all riparian owners equal use of the flowing stream sufficed for resource allocation. The benefits from changing the existing institutions governing water were not sufficient compensation for the time and effort required to initiate the change.

As the settlement pressure increased, however, so too did these bene-fits. Especially in the states on the western edge of the Plains, land with available water became increasingly scarce. The value of water rights was rising in this arid country where water was an absolute necessity for raising any crops or livestock. Moreover, in areas where gold mining was prevalent, water was required at the mine site, which was often far from the nearest stream. The value of the marginal product of water in mining was high. As our theory predicts, these conditions induced individuals to devote more resources to the redefinition of property rights in water. For example, in the mining regions (especially California), there was no established customs of mining and no recognized laws. Hence, the miners set up mining districts, formed miners' associations, and established mining courts which provided laws.

> These miner's rules and regulations . . . were very simple and as far as property rights were concerned related to the acquisition, working, and retention of their mining claims, and to the appropriation and diversion of water to be used in working them. . . . There was one principle embodied in them all, and on which rests the "Arid Region Doctrine" of the ownership and use of waters, and that was the recognition of discovery, followed by prior appropriation, as the inception of the possessor's title, and development by working the claim as the condition of its retention.[39]

Though advised by eastern lawyers, the miners recognized the need for an alternative system of water law in the West and worked hard in the California and United States courts to have their customs and regulations regarding water recognized.[40]

While precedent established in California in 1850 lowered the cost of establishing new property rights in water, the increasing scarcity of water increased the benefits to definition and enforcement activity on the Great Plains. Settlers moved toward a system of water laws that:

1. Granted to the first appropriator an exclusive right to the water, and to later appropriators rights conditioned upon the prior rights of those who have gone before;
2. Permitted the diversion of water from the stream so that it could be used on nonriparian lands;
3. Forced the appropriator of water to forfeit his right if the water was not used, and;
4. Allowed for the transfer and exchange of rights in water between individuals.[41]

Our theory predicts that activities designed to establish and enforce exclusivity will be strongest in areas where water is most scarce. Hence it is not surprising to find that in Montana, Wyoming, Colorado, and New Mexico, where rainfall averages 15 inches per year, the common law was eventually abrogated; in North Dakota, South Dakota, Nebraska, Kansas, Oklahoma, and Texas, where rainfall is greater, the common law was retained in a modified form.[42] The evolution of water law on the Great Plains was a response to the benefits and costs of defining and enforcing the rights to that valuable resource.

Conclusion

The analysis herein suggests that a comparison of the benefits and costs of defining and enforcing property rights helps explain the evolution of property institutions. We have argued that the social arrangements, laws, and customs which govern asset ownership and allocation are established on the basis of variables endogenous to the economic system. Surely there is tragedy in the commons, but the extent of that tragedy is limited by the ability of individuals to alter the nature of rights. As long as the benefits of eliminating the commons are low relative to the costs, there is little incentive for individuals to define and enforce private property rights; the tragedy of the commons is small. However, as this ratio of perceived benefits and costs changes, so will the level of definition and enforcement activity. On the benefit side of an individual's investment decision are the value of the asset and the productivity of the activity designed to establish or enforce property rights. The higher the value of the asset and the higher the probability of losing the right to use that asset, the greater the degree of definition and enforcement activity. On the cost side are the "production functions" for such activities and the opportunity costs of resources devoted to definition and enforcement. Technological change or lower resource prices will increase property rights activity. From our examination of the American West it is clear that as the ill effects of common ownership manifested themselves, individual efforts were channeled toward transforming the nature of ownership in land, livestock, and water.

Notes

1. Garrett Hardin, "The Tragedy of the Commons," *Science,* **162** (1968), 1243–1248; reprinted as Chapter 3 of this volume.
2. George F. Chaver, "Some Remarks on the Commerce of Salem from 1626 to 1740," *Historical Collections of the Essex Institute,* **1** (July 1859), 82.
3. For example, see Walter Prescott Webb, *The Great Plains* (New York: Grosset & Dunlap, 1931); and Carl Frederick Kraenzel, *The Great Plains in Transition* (Norman: University of Oklahoma Press, 1955).
4. Lance Davis and Douglass C. North, *Institutional Change and American Economic Growth* (Cambridge: Cambridge University Press, 1971); and Douglass C. North and Robert Paul Thomas, *The Rise of the Western World: A New Economic History* (Cambridge: Cambridge University Press, 1973).
5. See, for example, Steven S. Cheung, "The Structure of a Contract: The Theory for a Non-Exclusive Resource," *Journal of Law and Economics,* **13** (April 1971); Harold Demsetz, "Toward a Theory of Property Rights," *American Economic Review,* **57** (May 1967); Douglass C. North, "The Creation of Property Rights in Europe, 900–1700 A.D.," unpublished manu-

script (University of Washington, 1972); and Svetozar Pejovich, "Towards an Economic Theory of the Creation of Property Rights," *Review of Social Economy*, **30** (1972), 309-325.

6. Demsetz, p. 354.
7. Pejovich, pp. 310, 316.
8. Our unit of measure on the x-axis is essentially the same as that used in information theory where a rightward shift implies an increase in search activity and not necessarily an increase in information. See for example, Armen Alchian and William Allen, *University Economics*, 3rd ed. (Belmont, Calif.: Wadsworth, 1972), pp. 137-155; or Paul Heyne, *The Economic Way of Thinking* (Chicago: Science Research Associates, 1973) p. 86.
9. We have drawn the MB and MC curves, with negative and positive slopes, respectively, but the sufficient condition for stable equilibrium only requires that the MC curve cross the MB curve from below. Hence, it is permissable that over some range the marginal benefits may be rising and the marginal cost may be falling.
10. Alchian and Allen, p. 141.
11. We say "usually" will increase the productivity, because, although one would expect that an increased probability of loss would make a given activity more productive, situations are conceivable where that doesn't happen. For instance, if one discovered that one lived on an earthquake fault, the probability of loss would be greater, but one also might entirely cease definition and enforcement.
12. Professor Douglass North has stated, "a theory of property rights and of their creation is certainly incomplete without a theory of the state." As the evolution of institutions that influence the marginal gain from private definition and enforcement activity fits into the theory of collective property rights decisions, an understanding of individual decisions is imperative. See Douglass C. North, "The Creation of Property Rights in Europe, 900-1700 A.D."
13. See Alchian and Allen, p. 141.
14. Most of our information is from Montana and Wyoming but many of the same trends were experienced throughout the region between the 98th meridian and the Rocky Mountains.
15. Webb, p. 206.
16. There are other property rights questions of interest in the Plains that we do not consider here. For instance, the conflict between the Indian and the settler was obviously a question of defining property rights. The near-extermination of the buffalo is a good example of what can happen to a common property resource.
17. Webb, p. 17.
18. Ernest Staples Osgood, *The Day of the Cattleman* (Minneapolis: University of Minnesota Press, 1929), p. 182.
19. For a discussion of crowding on the open range see Osgood, pp. 181-183.
20. Webb, p. 229.
21. Osgood, pp. 21, 201.

22. Maurice Frink, W. Turrentine Jackson, and Agnes Wright Spring, *When Grass Was King* (Boulder: University of Colorado Press, 1956), pp. 98–99.

23. The stockgrowers' organizations were created to define rights in both land and livestock. The winter of 1886–1887 had the effect of decreasing enforcement and definition activity in both assets. W. Turrentine Jackson points out, for instance, that because of the decreased lobbying power of the stockgrowers, many stock laws were repealed in the legislature of 1888. See Jackson, "The Wyoming Stock Growers Association, Its Years of Temporary Decline, 1886–1890," *Agricultural History*, **22** (October 1948), 269.

24. Jackson, "The Wyoming Stock Growers Association," p. 265.

25. Minutes of the Montana Stockgrowers Association, 1885–1889, as quoted by Ray H. Mattison, "The Hard Winter and the Range Cattle Business," *The Montana Magazine of History*, **1**, no. 4 (October 1951), 18.

26. Alistair Cooke, *Alistair Cooke's America* (New York: Knopf, 1973), p. 237.

27. Jay Monaghan, ed., *The Book of the American West* (New York: Bonanza, 1963), p. 292.

28. Osgood, p. 193.

29. Osgood, p. 33.

30. Osgood, p. 114.

31. Frink et al., p. 12.

32. *Laws of the Montana Territory, 1864–1865*, Session I, p. 401; *Laws of Wyoming Territory, 1869*, Session I, chap. 62, pp. 426–427.

33. Osgood, pp. 124–126.

34. Osgood, p. 187.

35. For a complete account of the use of barbed wire over time see Webb, p. 309.

36. As quoted in Webb, p. 434.

37. For a discussion and map of settlement along streams see Webb, p. 433.

38. For a discussion of the importance of this historical precedent see Webb, p. 447.

39. Clesson S. Kinney, *Law of Irrigation and Water Rights and the Arid Region Doctrine of Appropriation of Waters*, vol. 1 (San Francisco: Bender-Moss, 1912), sec. 598.

40. See Webb, pp. 444–448.

41. For a discussion of the rights of property under prior appropriation see Wells A. Hutchins, *Water Rights Laws in the Nineteen Western States*, Natural Resource Economics Division, U.S.D.A., Miscellaneous Publication no. 1206, vol. 1, pp. 442–454.

42. See Webb, p. 446.

21

Environmental Resource Management: Public or Private?

Robert L. Bish

Recent interest in the environment, accompanied by predictions of imminent destruction, has led to a crisis atmosphere with requests for government prohibition of some resource uses, government regulation of other uses, and government ownership of natural areas such as wild life refuges and biologically productive salt marshes. Requests are common for regulation of environmental and natural resources by public agencies, as if regulation itself could solve the problems.

This essay claims that environmental resource problems are not new, that similar problems have been faced and resolved historically, and that there are a variety of alternative institutional arrangements for managing environmental resources efficiently and preventing their destruction. Furthermore, a good understanding of the relationship between institutional arrangements and environmental consequences carries one considerably further than a simple private greed–public good dichotomy analysis. The approach will be first to indicate the critical resource problems and institutions for efficient use and prevention of environmental destruction; second, to analyze alternative institutional arrangements with regard to the critical issues; and finally to consider the relevance of the public–private dichotomy in institutional arrangements for environmental control.

This essay is a summary of some of the points raised in lectures at a Utah State University Special Summer Curriculum in Public Policy and Environment.

Critical Issues in Environmental Management

The most critical issue in environmental management is that users of environmental resources do not see that their use imposes costs on others, either directly or indirectly. The costs may accrue at different times or in different places, or the costs of any individual's use may be so small that he does not notice them, while the cumulative costs of many users yield destructive consequences. Costs may involve such a large group of individuals that no single affected person has the incentive to do something about costs imposed upon him alone. These cost problems are magnified if individuals have no legal means of forcing modification of the actions of the cost generator, and if there is a lack of valid scientific information about environmental consequences.

External Effects and Common Pools

External effects are consequences, either beneficial or harmful, accruing to third parties from the use or sale of economic resources. However, the simple existence of negative external effects does not indicate that a problem needs correction if the costs of correction would exceed the benefits to be gained by removing the effects.

A special kind of external effect occurs in common pool resources. In a common pool resource each individual's use increases the costs or decreases the value to other users. An example of a common pool is a water basin: each user's pumping lowers the water table and makes the use of the resource more costly for other pumpers. A major risk with common pools is that overuse may result in destruction of the resource. For example, if pumping from a water basin exceeds the safe annual yield, the basin may become compacted and cease to store water; or if a fishery is overfished, it may be completely eliminated. The effects common pool users have on one another are external effects, but the large number of individual users and the potential destructibility of the resource constitute a specialized case of externality problems.[1]

Property Rights

If there existed easily enforceable property rights (including liability for damages imposed on others) to all resources, the allocation of environmental resources could function efficiently within the traditional private market system. The issue of property rights is important for two reasons: first, it is not always clear who possesses "rights" to limit the use of environmental resources; and second, the costs of enforcing these rights may be extremely high.

The existence of valuable unowned resources provides an incentive for individuals to try to capture the resource before other potential users can do so. This is likely to lead to premature use of the resource and increase the possibility of its destruction. Also, the lack of firm property rights makes it more costly for an individual to enter in a private agreement for managing the resource. For example, even if one has a right to fish in a common fishery forever, it may not be wise to limit one's own fishing in order to preserve the fishery if others do not do likewise. Even if all fishermen agree to limit their activities, a fisherman could come along in the future and negate the agreement by overfishing.

Air, water, and many public land benefits are not easy to capture; and exclusion or limitation of users, a necessary condition for preservation of an overused common pool, would require considerable expenditure. Technology is available to enforce virtually any kind of property right; however, the cost of enforcement may exceed the value of the preserved resource.

If enforceable property rights exist, the possessor of those rights has an incentive either to use the resource in such a manner that it provides the highest benefits and is not destroyed, or to sell the rights for beneficial nondestructive use to another who values them more. Thus an individual pursuing his own interests can be expected to utilize efficiently resources that carry firm property rights. This tendency, however, cannot be expected in individuals pursuing their own interests on unowned resources.[2]

Large Group Problems

The use of resources by many individuals, or external effects accruing to many individuals, complicate resource management problems even when property rights are specific. This is due to the time and effort needed for effective cooperation among large groups of people, especially if the group is so large that any individual sees the costs of participating in group decision making as greater than his benefits.[3]

Both common pool and environmental externality problems are likely to involve large groups. For example, 100,000 sportsmen fish for salmon on Puget Sound, or 10,000 farmers draw water from the same water basin in West Texas; air pollution may affect six million people in the Los Angeles Basin, or pesticide runoff from agriculture may contaminate much of Lake Michigan.

Externality problems also may be caused by individuals; the externality becomes a problem only when many individuals engage in the same activity at the same time and in the same place. For example, 1 or even 100,000 cars on the Los Angeles freeway system would not make the air unbreathable; but several million automobiles cause severe smog problems.

These large group problems provide the most significant rationale for dealing with environmental problems in the public rather than the private sector. However, the use of political organization to reduce decision-making costs so that large groups can better indicate their preferences is primarily a demand aspect rather than a supply or management aspect of resource use; therefore, it is not relevant for determining whether supply or management should be private or public. Political units can lease or buy without assuming direct management of basic resources, and many questions of political organization would be much clearer if the differences between demand and supply functions were made explicit in analysis of the public sector.[4]

Information

Two information problems are significant in efficient environmental resource use. First, it may be very costly or impossible to determine the full effects of environmental resource use because their occurrence is distant in either space or time. Furthermore, many effects are indirect; i.e., smog itself is not released into the air but rather occurs as a result of photochemical reactions. It is unlikely that any single resource user will undertake to study effects of use because the cost of acquiring information compared to his personal gain is very small. Thus some kind of cooperative or political action may well be necessary to finance scientific research on environmental uses.

A second problem is weighing the benefits of information on resource use against the costs.[5] This is difficult to estimate, because users are not forced to be accurate in their evaluations. If one individual benefits more than another from using a resource, he will be willing to pay a high price to compensate the second in exchange for his rights. Therefore, it is to the advantage of each to overstate the value of the resource to him in order to benefit as much as possible. Unless a mechanism exists to force each potential user to reveal the true value of the resource to him, allocation is difficult and arbitrary.[6]

The critical nature of environmental resources and the problems of information and enforcement of property rights have now been identified. In the following section each issue will be considered in relation to alternative arrangements for environmental management.

Institutional Alternatives

Any proposal for environmental resource management is unlikely to be successful if it does not specify property rights; or, when large groups are involved, provide a mechanism to reduce the decision-making costs among the group members. However, within these constraints a variety of institutional arrangements are feasible—including the classic dichotomy of private or public ownership and management. Both of these general alternatives will be examined to determine if the public-private distinction is relevant or whether it is simply a screen which hides the crucial issues of environmental resource management.

Private Ownership

Many natural resources are privately owned, including land, mines, forests, and beaches. In exchange for his management of the resources, the owner receives payment from users. Part of the payment may be seen as compensation for his managerial function and part as an "unearned" rent, accruing simply because the resource is scarce.[7] If it is decided in the political process that the owner has no special claim to the rents, they may be taxed away with no effect on the allocation or use of the resources.[8] Private ownership of natural resources leads to the most efficient resource use when there are no third party effects from use, and when users of the resource can easily be charged. The owner, in seeking to maximize his return, will sell the resource to the individual who places the highest value on it and excludes potential users who are not willing to pay the market clearing price. Thus the difficult problem of identifying the value of a resource is overcome when the users reveal their preferences by paying the market price. There is then no need for an administrative official to determine how much each potential user values the resource and to administer it accordingly. This is the usual process through which resources are allocated in a private property economy.[9]

A good example of privatization of a publicly owned natural resource was the enclosure movement in medieval England. An increase in the demand for wool stimulated peasants to graze a large number of sheep on common pasture lands, with the result of overgrazing and destruction of the pasturage. From each peasant's point of view, adding another sheep would not increase destruction noticeably, and besides, he reasoned, if he did not add sheep, his neighbor probably would. However, all the peasants' actions taken together had the potential for destroying the valuable resource. Partially to preserve pasture lands, but mostly to obtain the increases in the value of pasturage as wool became more valuable, the stronger lords and nobles undertook to exclude peasant flocks from what had formerly been common land, and eventually they turned most of the land into private property under their control. The new owners then had an incentive to limit the number of sheep permitted to graze the land in order to prevent overgrazing. In some cases, peasants were permitted to graze specified numbers of sheep for a fee; in other cases owners grazed only their own flocks. Once the land was private, its use was also no longer restricted to pasturage. If the demand for wool fell, less land would be needed for grazing sheep, and the owner could turn the land to the production of grain. On the other hand, if the demand for wool increased, potential sheep raisers had an incentive to purchase or rent privately owned land from nonsheep raisers and turn that land into pasturage. Once the resource was private, the owner could be expected to put the land to its best use in response to changing social demands.

The income distribution effects of the enclosure movement were extremely unfavorable to peasants and provided windfall gains to lords and nobles. However, in a society regulated more by justice than police power, it would be possible either to sell natural resources, with the proceeds going to the general public treasury or to former users, or to tax the rents away from the owners, leaving only sufficient returns to compensate for their management.

Other examples of privatization of natural resources include grants of large timber acreages to the railroads and private control of ocean or waterfront beaches in much of the United States. If the resource had a very low value, a private owner might find it in his interest to use the resource up—as happened with the cut-and-run logging practices of the last century. But when the resource has a high value, the owner has an incentive to manage it for highest possible returns, as is done with the vast tree farms owned by timber companies, especially in the Northwest and the Southeast. Privately owned ocean beaches are less common, but it is not clear that the only way to preserve natural amenities and high quality recreational land is to make beaches public rather than private. Where private beaches do exist, the owner limits his gathering of oysters and clams and regulates access to maintain low density use. Public beaches, especially those near large population concentrations, are often overrun with people, and they also become depleted of marine life. Making beaches public may mean simply that many features of the beaches are destroyed. Presumably, this result is not the objective of conservationists who recommend that natural resources be maintained in the public domain.

Ironically, some more socialized countries rely much more on private resource management than does the United States. For example, in England fishing rights to a good salmon stream belong to adjacent land owners. The rights cost over $2000 annually (taxed of course).[10] Also in England, surface rights to reservoirs are usually granted or sold to a "club" which then undertakes to manage all surface uses such as sailing and boating, thus putting the entire common pool under control of a single manager. Nonclub members have access, but they are charged on the basis of their use of the resource.[11] Having different resources managed by different organizations provides greater variety in the quality of resource usage than can be provided in a country where all resources are managed by a single public bureaucracy. Usage based on direct payment may well be the best way to prevent resource destruction in a small, densely populated country like England.

While many examples of efficient resource management through privatization exist, the cost of enforcing property rights, including the right not to be damaged, makes some resources unsuited for relatively unregulated, private management. For example, third party effects from private forestry, such as the siltation of salmon streams caused by logging, are not likely to be controlled without public regulation, unless, as in England, the landowner could receive payment from the fishermen too. Information regarding grazing, forestry, or beach use may be too costly for any individual owner to acquire, but it would be valuable to all if some joint financing could be arranged. Also, it may be more efficient for an owner to lower the value of his resource simply because of pricing convenience. The owner of a primitive area may rent his land for logging because stumpage can be sold, although hikers and campers place a higher value on the area remaining in a natural state. It would be virtually impossible for the owner to try to charge each individual user of the area. For cases of these kinds, it is necessary to examine public ownership and management and evaluate the alternatives.

Public Ownership

Public ownership and management is often advocated as a means of preserving environmental resources. However, public ownership does not necessarily mean that every member of the public can use the resource as often and as much as he wants. If public ownership did mean completely open and unrestricted access, common pool resources would quickly be destroyed from overuse because no single individual would see destructive consequences from his use, while the combined use by all individuals would likely exceed the capacity of the resource. Instead, public ownership and management means that some political official is going to decide by whom, how, and how much a resource is used, rather than private market transactions rationing the resource. That is, the political official rather than the private owner has been assigned the property rights. When a public official controls a resource the question becomes: What incentives does the official face? What benefits will he receive from alternative allocations of the resource that will influence or determine his decisions?

There are cases in which public officials are officially supposed to sell resources to gain revenue for general government.[12] Even here, a public official may not manage as efficiently as a private owner because he does not share the gains of increased revenues resulting from more efficient use, and he may find it in his interest to sell resources below their opportunity cost to politically powerful or friendly groups. If publicly owned resources are not sold, the rationale for public management is often that the nature of the resource makes direct sale unfeasible, even though the potential users still place a high value on the resource. Thus publicly owned resources are likely to generate high unearned rents, like any factor in fixed supply. The question then becomes: Who shall receive the rents?

First, it is not clear that a public official has any incentive to assign publicly owned resources to anyone who does not undertake the most political activity to obtain them; and second, it might not be possible to identify the value various users place on the resource because preferences are not revealed in market-like transactions. Instead, the public official is faced with competing claims, each potential user listing all the reasons he, rather than some other user, should be permitted to use the resource. Competing claims which exceed the capacity of the resource are exactly what can be expected when something valuable is given away.

A public official is also faced with the problem of the disposition of the rents. In general, the constitutions of government agencies in the United States specify that no profits may be made, and revenues are held down to a level just sufficient to cover the direct operating costs of the agency. A scarce resource should be generating large rents which could then be applied to the general costs of government. With prices much lower than they would be if the rents were obtained by a private owner, these potential rents go instead to the users of the resource, thus providing additional incentives for overstating benefits and undertaking political action to obtain larger shares of resource use.

Only limited consideration has so far been given to the allocation of publically owned resources in the United States.[13] Thus, while we know where problems of private ownership lie, it is difficult to draw firm conclusions about the effects of public ownership. However, the evidence available supports these observations:[14]

1. A majority of decisions in the public sector are bargained among administrative officials, between administrative and elected officials, or between administrative officials and private individuals, rather than made in voting or in direct formal administrative relationships.

2. The individuals in the public sector as well as those in the private sector appear to respond to immediate and direct incentives.

3. These incentives appear to be most effectively offered by well-organized groups rather than by unorganized individual citizens.

Most decisions on environmental resource use are also made in bargained agreements between administrative officials and individual representatives of well-organized groups. Elected officials tend to play only a minor role except for the legislation of some constraints as general policy guidelines. Organized groups such as timber interests, mining interests, and cattle ranchers have much more influence on national forest policy than would individual hikers, campers, and fishermen. Traditional marine users such as shippers, commercial fishermen, chambers of commerce, and allied industrial and commercial shoreline users exercise greater influence on shoreline use then swimmers, surfers, picnickers, duck hunters, and others who prefer the shoreline to be left in a relatively natural state.

Public ownership and management of resources will probably benefit well-organized groups as would the private assignment of property rights; although with public ownership valuable rents will be obtained by users instead of resource owners. Even public agencies may neglect third party interests. (For example, is the Army Corps of Engineers any better than Weyerhaeuser in this regard? Probably not.) Unless individual citizens become well organized and active in the political process, their interests are neglected. And even when citizens do become interested enough to organize, their political staying power is likely to be much weaker than that of well-organized economic interests whose welfare depends on the dominance of public agencies.[15]

If we return to the issues raised previously and ask what differences exist because of public rather than private ownership of natural resources, it appears that there are very few. The possibility of external effects and the common pool nature of the resource remain the same. Property rights must be allocated, in one case by a private owner and in the other case by public officials. The large group problem may or may not have been resolved in either case. Unless the political organization managing the resource is designed very carefully, large numbers of individual users are more likely to be neglected under public ownership. As for information, when the resource can be sold, a private owner will obtain the most accurate information available for evaluating alternative potential users. A public official, however, will have only equally competing demands to evaluate. If the scale is large, the public official may have an incentive to undertake research to learn the long range effects of alternative resource uses. However, in general, the American political process with its two- and four-year election cycles is not noted for long range planning or for sacrificing current benefits for greater future benefits.

All that really changes in converting resources from private to public ownership are the incentives faced by the managers of the resources. The private owner faces market demands (which can also be articulated by political groups), and the political official faces political demands. If anything, the private owner might respond to all potential user demands much more efficiently than the political official. He will certainly have better information on alternative values. Equally important, if private ownership does create negative external effects, individuals affected still have recourse to political officials and the courts to obtain compensation. If the effects are generated by a political official allegedly managing public resources in the public interest, recourse is much more difficult to obtain, as political units usually avoid being subjected to lawsuits without their permission.

In order to make a rigorous comparison of the expected consequences of private or public management of a natural resource, one has to examine the nature of the particular resource involved, the constraints and incentives that exist for either the private owner or the public official, and the ability of large groups to deal with private owners or to compete politically. In addition, one has to examine whether either private or public management would ever permit a single group or interest to obtain a monopoly over the resource use and exclude other users. And finally, one would have to determine just what kind of information would be produced in either market transactions or in the political bargains struck between the public manager and resource user. In none of these issues can one draw the conclusion that one form of ownership and management is unquestionably superior to the other.

Conclusions

Distinguishing between private and public resources management is usually meaningless in determining how effectively a resource will be used or preserved. Instead, one must look at the specific incentives either the private owner or the public manager faces in allocating the resources he controls. This leads to an entire range of questions about market structure and political structure within which private and public sectors interact in many complex ways. For example, even a private owner depends on governmentally enforced property rights, and the public manager depends on private rewards such as a salary increase or professional promotion. If the private owner can capture the gains from efficient resource management, there are reasons to expect he will manage and preserve the resource more efficiently than a public official. There is not justification for assuming that merely changing the ownership of a resource from private to public will result in more efficient usage or prevent its destruction.

Notes

1. Externality issues and their complications are treated in more detail in Robert L. Bish, *The Public Economy of Metropolitan Areas* (Chicago: Markham, 1971), chap. 2. For the classic statement on common pool resources see H. Scott Gordon, "The Economic Theory of a Common-Property Resource: The Fishery," *Journal of Political Economy*, **62** (April 1954), 124–142.

2. For an analysis of property rights and transaction costs, see R. H. Coase, "The Problem of Social Cost," *Journal of Law and Economics*, **3** (October 1960), 1–44; and N. S. Cheung, "The Structure of a Contract and the Theory of a Non-exclusive Resource," *Journal of Law and Economics*, **13** (April 1970), 49–70.

3. The classic analysis of group size in relation to undertaking action for individual benefit is Mancur Olson, *The Logic of Collective Action: Public Goods and the Theory of Groups* (Cambridge, Mass.: Harvard University Press, 1965).

4. For an analysis of the separation of demand and production factors in the urban public economy, see Robert Warren, "A Municipal Services Market Model of Metropolitan Organization," *Journal of the American Institute of Planners*, **30** (August 1964), 193–204. For an analysis of British Government demand articulation and private supply of parks, see Warren A. Johnson, *Public Parks on Private Lands in England and Wales* (Baltimore: Johns Hopkins Press, 1971).

5. These conclusions are based on the assumption that for prices to be meaningful in comparing gains and losses to different individuals, the prices must emerge from voluntary transactions which exhaust all potential gains from trade. That is a situation in which no one can benefit without someone else losing, each by their own evaluations of their own situation. For an analysis of efficiency conditions, see Francis M. Bater, "The Simple Analytics of Welfare Maximization," *American Economic Review*, **47** (March 1957), 22–49.

6. For further analysis of the relation between incentives and information, see F. A. Hayek, "The Use of Knowledge in Society," *American Economic Review*, **70** (September 1945), 519–530.

7. An "economic rent" is the difference between the cost of providing the resource and the amount paid for its use. The cost of natural resources is very low, and yet high prices must be paid in order to bid them out of reach of destruction.

8. Economic rents are generally captured only by the first owner of a resource. For example, the discoverer of a mine may sell it for a high price, the difference between the cost of discovery and the selling price being a rent. Subsequent owners, however, do not receive rents as they pay for the value of the mine when they purchase it. Thus to tax rents, one must get at the first owner, who is not necessarily the current owner.

9. Ethical justification for resource allocation based on market forces depends on the competitive functioning of labor markets as well.
10. Johnson, p. 35.
11. Johnson, p. 79.
12. For example, the Washington State Department of Natural Resources manages state owned forests, tide lands, and subsurface lands with a maximizing revenue mandate.
13. See Vincent Ostrom, "Water Resource Development: Some Problems in Economic and Political Analysis of Public Policy", in Austin Ranney, ed., *Political Science and Public Policy* (Chicago: Markham, 1968), pp. 123–150.
14. One analysis that brings out these conclusions very well is Aaron Wildavsky, *The Politics of the Budgetary Process* (Boston: Little, Brown, 1964).
15. As mentioned in Part II, the primary role of political organization may be to overcome the cost–benefit problems of large groups. For further analysis of the use of political organizations to resolve large group problems, see Bish, chap. 3; and James M. Buchanan and Gordon Tullock, *The Calculus of Consent* (Ann Arbor: University of Michigan Press, 1962).

22

Property Rights, Environmental Quality, and the Management of National Forests

John Baden and Richard Stroup

The Conventional View on Property Rights

It is commonly asserted that American society places too much value on property rights, too many of these property rights are in private hands, and much too little value is placed on human rights. Variants of this view are associated with liberal and radical politics. They were extremely common in the flood of environmental crisis literature after Earth Day, 1970. This position is overly simplistic and betrays a gross and perhaps dangerous ignorance of the social functions of property rights and the forces that determine their evolution.

We hope to explain here that a fundamental cause of inefficient resources use is an institutional structure that underweights, assigns to wrong parties, neglects, or otherwise fails to include, certain existing or potential property rights. We suggest efforts to modify rights in the national forests. In brief, we suggest that net improvements in both efficiency and equity are likely to result if certain of the property rights in the national forests are sold to private parties.

This article has been revised from an earlier version by the same authors entitled "Private Rights, Public Choices, and the Management of National Forests," which appeared in *Western Wildlands*, **2**, no. 4 (Autumn 1975), 5–13.

The Evolution of Property Rights

In an extremely simple social environment property rights are of little importance. For a pure hermit like Robinson Crusoe before Friday, property rights were simply irrelevant. Property rights are tools used to organize society. They encourage constructive behavior, reduce uncertainty, and have a capacity for prediction that can result in long-range productive activities with a promise of potential rewards.

In effect, property rights specify how persons may be benefited or harmed. There is a clear relationship between the structure of property rights and the lawful ability of an individual to impose costs or external effects on others. An obvious example would be that of the paper company which, under one system of rights, may have society's implicit permission to use the atmosphere or watershed as an environmental sink for its wastes.

It is our basic argument that cultural shifts (or changing beliefs and values), changes in the relative values of resources, new technology, and increased social interdependence all may require the development of new property rights. With such changes, property rights can account for externally imposed costs to which the old system was insensitive. The movement in this direction is a primary thrust of the environmental movement. Further, it has historic precedents. New property rights will develop when relative values shift to make defining and enforcing these rights worthwhile.

For example, anthropological evidence establishes a close link between the development of private rights to land and the commercial fur trade involving the Indians of Northeastern North America. Property rights were modified by the Indians to reduce externalities, in this case the overhunting of game.

In the absence of property rights to animals or their habitat there is no sanctioned ability to control hunting and trapping. Under conditions of high demand, overkill or hunting beyond sustained yield would take place. Thus, success by one party on the trapline imposed external costs on following trappers.

Prior to the establishment of the fur trade, hunting and trapping were for domestic consumption only. Hence, demand for the game resource was low and externalities or imposed costs were negligible. Thus, there was no reason to have recognized property rights in land and associated resources.

With the development of the fur trade, the value of furs increased dramatically and as a result the scale of hunting increased. The negative externalities associated with free hunting became more than trivial and as a consequence, the property rights system was modified.

By the early 1700s territorial hunting and trapping arrangements based on kin ties developed in Quebec and Newfoundland. The Iroquois, for example, appropriated land two leagues square for each group. Similar developments were found among the coastal tribes of the North-west. Rights among some of the latter tribes included inheritance.

In sum, property rights changed with changing conditions, especially the changing value of a resource. When it became economically beneficial, property rights developed that encouraged the conservation of fur-bearing animals, with the concomitant ability and incentive to prevent poaching.[1]

Implications of Property Rights for Forest Use

Economic growth and development fundamentally involve the manner in which resources are used, producing utilities and disutilities. The re-sponse of decision makers to the opportunities for development are determined by the "rules of the game," or public laws and contracts. An important concern when considering the proposed development of Western lands is that certain important property rights will be unassigned, that the costs of negotiating these rights will be so high as to preclude efficient use of the resources, or that the structure of rights preclude optimum use of the resource. It can be demonstrated that without the cost of negotiation and transaction, production outcome would be identi-cal regardless of who has rights to air and watersheds.[2] On the other hand, high costs of negotiating and enforcing rights can yield inefficient allocations. Other inefficiencies can be expected if the structure of prop-erty rights insulate resource managers from market or other public forces.

In the United States the rules of the game have traditionally fostered economic development, often at the expense of amenity resources. When resources were abundant and population low, this was socially optimal. There comes a time, however, when it is preferable to modify this bias and grant people rights to amenities.

Generally, then we face two related problems. First, some rights such as amenities, may be either unassigned or difficult to enforce. Second, management responsibilities may be assigned to those insulated from the preference of potential consumers. There is then less of a cushion to absorb the opportunity costs of providing amenities.

The pressure for changing the rules of the game will arise when the costs of these changes are outweighed by the projected benefits from the new rules. Thus, attempts to change the rules are productive activities to which resources can be devoted. As culture and technology change, increasing the value of a bundle of rights, the return on defining and enforcing these rights becomes greater. As high quality air, water, scenery, and back country have become scarce, and thus more valuable, individuals have attempted to better define their rights to these resources. This process will be a critical feature of the struggle for control of Western lands and resources. A failure to understand the importance of this contest over property rights will seriously disadvantage those of us interested in fostering quality management of our national forests. In terms of commodity production, a change in rules may lead to more nearly optimal regulation of the forests. Both of these advantages are likely to be lost through an inappropriate institutional structure.

Institutional Pathology and the Bureaucratic Management of National Forest Lands

A bureaucracy is defined as an organization that (1) receives at least part of its budget from grants rather than exclusively from the sale of packageable goods; and (2) has managers who neither receive a portion of its profits as personal income nor personally absorb any of its losses. From the standpoint of public welfare, these features create the possibility of a pathological institution, that is, one that does not serve its supposed purpose. In the area of forest management, the danger is especially great.

It is reasonable to assume that bureaucrats, like other people, are primarily self-interested. As a rule, both bureaucrats and businessmen generate public benefits primarily as byproducts of efforts to enhance their own well-being. The private businessman offering services and products for sale is far more likely to pay attention to the preferences of the consuming public than is his public servant counterpart.

We are not prepared to argue that the bureaucrat is either less moral or less intelligent than his counterpart in the private sector. Given that nonpriced products dominate the output of public agencies, it is exceedingly difficult to estimate the relative values of these products. No matter how intelligent or well-intended the public administrator, it is probably impossible for him to produce at the socially optimum level other than by luck. Without the benefit of the high-quality information generated by the market, he has no easy way to determine what the optimum level is. In the auto industry, decisions on how many autos of each style, size, color, etc. are difficult, but executives get daily reality checks, in the form of relative sales information to tell them when and where corrections should be made. Each customer makes his choice, pays the price for added costs, and must live with his own decision. By contrast, the public sector consumer who has the same very small influence but will pay only a tiny share of added cost for added output, will typically be either apathetic or enthusiastically in favor of more of the goods *he* enjoys. Apathy, and indeed, ignorance on his part, is rational because in the public sector informed action will seldom influence what he is able to consume. He has to live with what the *public* chooses, regardless of his own actions.

In general, although there are massive amounts of waste in the public sector, and even some fraud and graft, the greatest inefficiency flows from very strong pressures on the bureaucrat to exceed the optimal size and scope, and hence the budget, of a public agency.[3]

For social efficiency, agencies should produce only to the point where the extra product is just worth the extra cost. Government agencies are fundamentally social tools to be employed when the opportunity costs of private action are excessive. Clearly then, the relative social value of any agency's production is a function of the state of the larger system. Budgets of the various bureaus should shift in response to changes in the relative social value of their products. It follows that the public spirited bureaucrat would occasionally argue that a portion of his budget should be allocated toward his competition in the public sector. As far as we know, this never happens. Pressures for growth apparently counter and swamp considerations of general welfare.

From the perspective of the self-interested administrator, there are very good reasons to argue for continuous expansion. The bureaucrat, because he lacks market information on the relative value of his product and those of other public agencies, suffers from the absence of an obvious and immediate reality check on what he wants to believe. Thus, it is easy for him to harbor the illusion that his agency has above average merit and therefore deserves above average budget increases.

If public welfare is to be optimized, public funds should be allocated in accord with the equimarginal principle. In the best of worlds funds would be shifted among agencies and their bureaus and offices in such a manner that the marginal benefits of those funds would be equal for each unit.

Unfortunately, however, in nonmarket activities we have only rough approximations of value produced. Hence, if there are systematic biases in the budgetary process, society would gain if certain functions were transferred from the political to the market allocation sector. This logic holds whether the agency's budget is either too large or too small. Many have argued, for example, that silvicultural segments of the Forest Service budget have been too small. Implicit in this position is the claim that the marginal benefits from additional investments are greater than those in alternative programs. This would imply that the private timber owner could increase his wealth by investing in more silvicultural practices.

In many cases waste is generated from the bureau being above optimum size, although substantial forces lead in this direction. For the bureau head, civil service rank, prestige, pay, and office amenities all are strongly related to the size of his bureau. (For example, in one university, for years only deans and above could have IBM typewriters.) In addition, expansion generates more possibilities for promotion. This enhances the ability to control those under his charge, since under Civil Service rules firings are nearly impossible to execute successfully. To gain control over inferiors the promise of promotions may be offered as inducements.

Of perhaps equal importance for the ambitious bureaucrat is the fact that a large proportion of his budget is "locked in" from previous years. This, of course, reduces the range of discretionary expenditures. New funds offer far more opportunities for flexibility and innovation.

Therefore, society may be better off if some public sector allocating functions were transferred to the private sector. Market forces could then determine the level of investment appropriate for the diverse preferences found in society. The problems of both over and under investment discussed above would be vitiated or, at the minimum, the costs of inappropriate investments would be borne by the private parties responsible for the errors. In the following section we consider some of the implications of selling property rights in the national forests.

Expected Impacts of Selling National Forests[4]

Proposed solutions to problems of managing the national forests range from small changes in criteria or practices to rather drastic changes in the form and function of management itself. Milton Friedman and others have suggested that government agencies should not manage these forests at all. Instead there would be private managers, and the present value of the forests would be captured for public use by auctioning off rights (title) to the lands in question.

The effectiveness of management, however measured, depends on the combination of information and incentives facing the decision maker, within his given context. In a market system with private ownership of rights, incentives and most information flow are handled through prices. We need not rely on good will, morality, or principle: greed will suffice. Within a market context people are of course free to ignore the wishes of others—expressed through bid and asked prices—but when prices are not distorted, resource users and owners sacrifice wealth exactly to the extent that they ignore those wishes. It is largely the efficiency of prices in transmitting information, and their effectiveness in providing incentive without coercion, which make the market system attractive.

The advantages claimed for this sort of resource management system include diversity, individual freedom, adaptiveness, the production of information, and a certain equity. Diversity is fostered because there is no single centralized decision maker, but many asset owners and entrepreneurs, each of whom can exercise his own vision. Those who correctly anticipate people's desires are most rewarded. Individual freedom is preserved as those who wish to participate in and support each activity may do so on the basis of willing consent. Adaptiveness is encouraged in both management and consumption, since prices provide immediate information and incentive. If only a few see scarcities or opportunities ahead, they can buy, sell, or provide expertise as a small group of consultants, and thus direct resource use without having to convince a majority. In this case profits will reward foresight and quick action, while losses discipline those who divert resources foolishly.

Production of information in a market situation is slowly being recognized for its own importance. Activities not marketed prove very difficult to manage rationally for there is little or no concrete evidence of how people really value them. We know, for example, how much people are willing to sacrifice for a thousand board feet of lumber, but how much would they pay for a day's access to a wilderness area? In the latter case we have only rough estimates. Even the most conscientious and competent manager cannot make good managment decisions without knowledge of the absolute and relative values of his various outputs.

Finally, there is a measure of equity in having those people who use a resource pay for it by sacrificing some of their wealth. The proceeds from the sale of public assets could be distributed, or invested and perpetually distributed to the poor, for example. Those using the forests would be required to pay, whether it be for recreation, timber harvest, or even research in a unique area.

Unfortunately, the orderly picture above does not fully describe all real world market situations. The prime villain in disturbing the beauty of the picture is what economists and political scientists call "externalities." Broadly, this means that asset owners or managers may not be in a position to capture all the benefits of their various actions. It is clear that in a market situation there is normally little incentive to provide goods or services that offer no return. If, for example, a forest owner could not (at low cost) exclude those recreationists who did not pay for access, receipts would understate recreational valuation, and he would have a diminished incentive to preserve or provide recreational opportunity. Among potential externalities are flood control, watershed provision, weather modification, animal habitat, biotic diversity, and environmental buffering. These effects might be partially internalized by placing restrictions on the title transfer, constraining the buyers to avoid certain socially costly decisions. But to the extent that this happens, the benefits of market organization and individually expressed preferences are eschewed. In practice management is generally left to those who have relatively little incentive to be guided by preferences expressed in relative prices. In sum, externality is recognized by many economists and political scientists as a necessary, but not sufficient, condition for government interference with markets. However, an important form of externality is pervasive also in all governmental forms of organization. At best, decision makers are held accountable by the threat of replacement. They do not directly receive the gains from better management (or costs from poor management) as private resource owners generally do.

Given the problems of market failures, people exercising "bad taste" or wanting "the wrong things," and the elimination of subsidy from those of us who now use the national forests at a reduced price, perhaps we should consider separating property rights from the land and selling only a portion of those rights now associated with the land. The rights sold would be those that can be effectively handled via market transaction.

Another fundamental law of political economy is that public goods, if privately supplied, tend to be under-supplied. The benefits of public goods cannot be captured via the market and people have a strong resistance to giving up valuable resources when the projected return is less than the cost. Thus, we should identify the public goods of the national forests and segregate them from the sale. Because the projected costs of enforcing property rights are so high, the provision of wilderness experiences is as much a public good as the examples given above. Thus if we want to prevent undervaluing these goods, we should keep them in the public sector and assign production responsibilities to a variety of competing agencies. The best argument for granting one agency a monopoly is one of economies of scale, and only occasionally would we anticipate such economies. Competition among the agencies, however, will benefit diverse public interests.

There are two obvious sets of rights that could be sold to private parties, rights to timber production and rights to grazing. However, there are interdependencies between these property rights and the public goods supplied by the forest. If general welfare is to be maximized, negative externalities must be controlled. Hence, the timber and grazing rights must be sold subject to constraints determined by potential impacts of harvesting and silvicultural practices upon the public goods.

Timber

Let us first consider selling timber rights. Note that it is not the land that would be sold, but rather the standing timber and the right to produce timber on some portion of the land. If the value of timber is expected to increase, then relatively intensive silviculture would be expected of the private operator, who had estimated both the costs and the benefits from various rates of harvest and levels of investment. The same incentives do not bear upon public managers insulated from market forces. The public manager is likely to find the prospect of increasing production more attractive than a rational consideration of the marginal benefits from this increase would indicate. Growing trees is fun. Growing more units per hectare is even more fun, and the implications of diminishing marginal returns are not very important to the bureaucratic silviculturalist.

Conversely, there are situations in which additional investments in silviculture are socially beneficial. Yet the bureaucrat must rely upon political allocations for budget increases. He is competing in the public sector with alternatives such as a space program, a foreign military adventure, or expanded welfare programs. The primary issues are not efficiency and equity, but rather skills of political mobilization and leverage. Because elections come every two, four or six years, the discount rate in the public sector may be very high. Thus there is under-investment in programs whose payoff is more than an election or two away. Until we achieve two-year rotations of Douglas fir we might expect this bias to be controlling.

It is also possible for environmental groups to dominate decisions to such a degree that timber harvest is scheduled at suboptimal phasings. This constitutes a transgenerational transfer. All we could expect from economic analysis is an explication of these shifts of benefit flow and an estimation of their consequences. Under the existing system, socially optimum use is largely a matter of luck.

It is, however, exceedingly important that the rights to produce timber not preclude production of public goods. For example, hunting, camping, and hiking rights would still be held by the public and the timber operator would be accountable for the costs of increased erosion. If property rights for fishing the drainage were sold to political districts or private groups such as Trout Unlimited or American Sportsman, then there would be a party with vested interest in protecting the quality of the watershed. More importantly, these sporting groups would have established, legally recognized property rights that could be protected by the legal process.

Selling timber rights to the national forests should not result in a shift to strictly short-sighted goals, such as immediate exploitation of logging to the detriment of long-run productivity. The owner of a forest may be 50 years old and expect to live only to 70; but, even if he wants to leave his heirs nothing, he will maximize his own returns by managing the forest in such a way as to maximize long-run expected value. He would thus sell out when he wants cash and would receive expected market value. Of course, if timber prices are expected to rise less rapidly than other prices, then immediate harvest may make sense both privately and socially, depending on timber growth rates and the effects of timber harvest on alternative forest land uses. Only in those cases when private owners cannot capture increased values of better management will they not be penalized for being short-sighted.

Grazing Rights

Substantial improvements could also be made in the allocation of rights to grazing and forage production. If demand for meat increases dramatically over the medium run, the value of forage will increase. Hence, the advantages from more effective management would be correspondingly greater. If the amenity values associated with wildlife populations, especially predators, increase, again greater advantages will come from improved property rights to these resources. In general, if either scarcity or culture increases the value of resources, then the payoffs from improved management also increase. In this section we argue that substantial improvements are likely to result from changes in the distribution of property rights for grazing on the national forests.

First, although existing practice suggests the contrary, subsidized rights for grazing privileges were not cast on gold tablets and distributed by God.* They represent an evolution, guided by the selective pressures of the political process, which transferred wealth from the general public to the holders of permits. The permittees then have been able to capitalize the value of these rights in the private lands which serve as a home base for their stock. Thus, the market value of a ranch with assigned AUMs is greater than an equally productive ranch that lacks AUMs on public lands. The maintenance of these rights is primarily, if not exclusively, a matter of administrative tradition rather than law. This tradition, however, is so well established that many western bankers will accept AUMs as partial collateral on a ranch mortgage. Normally, the government AUMs sell for much less than private AUMs, with the amount ranging from 10 percent to occasionally 100 percent of a market clearing price.

In the case we know best, one author of this essay receives about 700 percent more for the AUMs he sells from his land in Montana than does the Forest Service on land two to six miles away. Part of this difference may be due to the convenience afforded by corrals, loading chutes, etc., but most is accounted for by a windfall gain to the original holders of Forest Service AUMs. If the holder of Forest Service AUMs did not acquire them by buying a ranch with the value of the AUMs capitalized

---

*Such grazing privileges are measured in terms of "animal unit months" or AUMs. One AUM = pasture for one cow with calf for one month.

in its purchase price, he is being subsidized. If these values were capitalized in the sale of the ranch, the value of the AUMs constitutes a windfall gain to the original permittee.

Given that the holder of government AUMs has only imperfect property rights in his AUMs, he has a diminished incentive to make improvements on his land. Clearly these rights are politically determined and, hence, are inherently arbitrary. In the absence of clear and enforceable property rights in AUMs, we fully expect a suboptimal investment in long-run improvements. Further, the threat that these rights are temporary encourages overgrazing the land and treating it as a modified commons. Although the USFS regulates the number of animals permitted, many stockmen trespass additional animals on "their" unit. The costs of excessive use are distributed among the entire population in the form of diminished productivity of the land base. The costs of diminished wildlife habitat and increased erosion are entirely transferred to the general public.

Again, it seems reasonable to suggest that property rights to some of the forage produced by national forest lands be sold on the open market. Then the primary costs of overgrazing would be felt by those responsible for the errors. Furthermore, trespass animals would constitute theft from the federal government identical to other types of public theft and subject to the same range of criminal liabilities. When the property rights to government AUMs are sold, the public goods generated by these lands should be protected. If the domestic stock is sympatric with wildlife, some measures should be taken to protect the wildlife from competition. If an error is made in overestimating the number of AUMs sold for an area or if the value of wildlife increases relative to that of stock, then some of the AUMs could be bought back from the stockman at market value by exercising eminent domain. In contrast, if stock is symbiotic with valuable wildlife, as sometimes happens with deer and cattle, it may be efficient to subsidize stock. In the latter case, the stock produces positive externalities in terms of improved wildlife habitats.

Second, the stockman with grazing rights would have strong incentives to make production improvements. Improvements, however, would have to be restrained in order not to diminish other values without just compensation. For example, the holder of grazing rights would not be free to spray, chain, or otherwise decrease environmental quality.

The third advantage concerns a highly emotional topic, the predation of stock by wildlife. An increasing number of Americans place a growing value on such predators as lions and other cats, coyotes, wolves, and bears. Under current arrangements, individuals with subsidized grazing rights are free to kill these animals, and, moreover, this high social deprivation cost is subsidized by government hunters and trappers. Here economic inefficiencies are compounded by inequities.

Currently both interest and information are biased and concentrated in favor of the stockman. While a stockman is quite likely to attribute losses to predation, relatively few people will know that a government trapper took twenty lions from the Lincoln backcountry in one season. The public will be uninformed that twelve verified grizzly bears were killed for sheep predation on the Targhee since 1970 in a state that does not even have an open season on these bears and where the sheep holding pens were, for convenience, built near the center of the grizzly range.

If property rights in grazing were sold on the open market these conditions could improve substantially. Permits would be for forage and would not include any more rights to kill predators than those held by sport hunters. Violations of this provision of the sale would constitute poaching and could result in the forfeiture of grazing rights without compensation. While the remote stockman would still kill some predators and, hence, deprive the public of a valuable resource, the potential costs of his doing so would increase from near zero to something substantial. Some shooting in "self-defense" would doubtlessly occur, but it might be difficult to convince a jury. More importantly, the use of poison baits would be in clear violation of the sale. Predation history or folklore is well known in most local areas. Hence, when grazing rights were auctioned, traditionally high-predator areas would receive lower bids than low-predator lands.

As usual, when the full range of costs and benefits are included, the market would be an efficient allocating device. If this proposal were adopted, by changing the structure of property rights we could anticipate substantial improvements, in equity and efficiency, over the current system, which maximizes the negative features of both bureaucratic and market means of resource allocation.

Notes

1. To see how this process continued after the arrival of the white man, see "The Evolution of Property Rights: A Study of the American West," by T. Anderson and P. J. Hill, in *The Journal of Law and Economics,* **18** (April 1975).
2. See "The Problem of Social Cost," by R. Coase, in *The Journal of Law and Economics,* **3** (October 1960).
3. For a thorough treatment of this topic, see William Niskanen, *Bureaucracy and Representative Government* (Chicago: Aldine, 1971).
4. This section enlarges upon parts of Stroup and Baden, "Externality, Property Rights, and the Management of Our National Forests," *The Journal of Law and Economics,* **16** (1973), 303–312.

23

Neospartan Hedonists, Adult Toy Aficionados, and the Rationing of Public Lands

John Baden

Definitions and Comments

Several colleagues of a philosophical bent have assured me that there can be no such person as a spartan hedonist or a hedonistic spartan. Such constructs are in the same set as unicorns and centaurs. Positing an empty set and building a discussion around it may be taken as strong evidence of precocious senility or marked preference for a private language. I am prepared to argue, however, that while such charges may indeed be well founded, there can be at least modest utility in defining this set, examining it for members and, if any are found, predicting the land-use implications of there being such creatures as neospartan hedonists.

A spartan, briefly, is a person whose life style admits few luxuries and is conducted in a relatively unbuffered environment. He is subject to self-imposed discipline, and, in general, is oriented toward simplicity and physical exertion. In contrast to the spartan is the hedonist, a person oriented primarily toward the exploitation of the pleasure potential of his physical and social environments. The hedonist is associated with mental and physical softness and with the high consumption of material goods. The scion of a liquor, lightbulb, or pig iron dynasty, encysted in a yacht appointed with rich and tasty food and females, provides the paradigm of the hedonist. Given this background, there are obvious reasons for the conjunction of spartan and hedonist to be discounted as impossible. In principle, however, there is nothing to preclude the conjunction.

The neospartan hedonist is one who accepts Colin Fletcher's "law of inverse appreciation" as binding rather than merely descriptive. The law states: "The less there is between you and the environment, the more you appreciate that environment."[1] Hence, this person prefers cross-country skiing or snowshoeing to snowmobiling (or even riding lift chairs), boots to trail bikes, and canoes to motor boats. Material simplicity is highly valued for, among other things, being more consistent with mobility and freedom. For example, in and on the fringes of universities one commonly finds people self-consciously attempting to hold their possessions down to a jeepfull. Ideally, their possessions would all fit in a backpack and on a ten-speed bike. (A $600 stereo and a couple hundred feet of Perlon climbing rope preclude success.) For the ideal neospartan hedonist, most of the stuff that adds to the consumer's share of the GNP has very low or negative utility.

Many of these people favor activities such as climbing, backpacking, and mountain ski touring, whose severity is both demanding and unavoidable. The mere physics of gaining 4000 feet of altitude on skis while carrying a 30-pound pack suggests that such activities are not for the soft and mushy. I would even pose the above as a reasonably serious test of a marine or ranger fresh out of finishing school. For neospartan hedonists, these activities are not athletic events but experiences with high sensual content. Attention is on the fine tuning of a person to his environment rather than mastery over his environment.

The sensuality of the neospartan life style is apparent in the image created by the advertising beamed at this group. The spartan hike sustained by granola and energy bars (or other food that might pass as calf starter) ends in a gourmet dinner featuring wine or brandy followed by a plunge into a double-mummy sleeping bag with an attractive partner. Old-fashioned bundling is wedded to new-fashioned birth controls, thus keeping the future spartanly simple without foregoing present hedonism.

Shifts in Demands for Amenity Goods

Spokesmen for the extractive industries commonly counter the demands of recreationists with the rhetorical question, "Given the increasing demands for lumber (minerals, irrigation water, etc.), how can the U.S. afford to lock up more acres (rivers) in wilderness areas?" It is true that the derived demand for timber and minerals is expanding at a moderate

rate; this rate of expansion, however, is insignificant compared to the shifting demand for amenity goods. The Sierra Club response to the industrialists should be, "With demand for wilderness expanding at a rate of 10+ percent per year, how can the U.S. afford to eliminate any additional wilderness?"

This difference is based on the fact that amenities such as outdoor recreation goods are "superior" goods. In application, the actual demand for amenities such as outdoor recreation increases disproportionately with increases in income. In economic terms, when income is increased the demand curve for these goods (whatever its shape while sloping downward to the right) is shifted to the right and does not intersect the curve for demand before the increase. Given that the United States and other modernized societies will probably become increasingly affluent over at least the medium run, it appears that the demand for outdoor amenities will continue to increase, although not indefinitely, at the current rate of about 8 percent a year. This is substantiated by residential preferences for areas that offer ready access to outdoor recreation.

This argument can be expressed in terms of the shifting marginal utility of products directly consumed (recreation) versus those for which there is derived demand (for example, the demand for stumpage is derived from a demand for lumber and other forest products). Most simply, as the United States becomes increasingly wealthy and accumulates an ever greater volume of "stuff," the value of an additional unit of "stuff" declines. Concurrently, natural amenities are more rare and, hence, more valuable. Therefore, in terms of environmental values, Americans now face the problems of scarce natural amenities.

Direct consumers, the recreationists, do not comprise a homogeneous bunch, nor are their demands mutually harmonious. Those interested in the management of public land are accustomed to conflicts between the direct consumers and those who utilize the public resources in response to derived demand. While these conflicts will continue and increase in intensity with increased competition for resources, conflict among various types of recreational users will also increase.

Contrasting Types of Recreationists

We can better understand conflicts of use allocation among direct consumers if we identify their demands and inconsistencies. The recreationists described above do not use mechanized equipment; they are self-propelled. Their demands are for areas in which the impact of people is essentially unnoticed. Although this group is likely to support some site hardening, their primary management strategy is to disperse people and regulate their behavior to minimize environmental impact. Literature directed to recreationists often admonishes them to "Take nothing but pictures, leave nothing but foot prints." It is, of course, in the interest of recreational equipment firms to have their customers behave with such care. If they do, the carrying capacity of the wilderness, and thus the number of potential customers, will be increased.

In marked contrast are the aficionados of adult toys such as snowmobiles, trail bikes, 4 × 4s with or without campers, and the more exotic ATVs such as Coots. These are the people who, when "getting away from it all," take it all with them. They visit the national parks or TVA dams in a $\frac{3}{4}$-ton air-conditioned pickup, overburdened with a 10-foot cab-over camper, festooned with two trail bikes, and towing a 16-foot outboard speed boat. These are fundamentally the same people who form a club, charter a tractor-trailer rig to haul forty snowmobiles to the Intermountain West, and fly out to meet their snowmobiles, drink beer, and harass game on the winter range.Their spending prompts organizations such as the West Yellowstone Chamber of Commerce to put up 70 × 4-foot banners which read, "West Yellowstone—Snowmobile Capitol of the World—Welcomes Snowmobilers."

It is obvious that there is high potential conflict between these two groups of recreationists. Further, the inconvenience they generate are asymmetric; that is, cross-country skiers impose few externalities upon snowmobilers (or hikers upon trail bikers), but both of the latter disturb the former. On the basis of personal experience, I assure you that it is more than a nuisance to be run off trail by a pack of snowmobiles, and then, hours later, to find that the best camp site at the bottom of a snow bowl has been occupied. In addition to the tracks they leave, the party can be identified by their spoor of cans, Frito wrappers, and disposable aluminum charcoal grills.

The Development of a Bureaucratic Purgatory

Much of this conflict occurs on public land, and thus the issue is the managing of a common pool resource. Problems occur in managing such resources whenever the following conditions arise: first, ownership is held in common; second, users have independent rights to the resource; and third, demand for use of the resource exceeds the supply. Essentially, this is the situation found on much of the public land.

In the absence of regulation and management by the responsible agencies, one expects users to ignore the adverse effect of their action on others. If management is not imposed, the outcome of competition for this common pool resource will be a de facto monopoly of the resource by the group generating the largest negative externality. Skiers and hikers do not diminish the quality of the resource for the mechanized user, but the mechanized user greatly depreciates the quality of the experience for the self-propelled. Thus, the self-propelled, like the elk, are driven even further into the back country. In the absence of allocation by the agencies, resource utilization takes on the character of a negative or a zero-sum game.

Even the most conscientious and competent manager cannot make good decisions about resources without knowledge of the absolute and relative values of his various outputs. Activities not marketed are difficult to manage rationally, for there is little or no concrete evidence of how people really value them. We know, for example, how much people are willing to sacrifice to produce a herd of heifers, but how much will they pay for a sighting of mountain goats?

Agency data on amenity production has been sketchy at best. The management of the common pool resources used by recreationists is especially difficult because many of the values are not readily quantifiable —they are nonpackaged, difficult to market and, therefore, difficult to evaluate.

Although the market sometimes operates to foster coordination with minimum planning, a market solution seems inappropriate for many of the cases at hand. Governmental management and public planning are required, and with them comes conflict for the responsible agencies.

Given that the public lands are for multiple uses, relatively few of which can be easily marketed, the essential problem of balancing the various ecological tradeoffs with a mix of social values is difficult. A manager must not only understand the ecological impact of alternative management practices, he must also predict and incorporate, in the absence of full market pricing, the social values of various recreations sought by the public. This lack of objective, observable evaluations of resources and outputs, as well as market incentives, hampers efforts to achieve socially desirable results.

Until about 1940, managers of the public lands were mainly custodians. They were to stamp out bugs and fires, guard against timber and grass poachers, find the occasional lost tourist, and build roads and trails. They could rely on their professional judgment while playing the role of benevolent despots working for the public interest. Now, however, with demand exceeding supply in many areas, one type of use precludes others. As a result, the land manager has become the focus of cross-fire.

With crowding beyond carrying capacity there is a need to ration the utilization of facilities. Rationing, however, depends on enforcement mechanisms and a resultant diversion of agency time and money. Rather than being to Smokey the Bear as elves are to Santa Claus, land managers become policers and enforcers. This is likely to be an unpleasant duty for a person whose training is wholly in the natural sciences.

Rationing

If efficiency is the criterion, there is a social justification for rationing whenever excess demand diminishes aggregate satisfaction. In other terms, if one can move toward a Pareto optimal situation by modifying comsumption patterns, there is a justification for imposing a rationing system. There are several types of rationing that could be appropriate to the allocation problem. Any of them is consistent with management efforts to increase the supply of the scarce resource.

Garrett Hardin deserves substantial credit for broadcasting the classic wisdom of political arithmetic; that is, people in a commons have an incentive to ignore the social impact of private behavior. Given the problems of estimating values, a critical feature of any rationing scheme is the degree to which it provides information about the interdependence of competing demands and the opportunity cost of various actions.

From the perspective of the land manager, an acceptable rationing system would have one primary attribute. It would force each user to take the opportunity costs generated for others into account when using the common pool resource. Something analogous to a price system, which tells people that the opportunity cost of a Cadillac is 3.26 Datsuns or 74.61 Peugeot bicycles, would be useful to the bureaucrats responsible for allocating land.

In the happy situation when, at zero price, demand does not exceed supply, there is little need to pay much attention to demand. When this is not the case, and in the absence of equilibrium pricing, demands provide meaningful information only when considered in relation to supply. Otherwise, members of each user group will have incentives to allocate use so as to maximize the aggregate net benefit, and actual allocation will be made on the basis of political power and agency preference. There is reason to believe that the relationship between politically motivated allocation and aggregate net benefit is inverse.

In contrast, a rationing system that takes into account contending interests and their interdependence decreases the possibility of a monopoly developing in the common pool.

There are four rationing systems that might be employed to allocate land use among competing recreationists. In terms of aggregate net welfare, the system chosen would not increase one set of benefits without further decreasing others. There is little reason to believe that the bureaucracies involved would seek to maximize net social benefits. Bureaucracies tend to be run primarily for the bureaucrats, and the self-interest of the bureaucrats tends to be consistent with that of their stronger clients. Thus, a land manager would be expected to arrive at a system that is easy to administer and police, does not significantly disadvantage powerful groups in the political system, and improves the competitive position of the agency's stronger clientele groups. If there are several strong groups with competing and inconsistent demands, we would expect the agency to design a system that accommodated them all. If, however, the situation is in the form of a zero or negative-sum game, agency personnel will exist in a type of purgatory, and great emphasis will be placed on finding strategies to convert the situation into a positive-sum game. Given these conditions, we can consider alternative rationing schemes. In each case an effort is made to identify the group benefitted by the proposed scheme.

Rationing by Reservation

One of the most obvious rationing systems is by reservation. If the capacity of an area is set at 100 visitors per day, then visiting privileges are assigned to 100 visitors, presumably the first 100 to submit reservation forms. It is likely, however, that some of the visits will be reserved, on the basis of administrative discretion, for those persons especially important to the agency. I would be very surprised if a member of Congress or a heavy political contributor could not obtain a reservation for the time of his choosing. This could, of course, be done by expanding the quota for the day. Should this type of corruption become known, the agency would lose credit among the public.

This system is an advantage to those who think far enough ahead and who can plan their free time confidently. It is biased against the improvident, the spontaneous, and those who are suddenly granted vacations at unforeseen times.

If reservations are free or very cheap, people have an incentive to make reservations even if they may not be able to use their privilege. Then the facility will tend to be underutilized during a period of high demand.

This system is socially inefficient unless there is an open market for the reservations obtained. Under this system, for example, a person receiving 100 units of satisfaction from a wilderness experience could be precluded entry by one whom the experience yields only 1 unit of satisfaction if the former's reservation request were postmarked one day later than the latter's. If there were a well-functioning market for the reservations obtained, this source of inefficiency would be eliminated. In the process, however, one set of people would receive windfall gains.

Rationing by Random Selection

In this system, people would be assigned numbers, and then a set of numbers equal to the carrying capacity of the facility would be selected at random. In addition to having the disadvantages listed for the reservation system, this would require all people to postpone their final plans until the actual drawing of lots. This system appears to have worked fairly well in allocating big-game permits for such animals as moose and mountain goats. However, the issue there is not congestion but rather the number of animals taken during a season.

In terms of access to wilderness areas or national parks, the initial issue often is the peaking of demands. A random selection mechanism could function most smoothly if information were provided as to the probabilities of success as a function of time. If, for example, people were advised that, on the basis of previous years, the probability of obtaining a visiting permit was 0.01 for the 4th of July, 0.10 for the 4th of June and 1.00 for the 4th of October, people could be expected to weigh the advantages of visiting at a specific time against the probability of gaining admission, and then apply for the dates that would maximize their utility. The time demand curves might then smooth out considerably.

Rationing by Queuing

The "simple" system designed to ration by queuing is one of the most complex and highly misunderstood systems available. A queue is actually a price in terms of time. Smolensky has suggested that "Time prices also have an intuitive appeal because time as such is more equally distributed than money."[2] This suggestion neglects the fact that the amount of time available for future opportunities decreases with age.

Perhaps the greatest disadvantage of queuing is that the price of the good or service is time spent waiting, but no one receives the benefit of the price. Thus, potential revenue is not obtained by the suppliers of the resource. Obviously, this system discriminates against those for whom time has a high opportunity cost. To the degree that the opportunity cost of time is a function of wages per unit of time, this system in effect is a progressive tax on the use of facilities. Graphically then, one would expect the curve shown in Figure 23.1 for two people, H a person with a high wage rate and L, one with a low wage rate. In this example H would pay a high money price to use a facility because his time is dear, while L would be willing to pay a high time price because for him money is more dear than time.

It is important to remember that as long as there is competition for the use of the recreational resource base, for logging or mining, for example, capacity cannot be expanded indefinitely. Further, it would be difficult even for Disneyland to replicate Old Faithful or the Grand Canyon. Hence, at zero money price where demand exceeds supply, the queue filters out users for whom time has a high opportunity cost. Therefore, goods supplied publicly at congested facilities are not "public goods," but rather goods whose price is a function of opportunity costs of time.

This system of rationing is clearly an advantage to those whose time has a low opportunity cost. Perhaps most seriously disadvantaged are the

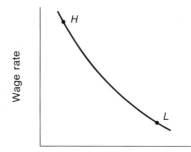

FIGURE 23.1
Time–money trade-offs.

lower-middle class and the working poor. Such a system would tend to keep these groups, now very significantly underrepresented in the national parks and wilderness areas, locked into their current position. In contrast, those who benefit the most from rationing by queuing are members of the professional class who have the freedom to schedule their visits when queues are very short, people such as students who have large amounts of discretionary time and relatively low opportunity costs for this time.

Rationing by Pricing at Equilibrium

Casual observation leads me to believe that there is considerable resistance to this method of rationing because it precludes access by the poor. This argument assumes that poor people currently do visit national parks and wilderness areas, and that alternative rationing systems would disadvantage the poor less than a system based on price. This second point suggests that for the poor, time has a low opportunity cost; that the poor can plan ahead better than the affluent and, hence, can submit their reservations earlier than others; or that the poor enjoy greater success at corrupting officials than the affluent. It is clear that the relatively wealthy are advantaged by a system that rations via pricing.

Recommendations

If current trends continue, there will be increased competition over the allocation of the public lands. Competition between recreational and extractive uses is a central problem, but it is discussed elsewhere. Allocation among the various incompatible recreational uses entails two fundamental issues.

First is the degree to which the uses generating the greatest social costs are permitted to dominate by making the area so unpleasant for other uses that the self-propelled—those with the light impact—are driven out. Numerous studies have indicated that the light users tend to have relatively high education and, aside from students, high incomes.[3] Comcomitantly, these people participate effectively in the political process. In the major work that has been done on political participation, Verba and Nie state that "social status has a closer relationship to political participation in the U.S. than in all but one of nine other countries for which it was possible to obtain data based on measurement similar enough to allow comparison."[4] The self-propelled, however, do not support industries nearly as large as the recreational vehicle industry. Further, the "soft" users are unlikely to spend as much on accommodations, lift tickets, fuel, and ritual apparel that changes style yearly. Hence, each group begins the political game with one advantage, making it very difficult to predict the outcome. One might note, however, that many of the light users are self-conscious regarding the role of people in the natural environment. Further, many of this group appear to view environmental issues as essentially religious in nature and are zealous in pursuing policies. In contrast, the mechanized seem to view their activities simply as a means of having a good time and, aside from sunk costs, may be indifferent between riding their trail bikes or watching a stock car race on a Sunday afternoon. In brief, the latter group is burdened with less ideological baggage.

The second issue in allocation involves the type of rationing employed. Rationing either by reservation or by random selection appears equitable and moderately easy to administer. Furthermore, bureaucrats, who by definition receive no portion of the difference between cost and revenue as personal income, have little incentive to increase net social benefit. Therefore, these two systems are likely to be preferred by the agencies.

When excess demand builds up, however, there will be increasing pressure to adopt one of the payment systems. People who want access badly will be willing to pay substantial amounts of either time or money to gain access; thus these are people who have the greatest incentive for the political action required to change the method of rationing. Although large centralized bureaucracies find it very difficult to make decisions that are time and place specific, I believe one can argue strongly that an allocation system combining time and money charges is most appropriate.

One justification for this argument is equity. The poor are underrepresented as visitors to parks and wilderness areas even though admission is available at no cost or a very low cost. The price of admission, however, represents only a very small portion of the total cost of access.

Given that major parks and wilderness areas are located at substantial distances from population concentrations, travel costs can be very high. If congested facilities were rationed by pricing, the revenue generated could be utilized by federal agencies to provide additional facilities near densely populated areas. Although the Tetons or the Canyonlands could not be replicated, they are only a portion of the variety of natural attractions.

Furthermore, when there is excess demand for a facility, the price paid by users has two components: the gate price in dollars and the price in time. The time price and the dollar price are inversely related; i.e., as the dollar price goes up, the line gets shorter. What one might call the total price (gate × time) is approximately a constant; it cannot sink to zero. (Smolensky makes the point that any price that results in a line is inefficient because the seller's price could be increased without affecting either the buyer's price or the quantity sold.)

Prices in time, like those in money, ration in terms of income, other opportunities, and preferences. In spite of the inefficiency discussed by Smolensky, queues can be used to increase the range of choice available. If the users of parks and wilderness areas divide, for example, into two groups of people—one group with low incomes and high amounts of discretionary time, and the other with high incomes and high opportunity costs for waiting—then any system that rationed either by time or by money alone would be seriously biased and discriminatory toward one of these groups. In brief, the range of choice is expanded when recreationists who prefer to pay with money can do so, while those who prefer to pay with time can also do so.

Notes

1. Colin Fletcher, *The Complete Walker* (New York: Knopf, 1968), p. 241.
2. Eugene Smolensky, "Waiting Time as a Congestion Charge," in Selma Mushkin, ed., *Public Prices for Public Products* (Washington D.C.: Public Affairs Press, 1972), pp. 95–108.
3. Between one-fourth and one-third of the wilderness users studied in California, Oregon, and Washington has done postgraduate work.
4. Sidney Verba and Norman H. Nie, *Participation in America: Political Democracy and Social Equality* (New York: Harper & Row, 1972), pp. 339–340.

24

Population, Ethnicity, and Public Goods: The Logic of Interest-Group Strategy

John Baden

Population control is essentially a problem of choice. All societies face the necessity of choosing their level of population; not to choose is in itself a choice.

There has been some controversy, particularly between Paul Ehrlich and Barry Commoner, centered around the methods to be employed in any attempt at population control. There are those who fear any suggestions that lead to institutionalized coercive methods as a threat of political repression. Barry Commoner, in *The Closing Circle*, has advanced the argument that if a substantial majority of society was to voluntarily accept a program for birth control, then coercion would be unnecessary.[1] However, there seems to be a flaw in this position. Garrett Hardin demonstrated that leaders of subgroups within a society have a vested interest in admonishing their followers to outbreed other subgroups.[2] Such admonitions potentially undermine voluntary cooperation in birth control, if loyalties to the subgroup can be directed. This brings us to the ways theories of population dynamics apply to issues of human population policy.

Competitive Exclusion

The competitive exclusion principle, also known as Gause's principle, states that complete competitors cannot coexist. Hardin, a biologist who has done us the service of straying into the area of political economy, elaborates on this scientific hypothesis and carries it into the area of population policy.[3] The hypothesized relationships are intuitively understood by the layman.

In biology it is held that if two noninterbreeding populations occupy the same ecological niche—if they are sympatric—and if one population multiplies at a faster rate than the other, ultimately the faster-growing population will completely displace the other. The logic remains consistent with multiple populations, but the complexity of relationships obviously increases.

Human populations are not perfectly analogous to animal communities. Human populations do interbreed, and differentiation of mixed or contiguous populations into subgroups is never perfect, over even the medium run. For example, Japanese in South Africa have been reclassified as White. Even in that rigid system the boundaries of subpopulations are in flux. Yet the similarity between nonhuman and human populations may be sufficiently close to merit examination. The mathematical truth of the proposition has been demonstrated by calculus and set theory.[4] The focus here is not on biology, but rather on the policy implications which arise from the potential application of the principle.

The Impossibility of Perpetual Growth

I assume that all moderately intelligent people not willing to rely on divine intervention will agree that the rate of human population growth must ultimately reach zero. With any positive rate of growth, whether it is only 1 percent per year or even .1 percent per year, a population approaches infinity in a relatively short period of time. The doubling time for a population is determined by dividing the rate of growth into the natural logarithm of 2, that is, $(.6931/r)$; roughly, one divides the percent growth rate into 70. Even a 1 percent growth rate will double a population in a mere human life-span. It is generally accepted that growth of this sort is intolerable in either biological or economic systems except in the short run. This realization is at last gaining general acceptance in human affairs.

This is not to suggest that we in the United States are nearing exhaustion of any essential resources such as water, fuel, or food, or that we are about to gag on pollution. Claims that we are in imminent danger are fundamentally silly and indicate a simple failure to appreciate the workings of resource allocating mechanisms. There are and will be adjustments that may be locally painful and could indeed lead to serious problems for particular organizations. The organizational problems, however, do not necessarily flow from a scarcity of resources.

In the immediate future we will confront increased congestion, dis-economies of scale in the operation of government units, and a diminution of natural amenities. These factors plus real, fancied, or contrived scarci-ties are likely to increase sensitivity to the issue of population growth. Migration to relatively undeveloped regions that offer a substantial supply of natural amenities is one secondary consequence.

We can also expect a general recognition that reduction of personal freedom necessarily accompanies high population density in a highly modernized, interdependent society. In brief, the personal costs of crowding become increasingly apparent, so that people should be more receptive to the ideal of a stable population size.

Tribalism and Population Policy

I have argued that population growth cannot ultimately be greater than zero, that within a finite system the subset that maintains the highest rate of growth will ultimately displace the others, and that the costs of growth will be come increasingly apparent. We can expect, then, that some peo-ple, out of a sense of responsibility and personal preference, will breed at replacement rates or lower. If one assumes that cultural values flow from parents to children, this leads to the self-elimination of conscience.[5] Should those exercising conscience in this direction be randomly dis-tributed, the above possibility would be of no concern. The fundamental assumption of social science research, however, is that human behavior is patterned rather than random.

In B. L. Crowe's response to Hardin, the issue of "tribalism" is intro-duced.[6] Although this term is uncertain even in anthropological literature and the concept may generate confusion, it does label a pattern of thought and behavior that is central to our concerns. Consistent with Crowe's usage we define a "tribe" as a group of people with the biological requi-sites of a society who perceive of themselves, and are perceived as, a distinct, endogamous group. From this perspective a tribe may be a race, a religious sect, or some other distinct subculture with an identity. Hardin notes that "The essential characteristic of a tribe is that it should follow a double standard of morality—one kind of behavior for in-group rela-tions, another for out-group."[7]

In a tribally heterogeneous society where political power is a positive function of group size, tribal members, or some of their leaders, will be tempted to foster some form of "breeding war." Thus, the pillow and the pill will be perceived as political weapons.

Fundamentally, policy is important to people because it shifts costs and benefits, and hence relative advantages, among individuals. Thus, in our context, where ethnic, racial, or religious group membership and identification are important and the welfare of the members of one's tribe is more important than the welfare of an anonymous outsider, we can expect:

1. Group leaders advocating political action that tends toward the socialization of costs and the localization of benefits with the group taken as the focus.
2. A realization that political power is partially determined by group size.
3. Admonitions to fellow tribal members to increase group size as an act of loyalty.
4. Group leaders discouraging factors that would produce a declining, or even stable, population of their group.
5. Neutrality toward or support for population limitation measures directed toward people who are not members of the tribe.

There is substantial casual data supporting these hypotheses. Some of the advocates of Black Power, for example, have argued that proposals to establish family planning clinics in Black ghettoes are precursors of genocide, and they have admonished their followers to engage in a breeding war.

Within the Black community a group with the acronym EROS (Efforts to Increase Our Size) developed the theme that babies grow into soldiers. Hence, there was open opposition to birth control clinics. Nathan Wright noted that "Opposition to birth control has been one of the manifestations of Black pride and Black efforts for survival and self-protection."[8] The same theme was enunciated on the 1972 television program "The Report of Population and the American Future" by Jesse Jackson, who argued that the safety of Blacks in America is dependent on the size of their population. During the fall of 1972, Dick Gregory stated with pride that he had nine children, planned to have more, and felt that birth control was not appropriate for his race.[9] Stokely Carmichael is well remembered for his statement that the proper position of women in the Black Power Movement is supine.[10]

My research among the Hutterites of the Northern Great Plains, a group whose doubling time due to natural increase is approximately 18 years, strongly suggests that many of the Hutterite elders are highly conscious of the political power associated with their very rapidly increasing members. Although doctrinal support of political participation in the larger system is uncertain, many colony members registered to vote in the late 1960s in response to proposed laws that would disadvantage the colonies.[11] Similar tribal responses have been reported in French

Canada and Ceylon while Hardin notes the same dynamics in Northern Ireland and Belgium.[12]

The main thrust here is simple: in a tribalized society *voluntary* birth control measures are inconsistent with the attainment of population stability at the optimum level. Thus, members of the several tribes find themselves locked into a game that is decidedly negative-sum. According to this logic, we are bound for a classic "tragedy of the commons" if compulsory birth control is not introduced.

The beginnings of this situation are seen clearly in Ceylon. During the 1960s the government of Ceylon fostered family planning in the hope of achieving population stability. Governmental support was withdrawn at the end of the decade; the rationale for such a policy change is consistent with the above logic. The Sinhalese, who make up 70 percent of the population and were the dominant group, became convinced that the Tamil minority was not cooperating with the voluntary birth control program. Thus, if the Tamils reproduced more rapidly, they would some day become a majority and might seize political power. As a result of this logic, Hardin concludes that "a purely voluntary system of population control can fail even if it is only a minority group that fails to cooperate. Simple mathematical analysis shows that it does not matter how small this minority is, so long as it exists."[13]

The Logic of Groups

I have indicated that there are strong pressures for a tragedy of the commons outcome in culturally nonhomogeneous, tribalized societies. Nearly all will agree that the implications of the possibility are serious in both domestic and international affairs.[14] Though the logic is sound and the problem ever more pressing, I hope to show that the predicted outcome is, if not wrong, seriously overstated. This conclusion is based on the logic of groups as developed by Mancur Olson.[15]

I assume the following. First, that members of a group (tribe) benefit from the increased power associated with the relative increase in group size. Second, that the net benefits associated with this increase remain positive even after the increased family costs are subtracted. Third, that decisions such as whether to produce the Nth child are a function of information and incentives. (Of course, information may not be perfect.)

The production of more children than are preferred by the decision makers (the prospective parents) as a contribution to the relative power position of the group follows the same logic as does private production of other public goods, labor union membership, or participation in a revolution. Nearly all economists would be highly skeptical if told that large numbers of people will sacrifice personal benefits to provide public goods. For example, in the absence of individual inducements, we expect very low rates of active and "expensive" participation in revolutions. The problem faced by the organizers of revolutions is largely that of the free rider. While the vast majority may benefit from the revolution, the benefits from success would remain constant whether or not one invested his personal resources in it. Lenin understood this problem, as have other successful revolutionaries.[16] Olson's statement on this organizational problem would be hard to improve upon: "So in any large, latent group, each individual in the class will find it to his advantage if all of the costs of sacrifice necessary to achieve the common goal are borne by others."[17] This tendency is the bane of radical organizers who condemn American workers as essentially selfish and materialistic. An engaging collection of these complaints is offered in Arnold Beichman's *Nine Lies About America.*[18]

The same logic can be applied to the organization of labor. At least over the short run, workers might be financially better-off if they are organized into a union (or somehow receive union benefits). In the absence of compulsion (or selective benefits), however, each individual worker has an incentive to avoid paying the various time and money costs associated with membership. "Labor associations can do nothing to raise wages but by force; it may be force applied passively, or force applied actively, or force held in reserve, but it must be force . . . they *must* coerce those among their members disposed to straggle; they *must* do their best to get into their hands the whole field of labor they seek to occupy and to force other working men either to join them or starve. Those who tell you of trades unions bent on raising wages by moral suasion alone are like those who would tell you of tigers who live on oranges."[19]

Increased political power for a group has the attributes of a public good for members of that group. Thus we are led to recall a fundamental law of political economy: public goods if supplied privately are undersupplied. While leaders of the various tribes may admonish their followers to breed beyond the level of individual preference, the admonition runs counter to the incentives faced by the decision makers.

This issue has caused some dissension between the sexes among Blacks. Many Black women resent being viewed and employed as baby factories. To the individual woman, charges that she is hindering growth of the revolution are not always sufficient to motivate change in breeding patterns. Consider this testimony:

> Finally, one tall, lean dude went into deep knee-bends as he castigated the sisters to throw away the pill and hop to the mattresses and breed

revolutionaries and mess up the (white) man's genocidal program. A slightly drunk lady from the back row kept interrupting with, for the most part, incoherent and undecipherable remarks. But she was encouraged finally just to step into the aisle and speak her speech, which she did, shouting the brother down in gusts and sweeps of historical, hysterical documentation of mistrust and mess-up, waxing lyric over the hardships, the oatmeal, the food stamps, the diapers, the suffering, the bloody abortions, the mangled births. She was mad as hell and getting more and more sober. She was righteous and beautiful and accusatory, and when she pointed a stiff finger at the brother and shouted "And when's the last time you fed one of them brats you've been breeding all over the city, you jive-ass so-and-so?" she tore the place up.[20]

Strategies for Tribal Leaders

If group leaders are to successfully foster larger than average population increases (or smaller decreases) there are several strategies available. Most basic would be a program to socialize the costs of having children, if not over the entire society then among the tribe.

The purest example of this is found among the Hutterites of North America. The Hutterites are organized into nuclear families and are assigned apartments in what is usually a quadplex. Housing and furnishings are supplied by the colony corporations; medical care, food, clothing, education, and nursery schools are also supplied by the colony. The benefits of a larger population are captured by the family but the costs are born by the corporation. Although the Hutterites and the Amish, another traditional Anabaptist sect, have similar theological views toward birth control, the birth rate of the noncommunal Amish is only about 72 percent as high as that of the Hutterites.[21]

Although this case is clearly an anomaly because of its completely communal organization, it is merely the application of the principle carried to its logical extreme. If a tribe were geographically centralized it could subsidize the costs of childrearing with low maternity rates in hospitals, day care centers, school lunches, and other welfare. These programs would be especially attractive if their costs were spread over the entire society, while the benefits were localized. Such a policy would be more effective if birth control technology was relatively inaccessible to members of the tribe. The common justification for lack of birth control is likely to be moral or religious rather than political, but the impact remains similar regardless of the rationale. Although I do not care to publicize an elaborate plan for "tribal" leaders, further development of these strategies would appear to be a fairly easy task.

Conclusion: Policy Recommendations

A true conservative is one who has a preference for preserving valued features of the social system, including the environmental system on which we are dependent. And an ever increasing human population is clearly inconsistent with the maintenance or improvement of the natural environment. While increased economic production could foster optimum management of the environmental system, population increases carry no similar advantage. Thus, conservatives have a strong incentive to bring population growth down to zero.

The population implications of tribalism constitute a threat to this goal if tribal leaders are successful in commanding strong loyalties from their group, and if the costs of having children are spread throughout society. Attempts to nullify this threat may entail a policy of overt coercion. However, strategies can be designed that would lead prospective parents into making voluntary decisions consistent with the goals of population control. This would involve either increasing the costs of having children, decreasing the benefits, or both.

Two policy recommendations result from the above considerations. The first is elemental; privatize the costs of having children. Demand curves for children, like everything else, slope downward and to the right. In the absence of government subsidies for childrearing, these curves will exhibit sharper profiles. Prospective parents can be expected to take the relative cost of children into account when determining their optimum family size. Significantly increased costs resulting from each additional child would act as a strong deterrent to large families. For the success of this policy, of course, birth control technology must be made available to all prospective parents.

The second recommendation is more difficult to explain and enforce. Discrimination against tribal members by the encompassing society must be reduced. When the larger society is nonthreatening, identification with some subgroup is of less practical importance. Strong group identity, perceived by both the society and the members of the group, would tend to dissolve. Hence, the advantages of high degrees of ingroup loyalty and participation would decrease substantially. Fewer group members would consider increased tribal strength as a significant benefit of an additional child. This suggestion, unlike the previous one, is consistent with the direction of American society and is likely to be unquestioned except by those tribal leaders whose position and power would be eroded by a hospitable social environment.

Notes

1. Barry Commoner, *The Closing Circle* (New York: Knopf, 1971).
2. G. Hardin, "Population Skeletons in the Environmental Closet," *Bulletin of the Atomic Scientists,* **28** (1972), 37–41.
3. G. Hardin, "The Competitive Exclusion Principle," *Science,* **131** (April 1960), 1292–1297.
4. A. J. Lotka, Jr., *Journal of the Washington Academy of Science,* **22** (1932), 469; G. E. Hutchinson, *Cold Spring Harbor Symposia in Quantitative Biology,* **22** (1957), 415 (Cold Spring Harbor, N.Y.: Laboratory of Quantitative Biology).
5. See G. Hardin, "The Tragedy of the Commons," *Science,* **162** (1968), 1243–1248 (reprinted in this volume as Chapter 3) for the classic discussion of this point.
6. B. L. Crowe, "The Tragedy of the Commons Revisited," *Science,* **166** (1969), 1103, reprinted in this volume as Chapter 8.
7. G. Hardin, *Stalking the Wild Taboo* (Los Altos, Calif.: William Kaufmann, 1973), p. 215.
8. Nathan Wright, "Black Power vs. Black Genocide," *The Black Scholar,* **1,** no. 2 (1969), 47–52.
9. "Heat, Light, and Values," a conference held at Utah State University, Logan, Utah, October 1972.
10. For a discussion of these views, see Maxine Williams, "Why Women's Liberation Is Important to Black Women," in *Feminism and Socialism* (New York: Pathfinder Press, 1972), pp. 40–47.
11. For a brief discussion on this group, see John Baden and Richard Stroup, "Choice, Faith, and Politics: The Political Economy of Hutterian Communes," *Public Choice,* Spring 1972, 1–11.
12. Hardin, "Population Skeletons," pp. 37–41.
13. Hardin, *Stalking the Wild Taboo,* p. 214. Thus, in the absence of compulsory birth control, the prognosis is disaster.
14. For one of many examples see Harold and Margaret Sprout, *Toward a Politics of the Planet Earth* (Princeton, N.J.: Van Nostrand, 1971), pp. 298–327.
15. Mancur Olson, Jr., *The Logic of Collective Action: Public Goods and the Theory of Groups* (Cambridge, Mass.: Harvard University Press, 1965).
16. V. I. Lenin, *What Is to Be Done?* (New York: International Publishers, 1929).
17. Olson, p. 106.
18. Arnold Beichman, *Nine Lies About America,* rev. ed. (New York: Pocket Books, 1973), chap. 4.
19. Henry George, *The Condition of Labor: An Open Letter to Pope Leo XIII* (New York: U.S. Book Co., 1891), p. 86, quoted in Olson, p. 71.
20. Toni Cade, "The Pill: Genocide or Liberation," *The Black Woman, An Anthology* (New York: Signet Classics, 1970), pp. 162–169.
21. Population Reference Bureau, *Population Bulletin,* **24,** no. 2 (November 1968), 25.

25

Living on a Lifeboat

Garrett Hardin
(1974)

Susanne Langer[1] has shown that it is probably impossible to approach an unsolved problem save through the door of metaphor. Later, attempting to meet the demands of rigor, we may achieve some success in cleansing theory of metaphor, though our success is limited if we are unable to avoid using common language, which is shot through and through with fossil metaphors. (I count no less than five in the preceding two sentences.)

Since metaphorical thinking is inescapable it is pointless merely to weep about our human limitations. We must learn to live with them, to understand them, and to control them. "All of us," said George Eliot in *Middlemarch,* "get our thoughts entangled in metaphors, and act fatally on the strength of them." To avoid unconscious suicide we are well advised to pit one metaphor against another. From the interplay of competitive metaphors, thoroughly developed, we may come closer to metaphor-free solutions to our problems.

No generation has viewed the problem of the survival of the human species as seriously as we have. Inevitably, we have entered this world of concern through the door of metaphor. Environmentalists have emphasized the image of the earth as a spaceship—Spaceship Earth. Kenneth Boulding[2] is the principal architect of this metaphor. It is time, he says, that we replace the wasteful "cowboy economy" of the past with the frugal "spaceship economy" required for continued survival in the limited world we now see ours to be. The metaphor is notably useful in justifying pollution control measures.

Reprinted from *BioScience* **24**:10 (October 1974) with permission of the American Institute of Biological Sciences. A shorter, somewhat different version was published earlier in *Psychology Today,* under an inflammatory heading. The title I furnished the editor was "Lifeboat Ethics." But without consultation he added a subtitle: "The Case Against Helping the Poor." Since the subtitle was in much larger type than the title, it largely determined the overwhelmingly negative response, which was in sharp contrast to the subsequent reaction to the *BioScience* version.

Unfortunately, the image of a spaceship is also used to promote measures that are suicidal. One of these is a generous immigration policy, which is only a particular instance of a class of policies that are in error because they lead to the tragedy of the commons.[3] These suicidal policies are attractive because they mesh with what we unthinkingly take to be the ideals of "the best people." What is missing in the idealistic view is an insistence that rights and responsibilities must go together. The "generous" attitude of all too many people results in asserting inalienable rights while ignoring or denying matching responsibilities.

For the metaphor of a spaceship to be correct the aggregate of people on board would have to be under unitary sovereign control.[4] A true ship always has a captain. It is conceivable that a ship could be run by a committee. But it could not possibly survive if its course were determined by bickering tribes that claimed rights without responsibilities.

What about Spaceship Earth? It certainly has no captain, and no executive committee. The United Nations is a toothless tiger, because the signatories of its charter wanted it that way. The spaceship metaphor is used only to justify spaceship demands on common resources without acknowledging corresponding spaceship responsibilities.

An understandable fear of decisive action leads people to embrace "incrementalism"—moving toward reform by tiny stages. As we shall see, this strategy is counterproductive in the area discussed here if it means accepting rights before responsibilities. Where human survival is at stake, the acceptance of responsibilities is a precondition to the acceptance of rights, if the two cannot be introduced simultaneously.

Lifeboat Ethics

Before taking up certain substantive issues let us look at an alternative metaphor, that of a lifeboat. In developing some relevant examples the following numerical values are assumed. Approximately two-thirds of the world is desperately poor, and only one-third is comparatively rich. The people in poor countries have an average per capita GNP (Gross National Product) of about $200 per year; the rich, of about $3,000. (For the U.S. it is nearly $5,000 per year.) Metaphorically, each rich nation amounts to a lifeboat full of comparatively rich people. The poor of the world are in other, much more crowded lifeboats. Continuously, so to speak, the poor fall out of their lifeboats and swim for a while in the water outside, hoping to be admitted to a rich lifeboat, or in some other way to benefit from the "goodies" on board. What should the passengers on a rich lifeboat do? This is the central problem of "the ethics of a lifeboat."

First we must acknowledge that each lifeboat is effectively limited in capacity. The land of every nation has a limited carrying capacity. The

exact limit is a matter for argument, but the energy crunch is convincing
more people every day that we have already exceeded the carrying capacity of the land. We have been living on "capital"—stored petroleum and
coal—and soon we must live on income alone.

Let us look at only one lifeboat—ours. The ethical problem is the same
for all, and is as follows. Here we sit, say 50 people in a lifeboat. To be
generous, let us assume our boat has a capacity of ten more, making 60.
(This, however, is to violate the engineering principle of the "safety factor." A new plant disease or a bad change in weather may decimate our
population if we don't preserve some excess capacity as a safety factor.)

The 50 of us in the lifeboat see 100 others swimming in the water
outside, asking for admission to the boat, or for handouts. How shall we
respond to their calls? There are several possibilities.

One. We may be tempted to try to live by the Christian ideal of
being "our brother's keeper," or by the Marxian ideal of "from each
according to his abilities, to each according to his needs." Since the needs
of all are the same, we take all the needy into our boat, making a total of
150 in a boat with a capacity of 60. The boat is swamped, and everyone
drowns. Complete justice, complete catastrophe.

Two. Since the boat has an unused excess capacity of 10, we admit
just 10 more to it. This has the disadvantage of getting rid of the safety
factor, for which action we will sooner or later pay dearly. Moreover,
which 10 do we let in? "First come, first served?" The best 10? The need-
iest 10? How do we *discriminate?* And what do we say to the 90 who
are excluded?

Three. Admit no more to the boat and preserve the small safety
factor. Survival of the people in the lifeboat is then possible (though we
shall have to be on our guard against boarding parties).

The last solution is abhorrent to many people It is unjust, they say.
Let us grant that it is.

"I feel guilty about my good luck," say some. The reply to this is
simple: *Get out and yield your place to others.* Such a selfless action might
satisfy the conscience of those who are addicted to guilt but it would not
change the ethics of the lifeboat. The needy person to whom a guilt-addict
yields his place will not himself feel guilty about his sudden good luck. (If
he did he would not climb aboard.) The net result of conscience-stricken
people relinquishing their unjustly held positions is the elimination of
their kind of conscience from the lifeboat. The lifeboat, as it were, purifies
itself of guilt. The ethics of the lifeboat persists, unchanged by such
momentary aberrations.

This then is the basic metaphor within which we must work out our
solutions. Let us enrich the image step by step with substantive additions
from the real world.

Reproduction

The harsh characteristics of lifeboat ethics are heightened by reproduction, particularly by reproductive differences. The people inside the lifeboats of the wealthy nations are doubling in numbers every 87 years; those outside are doubling every 35 years, on the average. And the relative difference in prosperity is becoming greater.

Let us, for a while, think primarily of the U.S. lifeboat. As of 1973 the United States had a population of 210 million people, who were increasing by 0.8 percent per year, that is, doubling in number every 87 years.

Although the citizens of rich nations are outnumbered two to one by the poor, let us imagine an equal number of poor people outside our lifeboat—a mere 210 million poor people reproducing at a quite different rate. If we imagine these to be the combined populations of Colombia, Venezuela, Ecuador, Morocco, Thailand, Pakistan and the Philippines, the average rate of increase of the people "outside" is 3.3 percent per year. The doubling time of this population is 21 years.

Suppose that all these countries, and the U.S., agreed to live by the Marxian ideal, "to each according to his needs," the ideal of most Christians as well. Needs, of course, are determined by population size, which is affected by reproduction. Every nation regards its rate of reproduction as a sovereign right. If our lifeboat were big enough in the beginning it might be possible to live *for a while* by Christian-Marxian ideals. *Might.*

Initially, in the model given, the ratio of non-Americans to Americans would be one to one. But consider what the ratio would be 87 years later. By this time Americans would have doubled to a population of 420 million. The other group (doubling every 21 years) would now have swollen to 3,540 million. Each American would have more than eight people to share with. How could the lifeboat possibly keep afloat?

All this involves extrapolation of current trends into the future, and is consequently suspect. Trends may change. Granted: but the change will not necessarily be favorable. If—as seems likely—the rate of population increase falls faster in the ethnic group presently inside the lifeboat than it does among those now outside, the future will turn out to be even worse than mathematics predicts, and sharing will be even more suicidal.

Ruin in the Commons

The fundamental error of the sharing ethics is that it leads to the tragedy of the commons. Under a system of private property the man (or group of men) who own property recognize their responsibility to care for it, for if they don't they will eventually suffer. A farmer, for instance, if he is intelligent, will allow no more cattle in a pasture than its carrying capacity justifies. If he overloads the pasture, weeds take over, erosion sets in, and the owner loses in the long run.

But if a pasture is run as a commons open to all, the right of each to use it is not matched by an operational responsibility to take care of it. It is no use asking independent herdsmen in a commons to act responsibly, for they dare not. The considerate herdsman who refrains from overloading the commons suffers more than a selfish one who says his needs are greater. (As Leo Durocher says, "Nice guys finish last.") Christian-Marxian idealism is counterproductive. That it *sounds* nice is no excuse. With distribution systems, as with individual morality, good intentions are no substitute for good performance.

A social system is stable only if it is insensitive to errors. To the Christian-Marxian idealist a selfish person is a sort of "error." Prosperity in the system of the commons cannot survive errors. If *everyone* would only restrain himself, all would be well; but it takes *only one less than everyone* to ruin a system of voluntary restraint. In a crowded world of less than perfect human beings—and we will never know any other—mutual ruin is inevitable in the commons. This is the core of the tragedy of the commons.

One of the major tasks of education today is to create such an awareness of the dangers of the commons that people will be able to recognize its many varieties, however disguised. There is pollution of the air and water because these media are treated as commons. Further growth of population and growth in the per capita conversion of natural resources into pollutants require that the system of the commons be modified or abandoned in the disposal of "externalities."

The fish populations of the oceans are exploited as commons, and ruin lies ahead. No technological invention can prevent this fate: in fact, all improvements in the art of fishing merely hasten the day of complete ruin. Only the replacement of the system of the commons with a responsible system can save oceanic fisheries.

The management of western range lands, though nominally rational, is in fact (under the steady pressure of cattle ranchers) often merely a government-sanctioned system of the commons, drifting toward ultimate ruin for both the rangelands and the residual enterprisers.

World Food Banks

In the international arena we have recently heard a proposal to create a new commons, namely an international depository of food reserves to which nations will contribute according to their abilities, and from which nations may draw according to their needs. Nobel laureate Norman Borlaug has lent the prestige of his name to this proposal.[5]

A world food bank appeals powerfully to our humanitarian impulses. We remember John Donne's celebrated line, "Any man's death diminishes me." But before we rush out to see for whom the bell tolls let us recognize where the greatest political push for international granaries comes from, lest we be disillusioned later. Our experience with Public Law 480 clearly reveals the answer. This was the law that moved billions of dollars worth of U.S. grain to food-short, population-long countries during the past two decades. When P.L. 480 first came into being a headline in the business magazine *Forbes*[6] revealed the power behind it: "Feeding the World's Hungry Millions: How it will mean billions for U.S. business."

And indeed it did. In the years 1960 to 1970 a total of 7.9 billion dollars was spent on the "Food for Peace" program, as P.L. 480 was called. During the years 1948 to 1970 an additional 49.9 billion dollars were extracted from American taxpayers to pay for other economic aid programs, some of which went for food and food-producing machinery. (This figure does *not* include military aid.) That P.L. 480 was a give-away program was concealed. Recipient countries went through the motions of paying for P.L. 480 food—with IOUs. In December 1973 the charade was brought to an end as far as India was concerned when the U.S. "forgave" India's $3.2 billion debt.[7]

Though all U.S. taxpayers lost by P.L. 480, special interest groups gained handsomely. Farmers benefited because they were not asked to contribute the grain—it was bought from them by the taxpayers. Besides the direct benefit there was the indirect effect of increasing demand and thus raising prices of farm products generally. The manufacturers of farm machinery, fertilizers and pesticides benefited by the farmer's extra efforts to grow more food. Grain elevators profited from storing the grain for varying lengths of time. Railroads made money hauling it to port, and shipping lines by carrying it overseas. Moreover, once the machinery for P.L 480 was established an immense bureaucracy had a vested interest in its continuance regardless of its merits.

Very little was ever heard of these selfish interests when P.L. 480 was defended in public. The emphasis was always on its humanitarian effects. The combination of multiple and relatively silent selfish interests with highly vocal humanitarian apologists constitutes a powerful lobby for extracting money from taxpayers. Foreign aid has become a habit that can apparently survive in the absence of any known justification. A news commentator in a weekly magazine[8] in 1974, after exhaustively going over all the conventional arguments for foreign aid—self-interest, social justice, political advantage and charity—and concluding that none of the known arguments really held water, concluded: "So the search continues for some logically compelling reasons for giving aid . . ." In other words, *Act now, Justify later*—if ever. (Apparently a quarter of a century is too short a time to find the justification for expending several billion dollars yearly.)

The search for a rational justification can be short-circuited by interjecting the word "emergency." Borlaug uses this word. We need to look sharply at it. What is an "emergency"? It is surely something like an accident, which is correctly defined as *an event that is certain to happen, though with a low frequency.*[9] A well-run organization prepares for everything that is certain, including accidents and emergencies. It budgets for them. It saves for them. It expects them—and mature decision makers do not waste time complaining about accidents when they occur.

What happens if some organizations budget for emergencies and others do not? If each organization is solely responsible for its own wellbeing, poorly managed ones will suffer. But they should be able to learn from experience. They have a chance to mend their ways and learn to budget for infrequent but certain emergencies. The weather, for instance, always varies and periodic crop failures are certain. A wise and competent government saves out of the production of the good years in anticipation of bad years that are sure to come. This is not a new idea. Joseph taught this policy to Pharaoh in Egypt more than two thousand years ago. Yet it is literally true that the vast majority of the governments of the world today have no such policy. They lack either the wisdom or the competence, or both. Far more difficult than the transfer of wealth from one country to another is the transfer of wisdom between sovereign powers or between generations.

"But it isn't their fault! How can we blame the poor people who are caught in an emergency? Why must we punish them?" The concepts of blame and punishment are irrelevant. The question is, what are the operational consequences of establishing a world food bank? If it is open to every country every time a need develops slovenly rulers will not be motivated to take Joseph's advice. Why should they? Others will bail them out whenever they are in trouble.

Some countries will make deposits in the world food bank and others will withdraw from it: there will be almost no overlap. Calling such a depository-transfer unit a "bank" is stretching the metaphor of *bank* beyond its elastic limits. The proposers, of course, never call attention to the metaphorical nature of the word they use.

The Ratchet Effect

An "international food bank" is really, then, not a true bank but a disguised one-way transfer device for moving wealth from rich countries to poor. In the absence of such a bank, in a world inhabited by individually responsible sovereign nations, the population of each nation would repeatedly go through a cycle of the sort shown in Figure 25.1. P_2 is greater than P_1, either in absolute numbers or because a deterioration of the food supply has removed the safety factor and produced a dangerously low ratio of resources to population. P_2 may be said to represent a state of overpopulation, which becomes obvious upon the appearance of an "accident," e.g., a crop failure. If the "emergency" is not met by outside help the population drops back to the "normal" level—the "carrying capacity" of the environment—or even below. In the absence of population control by a sovereign, sooner or later the population grows to P_2 again and the cycle repeats. The long-term population curve[10] is an irregularly fluctuating one, equilibrating more or less about the carrying capacity.

A demographic cycle of this sort obviously involves great suffering in the restrictive phase, but such a cycle is normal to any independent country with inadequate population control. The third century theologian Tertullian[11] expressed what must have been the recognition of many wise men when he wrote: "The scourges of pestilence, famine, wars, and earthquakes have come to be regarded as a blessing to overcrowded nations, since they serve to prune away the luxuriant growth of the human race."

Only under a strong and farsighted sovereign—which theoretically could be the people themselves, democratically organized—can a population equilibrate at some set point below the carrying capacity, thus avoiding the pains normally caused by periodic and unavoidable disasters. For this happy state to be achieved it is necessary that those in power be able to contemplate with equanimity the "waste" of surplus food in times

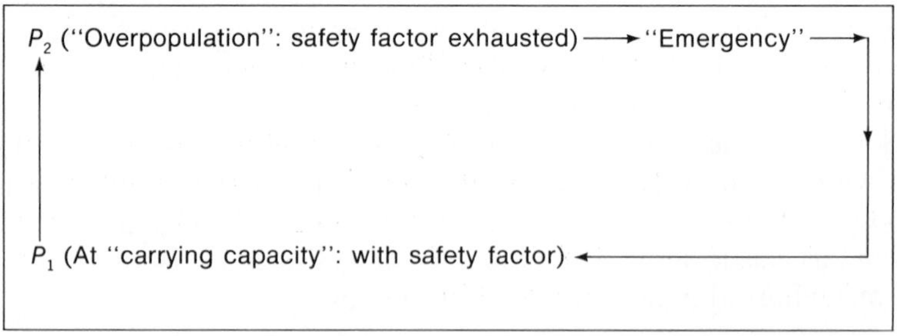

FIGURE 25.1

The population cycle of a nation that has no effective, conscious population control and that receives no aid from the outside. P_2 is greater than P_1.

of bountiful harvests. It is essential that those in power resist the temptation to convert extra food into extra babies. On the public relations level it is necessary that the phrase "surplus food" be replaced by "safety factor."

But wise sovereigns seem not to exist in the poor world today. The most anguishing problems are created by poor countries that are governed by rulers insufficiently wise and powerful. If such countries can draw on a world food bank in times of "emergency," the population *cycle* of Figure 25.1 will be replaced by the population *escalator* of Figure 25.2. The input of food from a food bank acts as the pawl of a ratchet, preventing the population from retracing its steps to a lower level. Reproduction pushes the population upward; inputs from the world bank prevent its moving downward. Population size escalates, as does the absolute magnitude of "accidents" and "emergencies." The process is brought to an end only by the total collapse of the whole system, producing a catastrophe of scarcely imaginable proportions.

Such are the implications of the well-meant sharing of food in a world of irresponsible reproduction.

I think we need a new word for systems like this. The adjective "melioristic" is applied to systems that produce continual improvement; the English word is derived from the Latin *meliorare*, to become or make

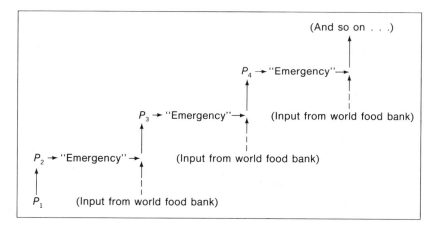

FIGURE 25.2

The population escalator. Note that input from a world food bank acts like the pawl of a ratchet, preventing the normal population cycle shown in Figure 25.1 from being completed. P_{n+1} is greater than P_n, and the absolute magnitude of the "emergencies" escalates. Ultimately the entire system crashes. The crash is not shown, and few can imagine it.

better. Parallel with this it would be useful to bring in the word *pejoristic* (from the Latin *pejorare,* to become or make worse). This word can be applied to those systems which, by their very nature, can be relied upon to make matters worse. A world food bank coupled with sovereign state irresponsibility in reproduction is an example of a pejoristic system.

This pejoristic system creates an unacknowledged commons. People have more motivation to draw from than to add to the common store. The license to make such withdrawals diminishes whatever motivation poor countries might otherwise have to control their populations. Under the guidance of this ratchet, wealth can be steadily moved in one direction only, from the slowly-breeding rich to the rapidly-breeding poor, the process finally coming to a halt only when all countries are equally and miserably poor.

All this is terribly obvious once we are acutely aware of the pervasiveness and danger of the commons. But many people still lack this awareness and the euphoria of the "benign demographic transition"[12] interferes with the realistic appraisal of pejoristic mechanisms. As concerns public policy, the deductions drawn from the benign demographic transition are these:

1. If the per capita GNP rises the birth rate will fall, hence the rate of population increase will fall, ultimately producing ZPG (Zero Population Growth);
2. The long term trend all over the world (including the poor countries) is of a rising per capita GNP (for which no limit is seen);
3. Therefore all political interference in population matters is unnecessary; all we need to do is foster economic "development"—*note the metaphor*—and population problems will solve themselves.

Those who believe in the benign demographic transition dismiss the pejoristic mechanism of Figure 25.2 in the belief that each input of food from the world outside fosters development within a poor country thus resulting in a drop in the rate of population increase. Foreign aid has proceeded on this assumption for more than two decades. Unfortunately it has produced no indubitable instance of the asserted effect. It has however produced a library of excuses. The air is filled with plaintive calls for more massive foreign aid appropriations so that the hypothetical melioristic process can get started.

The doctrine of demographic laissez faire implicit in the hypothesis of the benign demographic transition is immensely attractive. Unfortunately there is more evidence against the melioristic system than there is for it.[13] On the historical side there are many counterexamples. The rise in per capita GNP in France and Ireland during the past century has been accompanied by a rise in population growth. In the twenty years following the Second World War the same positive correlation was noted almost everywhere in the world. Never in world history before 1950 did the worldwide population growth reach one percent per annum. Now the average population growth is over two percent and shows no signs of slackening.

On the theoretical side, the denial of the pejoristic scheme of Figure 25.2 probably springs from the hidden acceptance of the "cowboy economy" that Boulding castigated. Those who recognize the limitations of a spaceship, if they are unable to achieve population control at a safe and comfortable level, accept the necessity of the corrective feedback of the population cycle shown in Figure 25.1. No one who knew in his bones that he was living on a true spaceship would countenance political support of the population escalator shown in Figure 25.2.

Eco-Destruction via the Green Revolution

The demoralizing effect of charity on the recipient has long been known. "Give a man a fish and he will eat for a day: teach him how to fish and he will eat for the rest of his days." So runs an ancient Chinese proverb. Acting on this advice the Rockefeller and Ford Foundations have financed a multi-pronged program for improving agriculture in the hungry nations. The result, known as the "Green Revolution," has been quite remarkable. "Miracle wheat" and "miracle rice" are splendid technological achievements in the realm of plant genetics.

Whether or not the Green Revolution can increase food production is doubtful,[14–16] but in any event not particularly important. What is missing in this great and well-meaning humanitarian effort is a firm grasp of fundamentals. Considering the importance of the Rockefeller Foundation in this effort it is ironic that the late Alan Gregg, M.D., a much-respected vice president of the Foundation, strongly expressed his doubts of the wisdom of all attempts to increase food production some two decades ago. (This was before Borlaug's work—supported by Rockefeller —had resulted in the development of "miracle wheat.") Dr. Gregg[17] likened the growth and spreading of humanity over the surface of the earth to the metastasis of cancer in the human body, wryly remarking that "Cancerous growths demand food; but, as far as I know, they have never been cured by getting it."

"Man does not live by bread alone"—the scriptural statement has a rich meaning even in the material realm. Every human being born constitutes a draft on all aspects of the environment—food, air, water, unspoiled scenery, occasional and optional solitude, beaches, contact with wild animals, fishing, hunting—the list is long and incompletely known. Food can, perhaps, be significantly increased: but what about clean beaches, unspoiled forests, and solitude? If we satisfy the need for food in a growing population we necessarily decrease the supply of other goods, and thereby increase the difficulty of equitably allocating scarce goods.[18,19]

The present population of India is 600 million, and it is increasing by 15 million per year. The environmental load of this population is already great. The forests of India are only a small fraction of what they were three centuries ago. Soil erosion, floods, and the psychological costs of crowding are serious. Every one of the net 15 million lives added each year stresses the Indian environment more severely. *Every life saved this year in a poor country diminishes the quality of life for subsequent generations.*

Observant critics have shown how much harm we wealthy nations have already done to poor nations through our well-intentioned but misguided attempts to help them.[20] Particularly reprehensible is our failure to carry out post-audits of these attempts.[21] Thus have we shielded our tender consciences from knowledge of the harm we have done. Must we Americans continue to fail to monitor the consequences of our external "do-gooding"? If, for instance, we thoughtlessly make it possible for the present 600 million Indians to swell to 1,200 millions by the year 2001—as their present growth rate promises—will posterity in India thank *us* for facilitating an even greater destruction of *their* environment? Are good intentions ever a sufficient excuse for bad consequences?

Immigration Creates a Commons

I come now to the final example of a commons in action, one for which the public is least prepared for rational discussion. The topic is at present enveloped by a great silence which reminds me of a comment made by Sherlock Holmes in A. Conan Doyle's story "Silver Blaze." Inspector Gregory had asked, "Is there any point to which you would wish to draw my attention?" To this Holmes responded:

> "To the curious incident of the dog in the night-time."
> "The dog did nothing in the night-time."
> "That was the curious incident," remarked Sherlock Holmes.

By asking himself what would repress the normal barking instinct of a watch dog Holmes realized that it must be the dog's recognition of his master as the criminal trespasser. In a similar way we should ask ourselves what repression keeps us from discussing something as important as immigration?

It cannot be that immigration is numerically of no consequence. Our government acknowledges a *net* inflow of 400,000 a year. Hard data are understandably lacking on the extent of illegal entries, but a not implausible figure is 600,000 per year.[22] The natural increase of the resident population is now about 1,700,000 per year. This means that the yearly gain from immigration is at least 19 percent, and may be 37 percent, of the total increase. It is quite conceivable that educational campaigns like that of Zero Population Growth, Inc., coupled with adverse social and economic factors—inflation, housing shortage, depression and loss of confidence in national leaders—may lower the fertility of American women to a point at which all of the yearly increase in population would be accounted for by immigration. Should we not at least ask if that is what we want? How curious it is that we so seldom discuss immigration these days!

Curious, but understandable—as one finds out the moment he publicly questions the wisdom of the status quo in immigration. He who does so is promptly charged with *isolationism, bigotry, prejudice, ethnocentrism, chauvinism* and *selfishness.* These are hard accusations to bear. It is pleasanter to talk about other matters, leaving immigration policy to wallow in the cross-currents of special interests that take no account of the good of the whole—*or the interests of posterity.*

We Americans have a bad conscience because of things we said in the past about immigrants. Two generations ago the popular press was rife with references to *Dagos, Wops, Pollacks, Japs, Chinks* and *Krauts* —all pejorative terms which failed to acknowledge our indebtedness to Goya, Leonardo, Copernicus, Hiroshige, Confucius and Bach. Because the implied inferiority of foreigners was *then* the justification for keeping them out, it is *now* thoughtlessly assumed that restrictive policies can only be based on the assumption of immigrant inferiority. *This is not so.*

Existing immigration laws exclude idiots and known criminals; future laws will almost certainly continue this policy. But should we also consider the quality of the average immigrant, as compared with the quality of the average resident? Perhaps we should, perhaps we shouldn't. (What is "quality" anyway?) But the quality issue is not our concern here.

From this point on, *it will be assumed that immigrants and native-born citizens are of exactly equal quality,* however quality may be defined. The focus is only on quantity. The conclusions reached depend on nothing else, so all charges of ethnocentrism are irrelevant.

World food banks move food to the people, thus facilitating the exhaustion of the environment of the poor. By contrast, unrestricted immigration moves people to the food, thus speeding up the destruction of the environment in rich countries. Why poor people should want to make this transfer is no mystery: but why should rich hosts encourage it? This transfer, like the reverse one, is supported by both selfish interests and humanitarian impulses.

The principal selfish interest in unimpeded immigration is easy to identify: it is the interest of the employers of cheap labor, particularly that needed for degrading jobs. We have been deceived about the forces of history by the lines of Emma Lazarus inscribed on the Statue of Liberty:

> Give me your tired, your poor
> Your huddled masses yearning to breathe free,
> The wretched refuse of your teeming shore,
> Send these, the homeless, tempest-tossed, to me:
> I lift my lamp beside the golden door.

The image is one of an infinitely generous earth-mother, passively opening her arms to hordes of immigrants who come here on their own initiative. Such an image may have been adequate for the early days of colonization, but by the time these lines were written (1886) the force for immigration was largely manufactured inside our own borders by factory and mine owners who sought cheap labor not to be found among laborers already here. One group of foreigners after another was thus enticed into the United States to work at wretched jobs for wretched wages.

At the present, it is largely the Mexicans who are being so exploited. It is particularly to the advantage of certain employers that there be many illegal immigrants. Illegal immigrant workers dare not complain about their working conditions for fear of being repatriated. There presence reduces the bargaining power of all Mexican-American laborers. Cesar Chavez has repeatedly pleaded with Congressional committees to close the doors to more Mexicans so that those here can negotiate effectively for higher wages and decent working conditions. Chavez understands the ethics of a lifeboat.

The interests of the employers of cheap labor are well served by the silence of the intelligentsia of the country. WASPS—White Anglo-Saxon Protestants—are particularly reluctant to call for a closing of the doors to immigration for fear of being called ethnocentric bigots. It was, therefore, an occasion of pure delight for this particular WASP to be present at a meeting when the points he would like to have made were made better by a non-WASP speaking to other non-WASPS. It was in Hawaii, and most of the people in the room were second-level Hawaiian officials of Japanese ancestry. All Hawaiians are keenly aware of the limits of their environment, and the speaker had asked how it might be practically and constitutionally possible to close the doors to more immigrants to the islands. (To Hawaiians, immigrants from the other forty-nine states are as much of a threat as those from other nations. There is only so much room in the islands, and the islanders know it. Sophistical arguments that imply otherwise do not impress them.)

Yet the Japanese-Americans of Hawaii have active ties with the land of their origin. This point was raised by a Japanese-American member of the audience who asked the Japanese-American speaker: "But how can we shut the doors now? We have many friends and relations in Japan that we'd like to bring to Hawaii some day so that they can enjoy this beautiful land."

The speaker smiled sympathetically and responded slowly: "Yes, but we have children now and someday we'll have grandchildren. We can bring more people here from Japan only be giving away some of the land that we hope to pass on to our grandchildren some day. What right do we have to do that?"

To be generous with one's own possessions is one thing; to be generous with posterity's is quite another. This, I think, is the point that must be gotten across to those who would, from a commendable love of distributive justice, institute a ruinous system of the commons, either in the form of a world food bank or that of unrestricted immigration. Since every speaker is a member of some ethnic group it is always possible to charge him with ethnocentrism. But even after purging an argument of ethnocentrism the rejection of the commons is still valid and necessary if we are to save at least some parts of the world from environmental ruin. Is it not desirable that at least some of the grandchildren of people now living should have a decent place in which to live?

The Asymmetry of Door-Shutting

We must now answer this telling point: "How can you justify slamming the door once you're inside? You say that immigrants should be kept out. But aren't we all immigrants, or the descendants of immigrants? Since we refuse to leave, must we not, as a matter of justice and symmetry, admit all others?"

It is literally true that we Americans of non-Indian ancestry are the descendants of thieves. Should we not, then, "give back" the land to the Indians, that is, give it to the now-living Americans of Indian ancestry? As an exercise in pure logic I see no way to reject this proposal. Yet I am unwilling to live by it; and I know no one who is. Our reluctance to embrace pure justice may spring from pure selfishness. On the other hand, it may arise from an unspoken recognition of consequences that have not yet been clearly spelled out.

Suppose, becoming intoxicated with pure justice, we "Anglos" should decide to turn our land over to the Indians. Since all our other wealth has also been derived from the land, we would have to give that to the Indians, too. Then what would we non-Indians do? Where would we go? There is no open land in the world on which men without capital can make their living (and not much unoccupied land on which men with capital can either). Where would 210 million putatively justice-loving, non-Indian, Americans go? Most of them—in the persons of their ancestors—came from Europe, but they wouldn't be welcomed back there. Anyway, Europeans have no better title to their lands than we to ours. They also would have to give up their homes. (But to whom? And where would *they* go?)

Clearly, the concept of pure justice produces an infinite regress. The law long ago invented statutes of limitations to justify the rejection of pure justice, in the interest of preventing massive disorder. The law zealously defends property rights—but only *recent* property rights. It is as though the physical principle of exponential decay applies to property rights. Drawing a line in time may be unjust, but any other action is practically worse.

We are all the descendants of thieves, and the world's resources are inequitably distributed, but we must begin the journey to tomorrow from the point where we are today. We cannot remake the past. We cannot, without violent disorder and suffering, give land and resources back to the "original" owners—who are dead anyway.

We cannot safely divide the wealth equitably among all present peoples, so long as people reproduce at different rates, because to do so would guarantee that our grandchildren—everyone's grandchildren—would have only a ruined world to inhabit.

Must Exclusion Be Absolute?

To show the logical structure of the immigration problem I have ignored many factors that would enter into real decisions made in a real world. No matter how convincing the logic may be it is probable that we would want, from time to time, to admit a few people from the outside to our lifeboat. Political refugees in particular are likely to cause us to make exceptions: we remember the Jewish refugees from Germany after 1933, and the Hungarian refugees after 1956. Moreover, the interests of national defense, broadly conceived, could justify admitting many men and women of unusual talents, whether refugees or not. (This raises the quality issue, which is not the subject of this essay.)

Such exceptions threaten to create runaway population growth inside the lifeboat, i.e., the receiving country. However, the threat can be neutralized by a population policy that includes immigration. An effective policy is one of flexible control.

Suppose, for example, that the nation has achieved a stable condition of ZPG, which (say) permits 1,500,000 births yearly. We must suppose that an acceptable system of allocating birth-rights to potential parents is in effect. Now suppose that an inhumane regime in some other part of the world creates a horde of refugees, and that there is a widespread desire to admit some to our country. At the same time, we do not want to sabotage our population control system. Clearly, the rational path to pursue is the following. If we decide to admit 100,000 refugees this year we should compensate for this by reducing the allocation of birth-rights in the following year by a similar amount, that is downward to a total of 1,400,000. In that way we could achieve both humanitarian and population control goals. (And the refugees would have to accept the population controls of the society that admits them. It is not inconceivable that they might be given proportionately fewer rights than the native population.)

In a democracy, the admission of immigrants should properly be voted on. But by whom? It is not obvious. The usual role of a democracy is votes for all. But it can be questioned whether a universal franchise is the most just one in a case of this sort. Whatever benefits there are in the admission of immigrants presumably accrue to everyone. But the costs would be seen as falling most heavily on potential parents, some of whom would have to postpone or forego having their (next) child because of the influx of immigrants. The double question *Who benefits? Who pays?* suggests that a restriction of the usual democratic franchise would be appropriate and just in this case. Would our particular quasi-democratic form of government be flexible enough to institute such a novelty? If not, the majority might, out of humanitarian motives, impose an unacceptable burden (the foregoing of parenthood) on a minority, thus producing political instability.

Plainly many new problems will arise when we consciously face the immigration question and seek rational answers. No workable answers can be found if we ignore population problems. And—if the argument of this essay is correct—so long as there is no true world government to control reproduction everywhere it is impossible to survive in dignity if we are to be guided by Spaceship ethics. Without a world government that is sovereign in reproductive matters mankind lives, in fact, on a number of sovereign lifeboats. For the foreseeable future survival demands that we govern our actions by the ethics of a lifeboat. Posterity will be ill served if we do not.

Notes

1. Susanne K. Langer, *Philosophy in a New Key* (Cambridge, Mass.: Harvard University Press, 1942).
2. Kenneth Boulding, "The Economics of the Coming Spaceship Earth," in Henry Jarrett, ed., *Environmental Quality in a Growing Economy* (Baltimore: Johns Hopkins Press, 1966).
3. Garrett Hardin, "The Tragedy of the Commons," *Science*, **162** (1968), 1243–1248.
4. William Ophuls, "The Scarcity Society," *Harper's*, April 1974, 47–52.
5. Norman Borlaug, "Civilization's Future: A Call for International Granaries," *Science and Public Affairs*, **29**, no. 8 (1973), 7–15.
6. William and Paul Paddock, *Famine—1975!* (Boston: Little, Brown, 1967), p. 188. This book is one of the few publications to point out the commercial roots of this humanitarian law.
7. *Wall Street Journal*, 19 February 1974. We can justifiably wonder why the release of the news of this government action was delayed for nearly two months.
8. Kermit Lansner, "Should Foreign Aid Begin at Home?" *Newsweek*, 11 February 1974, p. 32.
9. Garrett Hardin, *Exploring New Ethics for Survival* (New York: Viking, 1972), pp. 81–82.
10. Garrett Hardin, *Biology: Its Principles and Implications,* 2nd ed. (San Francisco: Freeman, 1966), chap. 9.
11. Garrett Hardin, ed., *Population, Evolution and Birth Control,* 2nd ed. (San Francisco: Freeman, 1969), p. 18.
12. Garrett Hardin, *Stalking the Wild Taboo* (Los Altos, Calif.: Kaufmann, 1973), chap. 23.
13. Kingsley Davis, "Population," *Scientific American*, **209**, no. 3 (1963), 62–71.
14. Marvin Harris, "How Green the Revolution," *Natural History*, **81**, no. 3 (1972), 28–30.
15. William C. Paddock, "How Green Is the Green Revolution?" *BioScience*, **20**, no. 16 (1970), 897–902.
16. H. Garrison Wilkes, "The Green Revolution," *Environment,* **14,** no. 8 (1972), 32–39.
17. Alan Gregg, "A Medical Aspect of the Population Problem," *Science*, **121** (1955), 681–682.
18. Garrett Hardin, "The Economics of Wilderness," *Natural History*, **78**, no. 6 (1969), 20–27.
19. Garrett Hardin, "Preserving Quality on Spaceship Earth," in James B. Trefethen, ed., *Transactions of the Thirty-Seventh North American Wildlife and Natural Resources Conference* (Washington, D.C.: Wildlife Management Institute, 1972).
20. William and Elizabeth Paddock, *We Don't Know How* (Ames: Iowa State University Press, 1973).

21. M. Taghi Farvar and John P. Milton, *The Careless Technology* (Garden City, N.Y.: Natural History Press, 1972).
22. William Buchanan, "Immigration Statistics," *Equilibrium*, **1**, no. 3 (1973), 16–19.

26

Commons and Community: The Idea of a Public

Kenneth E. Boulding

These are very powerful, insightful, and troubling essays. Anyone who reads them unmoved is either singularly insensitive to their implications or insensitive to what it means to be human. The authors of this volume are candid friends to the human race. They have every right to expect to be as popular as such friends usually are. What is being said here is of great importance for the future of humankind, perhaps even for our very survival. It will not be listened to with much pleasure. It is much pleasanter, in Garrett Hardin's useful term, to be a meliorist rather than a pejorist. It is agreeable to believe that if only we could do simple things like having a revolution or passing a law against evil, the world would immediately start going from bad to better.

There are circumstances, indeed, in which things do go from bad to better even if left to themselves. One has an uneasy feeling, however, that these circumstances are deplorably rare, and that if left to themselves, things tend to go from bad to worse. This is the law of moth and rust, the law of aging and decay. It is the Second law of thermodynamics. It can be generalized as the great Second Law: If anything happens it is because it had a potential for happening that overcame the resistance to its happening, and once it has happened that potential has been used up. Thinking of the law in terms of the diminution of potential rather than the increase in entropy gives it great generality at a certain cost in precision, which I am more than willing to pay. It also introduces a small element of what might be called "middle-run hope," that potential can be re-created and things can go on happening, and that they might even go from bad to better.

Every one of us started life as a fertilized egg, or so I am told by the biologists, and I believe them. This fertilized egg contained an enormous amount of genetic potential. It contained instructions for making us. That potential is slowly but surely exhausted as life proceeds. As we age the probability of our dying increases, until finally we die, and the genetic potential in our own bodies is exhausted. In the meantime, however, we may have fertilized another egg or had another egg fertilized. We create genetic potential and start the whole thing over again in our children. Furthermore, the genosphere itself, that fragile, discontinuous film of genetic know-how which spreads over the surface of the globe, seems to have increased its know-how over time, at least by human standards. It now knows how to make us, which it did not know how to do even ten billion years ago. There are two time's arrows—a downward-pointing one of entropy; and another, the arrow of evolution, which is the segregation of entropy, pointing, however crookedly, towards the better rather than the worse.

Garrett Hardin is enough of a master of metaphor to know how powerful and how dangerous it is. Knowledge grows by comparison, by perceiving what is like and what is unlike. Comparisons are also odious. The extraordinary process of change that began with Adam and Eve, whatever their names were, which is the story of the human race, is a process so much like biological evolution that we are justified in calling it social evolution, which in a sense is a metaphor. But then evolution itself is a metaphor, derived presumably from the act of unrolling a carpet.

The danger of metaphor is that it calls our attention to similarities but it is apt to divert us from differences. The similarities between social and biological evolution are profound; their differences are profound also. It is very dangerous to forget them. The greatest similarity is that each process is one of interacting species, each of which is a population of individuals, every member of which is "born," that is, comes into existence at a certain time, and "dies," goes out of existence at a later time, with a life span in between. The automobile is just as much a species as the horse. The earth is an ecosystem, perhaps we should say a network of interacting ecosystems, each of which consists of a set of populations—physical and chemical species like atoms of water, biological species like horses, and social species like automobiles and Mormon congregations. All species at a certain moment have a birth and death rate. If the birth rate exceeds the death rate, the species will grow; if the death rate exceeds the birth rate, it will decline. If it declines long enough, the population will be zero and the species will be extinct. The birth rate and the death rate of a species are functions of its own population and of all other populations with which it is in some kind of contact. These functions constitute an ecosystem. If the functions are such that there is a set of populations of different species for each of which the birth rate and death rate are equal and the population is constant, then we have ecological equilibrium. These never really exist in nature, but are approximated. There are quasi-equilibrium positions like a climactic ecosystem, but they change all the time through genetic mutation and environmental change. Evolution could almost be defined as ecological dynamics under conditions of constantly changing parameters.

There are some very fundamental differences, however, between social and biological evolution. One is that biological individuals are biparental at most, whereas social artifacts are multiparental; hence the birth of social artifacts is directly involved with large numbers of other species. A horse can be produced by another horse and a mare; an automobile is produced by the interaction of designers, architects, engineers, corporations, trade unions, mines, ore ships, assembly line workers, salesmen, lawyers, politicians, and so on, and so on. Its genetic structure involves not merely the blueprints in the drafting office, but the know-how of all people in organizations who cooperate in its production. The birth rate of automboiles, that is, the ratio of its production to its stock, is a function of markets, substitutes, its competitors, and its complements, like gasoline and gas stations. When gasoline becomes extinct, as it will, and if no other fuel is discovered, the automobile will likewise become extinct through reduction in its births, without much reduction in its deaths. The reduction in births will take place mainly because it is no longer profitable to produce it. Very few people will buy automobiles that cannot run.

Another very profound difference between biological and social systems is that in social systems human artifacts are made as a result of human decisions, which are very closely interrelated in human communities. Biologists call an ecosystem in a particular habitat a "community," but the word is a metaphor and a very misleading one. The populations of a biological ecosystem are related by such things as predation, utilization of common food supplies, and physical niches. One species may help create a niche for another, but they are not in any strict sense a community. They have no government, and no individual member of the system has an image of the total system, only of a very small fraction of it. Communities of human beings, because of their capacity for communication and shared images, have potentialities for conscious control which is not possessed by biological prehuman ecosystems.

It is a very interesting question as to whether there are parallels to the "tragedy of the commons" in prehuman ecosystems. There is a myth prevalent among amateur naturalists that nature somehow without the human race is infinitely wise and benevolent; that is, only human beings muck things up. It is the prize example of the "pathetic fallacy" that attributes human values to nonhuman structures. It is a survival indeed from the lovely, benign world of Isaac Watts, the hymn writer, in which:

> There's not a plant or flower below
> But makes Thy glories known
> And clouds arise and tempests blow
> By order from Thy throne.[1]

Tennyson 150 years later was much less sanguine:

> Are God and Nature then at strife,
> That Nature lends such evil dreams?
> So careful of the type she seems,
> So careless of the single life,
>
> 'So careful of the type?' but no.
> From scarped cliff and quarried stone
> She cries, 'A thousand types are gone;
> I care for nothing, all shall go.
>
> 'Thou makest thine appeal to me.
> I bring to life, I bring to death;
> The spirit does but mean the breath:
> I know no more.'[2]

Environmentalists today seem much closer to Isaac Watts than they do to Tennyson. Yet Tennyson's extraordinary insight (written, incidentally, a whole generation before *The Origin of Species*) cannot be sloughed off. If there is "wisdom" in prehuman nature, it is only the wisdom of ecological equilibrium and a special case of simultaneous differential equations. And ecological equilibrium, even when mathematically stable, is precarious and insecure, for there is always irresistible and irreversible change in the parameters of the system. For instance, we know very little about the sources of extinction. There are far more extinct species than extant ones. Species, like individuals, seem to have something like a life span, at the end of which their evolutionary potential is exhausted and they are displaced by species whose evolutionary potential is not yet exhausted.

It is very hard to find out about these systems, as often their significance lies in what did *not* happen rather than what did. Science has an extraordinary epistemological prejudice in favor of what does exist and what did happen, whereas what does not exist and did not happen are often much more significant for what they reveal about the nature

of the system. The great universe of the "might have been" has about
the same relation to a universe of what was and is as this little imperfect
sample that we call the present has to the great drama of the past and
future. It would be very hard to know, for instance, what niches were
not filled. There must have been many occasions in the process of evolution when a niche for a species developed but the mutation did not occur
that could have created the species to fill it. Similarly, it is very hard
to know how far extinction is a result of change in the equilibrium niche
structure itself, or is due to the dynamics of the system by which the
species overshoots a niche that it might have occupied in equilibrium
and so crashes to extinction.

The achieving of equilibrium depends very much on the timing
of the dynamic feedback to the system. Nature is only wise when feedbacks are rapid. Then each species expands soberly to its niche, at which
point its population ceases to grow. If it goes beyond this point, it is soon
cut back. As long as it has failed to reach this point, it will expand. Even
when all things work together for equilibrium, it is not necessarily for
good. In the strict sense, however, equilibrium is unknown in nature.
It is a figment of the human imagination, although it may be approximated. Even if parameters of the system that define the equilibrium
constantly change, moving it to new equilibria, they may prevent the
reaching of a potential equilibrium. The paradox here, one suspects,
is that in a world of catastrophe and uncertainty there is a strong survival
value in redundancy. Genetic redundancy, for instance, produces potential fertility far beyond what is necessary to sustain the population, from
the eggs of a cod to the sperms of man. Behavioral redundancy leads
to an enormous amount of just plain fooling around in the natural world,
by squirrels as well as by scientists, where idle curiosity has produced
the most fantastically unexpected payoffs.

If overshoot is the tragedy of the commons in the prehuman biosphere, territoriality seems to have been in part a strategy for the solution.
A population checked by a housing shortage, like robins, is likely to
enjoy better health, a larger food supply and more redundancy, and
therefore survival value, than populations of a Malthusian kind that
are limited only by the food supply. Malthusian species actually seem
to be rare in nature, perhaps because they do not develop enough redundancy to have survival value, so that even a quite small catastrophe
will wipe them out. It is only family territoriality, however, that really
pays off in terms of survival strategy. One suspects that group territoriality
is the worst of all possible worlds, as it involves both the expense of
fighting other groups for the territory and limitation by food supply.
Fighting is often unfriendly to survival. Any species that struggles too
hard for existence will very soon lose the struggle, so that conventional

substitutes for fighting have strong payoffs. Within a group territory, furthermore, there is always danger that the population may expand until it is limited by the food supply and all the advanatges of territoriality are lost.

Another strategy for survival is the predator–prey relationship. This is apt to be rather stable. The predator prevents the prey expanding to the limits of the prey's food supply, and the scarcity of the prey prevents the predator expanding to the limits of its food supply. Predation, again, is something of a substitute for the Malthusian tragedy.

Turning now to social systems, we also find a number of strategies for avoiding the Malthusian tragedy. One, of course, is property and primogeniture, which corresponds to family territoriality. If there is an expansion of population to more than the territory can hold comfortably, the surplus people are forced to emigrate. If they can find a niche elsewhere, that is fine; if not, they do not survive. Alfred Marshall has a beautiful example of two valleys in Germany, one of which stayed rich by practicing strong territorial primogeniture, driving out the younger sons to seek their fortunes in the world, the other of which practiced division of farms among minor children and ended up in Malthusian misery.[3] It is one of the great ironies of the French Revolution that the *égalité,* which really meant equal distribution of estates among children and the abolition of primogeniture along with other hallmarks of aristocracy, is a sure recipe for equality of misery if the surplus population that will inevitably result cannot be exported. For the earth as a whole, of course, the exporting of population is virtually impossible, unless Professor O'Neill comes along with his space colonies.[4]

It is not surprising, therefore, that a very common solution to the tragedy of the commons has been the appropriation of the commons and its division as private property among the appropriators. This is a process somewhat akin to Marx's "primary accumulation." It is not wholly surprising, incidentally, that Marxists hate Malthus so, even to the point sometimes of denying that there is any population problem at all. Malthus not only saw the great "miserific vision" of the tragedy of the "dismal theorem," as I have called it, but also had a very real answer to it, the trouble being that the answer is unacceptable.* The answer is the segregation of misery through a class structure. This has been a very common answer in the history of the human race. If we privatize the commons, we will create an upper class who owns and administers it. It will be administered well. There will be no overgrazing. The boundary between the well-managed private property and the ill-managed public

---

*The Dismal Theorem is that if the only thing that can check the growth of population is misery, the population will grow until it is miserable.

estate will stand out sharply as the famous irregular pentagon in the Sahel. Order and dignity will thrive in beautiful country houses, elegant gardens, productive farms within the boundary of class. Outside of this, the lower classes will breed themselves into egalitarian misery. If the upper class breeds too much it will chase out its youngest sons and un-marriageable daughters and will keep its population at the level at which it can enjoy per capita plenty. But outside this fence the lower class goes down to Hogarthian vice and misery. The pious and puritan middle class and upper working class may be admitted inside the territoriality fence and raise themselves above misery, restricting births, expelling the sur-plus, and catering to the rich, but there will always be the human cess-pool of the poor, whose population is checked only by misery or vice. If the class structure can be preserved, if the fences hold through a combination of the threat system, the police and the military, and the opiates of religion, nationalism, and ideology, the system is pretty stable. Up to now one can almost say that this has been the only successful answer to the tragedy of the commons. But its very success undermines its acceptability and the search for a better answer becomes a consuming passion for those whose minds and images are enlarged by empathy.

What, then, is the answer if it is not property, primogeniture, and class? The only other answer to the tragedy of the commons is the comedy of community. One is almost tempted to call it the Divine Comedy of community. Without some sort of sacredness, the comedy easily becomes black and obscene and returns once more to tragedy, either through incompetence or through tyranny.

There are some parallels perhaps between the human community and those of the termites, the bees, the ants, the beavers, and so on, but the differences are enormous. Insect communities have a division of labor on a modest scale. This is determined primarily by genetics, and there is virtually no learning of roles, though we cannot exclude the learning of behavior, as in the famous dance of the bees. The learning process, however, dominates in human society, human organization, and even human artifacts, which are merely realizations of the potential of human knowledge imposed on the physical world. It is the capacity of the human nervous system for enormously complex images extending far beyond the personal experience of the individual, and the corresponding capacity of language in communicating images among large numbers of indivi-duals, which make human society unique. Community is a phenomenon within human society, by no means universal or coextensive with it, by which the identity of the individual becomes bound up with identification with the group or community.

Identity is a very powerful source of decisional behavior. Decisions are of great importance in the behavior of human beings. Decisions are made according to the perception of images of the future and of the consequences of decisions, and they are made according to a value structure which is very largely learned, and which depends very much on the nature of the individual image of identity. A soldier behaves like a soldier, a barber like a barber, a child like a child, a lover like a lover, a president like a president, to a very large extent because each has an image of identity according to which only certain types of behavior are appropriate, that is, highly valued, and other types are not. In human societies, however, these identities are very largely learned; they are certainly not produced by genetics, which produces only the most undifferentiated potential, except in the case of characteristics recognized as defects, such as tone deafness or color blindness, which limits the ability of people to become musicians or painters. Apart from this, however, as Adam Smith himself pointed out, it is a learning process which makes the difference between the porter and the philosopher.[5]

We learn community as we learn everything else. It is a long and painful learning process. It begins in the hunting–gathering band. Everybody knows everybody and there is very general awareness of the nature and the resources of the community itself. Consequently, in spite of the fact that it operates usually in some sort of a commons, there is control of population, usually by infanticide, for everybody knows what the territory can support. The role of sacredness in the formation of communities, especially those of larger size, is an interesting and difficult question. Religion in some form seems to be universal in human culture, which makes one suspect that it is of great importance in the development of viable communities. Sacred sanctions that overcome the more self-centered images of individual interest might prevent the tragedy of the commons because of the community identity which the perception of sacredness creates in the individual. An illusion which seems to be common to both left and right is that individuals have some clearly identifiable objective interest which they readily perceive and act upon. In fact, interest, whether in the individual or in the group, is what is interesting and what the people are interested in, and this is enormously varied and highly learned within a very wide range of possibilities.

In larger groups, the identification of the individual with the group tends to break down. Larger groups, therefore, tend to spend more on threats to insure conformity and less on the creation of identity. The urban revolution and the invention of civilization about 3,000 B.C. or earlier was undoubtedly the result of the invention of organized threat systems, in the shape of either a priest or a king who could command either spiritual or material threat. Even here, however, threat has to be legitimated by identity and by symbols—the temple and the ritual, the impressive robes, the jewels, the crowns, the scepters, the ceremonies, the "state," as Adam Smith called it, of the ruler. The arts have played a crucial role in the development of buildings, paintings, rituals, music, and dance which carry conviction and establish legitimacy. Palaces and cathedrals say in no uncertain language "We are important and you belong to us." Within the framework of community either the commons can be privatized without the threat of disruption from those who are excluded from the property, or coercion (threat systems) in the administration of the public fief can be legitimized through taxes and regulations.

A very important dynamic in the building up of community is what I have called the "sacrifice trap."[6] Once people are coerced, or even better, persuaded, into making sacrifices, their identity becomes bound up with the community organization for which the sacrifices were made. Admitting to one's self that one's sacrifices were in vain is a deep threat to the identity and is always sharply resisted. Martyrs create the legitimacy, identity, and community of the church; dead soldiers on the battlefield perform the same function for the national state, as innumerable war memorials testify. The sacrifices which parents make for children, or children for parents, bind them to each other much more powerfully than either love alone or hatred and fear alone could possibly do. The strongest communities, indeed, are those towards which we feel ambivalent.

Where the boundaries of communities are not clearly defined and mutually accepted, the disputed space between communities becomes a commons which easily turns into a battlefield. War, indeed, is another example of the tragedy of the commons. In the absence of an overriding community, competing communities get into arms races and into conflict which is damaging to both sides. We see this also in the nonhuman biosphere where territoriality is apt to produce fighting. As noted earlier, there seem to be selective advantages in the development of ritual fighting and in the development of mutually recognized status, pecking orders, and so on. If the wolf has better conflict-resolution mechanisms than the dove, it is perhaps because the more territorial the species is, the more necessary it is for survival to have conflict-resolution machinery. How unfortunate it is, incidentally, that the dove—that dirty, disgusting bird without any mechanisms for conflict resolution—should have become the symbol of peace. Symbols often mean more than they say. It could be that there are deep subconscious reasons for this in our ambivalence towards peace. War, however, is costly and often irrelevant. From the point of view of the general evolutionary process it rarely matters who wins a fight. And persistent struggle often results in mutual exhaustion and even extinction, like the two cats of Kilkenny:

> There once were two cats of Kilkenny.
> Each thought there was one cat too many.
> So they they scratched and they bit.

> And they fought and they fit,
> Till instead of two cats there weren't any.

The effort to substitute ritual for actual fighting is a long-continued activity through human history. It results in the development of diplomacy, royal marriages, law courts, arbitration, ceremonies, treaties, all together comprising a very large range of human activity. As conflict becomes ritualized, the commons edges towards community.

A great problem of the human race at the present moment is that the world is becoming a single ecosystem, but is not a single community. There are grave dangers in becoming one world even if there were a world community. Evolution has persisted as long as it has on this planet probably because of geographical isolation. The world has not been a single ecosystem, but a mosaic of relatively isolated ecosystems with some possibilities of migration between them. Consequently, if a catastrophe wiped out one ecosystem, it did not wipe out all of them. Evolution was able to continue and eventually colonize the disaster area. The eruption of Krakatoa undoubtedly eliminated the total biological ecosystem of that island. Now after almost a hundred years it has been reestablished, perhaps not quite the same as it was before, but with innumerable species of all forms of life having colonized it from the undisturbed areas. Similarly, the Mayan civilization collapsed in about 900 A.D., quite irrecoverably, from the point of view of its own system. This did not affect either Europe or China, which knew nothing about it, and the catastrophe had very little impact on the general course of social evolution. On the other hand, if we have a single world ecosystem, a single world society, then if anything goes wrong, everything goes wrong; if there is any positive probability of irretrievable catastrophe, then if we wait long enough it is almost certain to happen.

This is not a trivial point. Suppose a particular system has a probability of P of irretrievable catastrophe in any one year. $\frac{1}{p}$ may be called the period of probability, which we use in an expression like "the 100-year flood," which is a level of flood, the probability of which in any one year is only 1 percent. Within any period of probability, the probability that the event will happen is about 63 percent. In 10 times the period of probability, the probability that it will happen is 99.9995 percent, which is a virtual certainty. A 100-year flood has about a 63-percent chance of happening within any given 100 years, and a 99.9995-percent chance of happening within 1,000 years. Suppose now that any one society has a period of probability of 1,000 years, which seems like about the right order of magnitude. It is virtually certain to suffer a fatal catastrophe in 10,000 years. If there are 100 such isolated societies, the chance of simultaneous catastrophe happening to all, which would be the only irretrievable catastrophe, would be .001100, which is very small indeed. The period of probability is now billions upon billions of years instead of a thousand. Even if 99 of the societies collapse simultaneously, the one society that does not collapse will continue the evolutionary process and will recolonize all the other societies. Over long periods of time, therefore, the role of isolation in the evolutionary process is extremely important, which is probably why it is just as well we don't have any intergalactic communications. The unification of the earth, however, into a single system would increase very substantially the probability of irretrievable catastrophe, unless something can be done to decrease the probability of catastrophe in that single system. To be all in one lifeboat may be as catastrophic as having all our eggs in one basket.

As Garrett Hardin well knows, metaphors are treacherous though necessary, and we have to be particularly careful of the lifeboat metaphor. A lifeboat that is not in some sense a community will not bring its human freight to shore, even if there is food for all; for collective decisions will have to be made and, if there is no community, they will not be made and the lifeboat will end up like Lebanon, with a community falling apart and everybody throwing everybody else overboard. We cannot assume, therefore, even if the resources are sufficient for the trip that the trip will be accomplished safely in the absence of community. There is a curious paradox here. The sense of a common threat from outside frequently increases the sense of community. It may temporarily make the problems of the internal commons easier, though often at a cost of making them more difficult later when the threat subsides. A community united only by a common threat will fall apart if the threat is removed. But the failure to fulfill a common obligation also destroys community and breaks it up into self-seeking individuals, and the internal problem of the commons becomes much harder.

The building of community is a process of appalling complexity which we understand very imperfectly, and which includes constant interaction between love and fear. There is a good deal in the proposition, for instance, that all nations have been created by their enemies. The English nation probably owes more to Joan of Arc than it does to William the Conqueror. Indeed, if it had not been for Joan of Arc, the English kings would have settled in the more agreeable part of their dominions, namely France, and England would have become like Brittany, a minor province of a great French empire. The United States is largely the creation of George III. Again, if it had not been for the American Revolution, as Adam Smith predicted, the British king would have moved to the most populous and prosperous part of his dominions—as the Portuguese king actually did!—and Britain, again, would have been a minor outpost of the great American empire. The process does not always work. Napoleon did not really create Germany, though he may have laid the foundations. France did not really create Italy.

If a community is to be established, there must be what Adam Smith called "the habit of subordination," which habit, he argued, accounted for the success of the American colonies against the Indians, who had no such habit and hence were incapable of uniting to form a community, in spite of the common threat of the European settlers. The great danger of the "lifeboat ethic," then, is that the metaphor may give aid and encouragement to those who deny community, who simply want to hold onto what they have and let the rest sink. Unfortunately for them, the devil does not always take the hindmost. Sometimes it is the foremost who plunge over the cliff in their proud and confident march to oblivion, and the hindmost scatter and survive.

Perhaps the cliff is a better metaphor than the lifeboat. We are on a pretty crowded mesa surrounded on all sides by cliffs. It doesn't matter much where we are on top of it; it matters enormously that we do not fall over the cliffs. On the other hand, it is just as easy to march over a cliff as it is to be pushed over it. The mesa metaphor can lead to a number of different models. In one, the Malthusian model, the rich occupy the middle of the mesa, with a barbed wire fence around them. They control their population and have a sustainable society, and do not exhaust their resources. Meanwhile the poor all around them multiply to the point where they push each other off the edge. In the second model, before the poor push each other off the edge, they pull down the fence, invade the preserve of the rich, and the whole mesa becomes one great mass of misery and poverty. This is all too apt to be the result of a revolutionary solution. In the third model, the rich gradually push their fence out, absorbing those poor who conform to the rules of a sustainable society. Chaos and misery characterize the edge of the mesa for a while, as the poor multiply indiscriminately, form nonsustainable societies, and push each other over the edge, but the fence gradually extends until finally it rims the whole mesa and the whole mesa is rich. This is certainly the most desirable scenario. At the moment, however, the rich, while they may inhabit the middle of the mesa, do not form a sustainable society. Their riches depend on inputs of energy and materials from exhaustible sources, many of which lie on the edge of the mesa rather than in the middle, and have to be imported. In a fourth model, perhaps a change in terms of trade pushes the fence out, so that more of the mesa becomes rich. This, unfortunately, is highly temporary, and unless new sources of energy and materials are discovered, the mesa again will soon fall back to universal poverty. In the fifth model, then, which is the only hopeful variant of the third, the center of the mesa devotes great effort to discovering nonexhaustible resources of energy and techniques of recycling, and becomes a sustainable society at a high level. Then it can expand its fence out and bring the rest of the mesa into its high-level, sustainable society, until the fence is again at the edge of the mesa.

It may be, however, that ultimate sustainability is not possible, simply because of the exhaustion of what might be called "social evolutionary potential" in any particular society or organization. It is strange how we take for granted that death is a universal law of living organisms and yet we deny this in the case of social organizations. It may indeed be that there is lurking in the wings a nonexistence theorem about the immortality of particular systems. The proof would involve a combination of the generalized Murphy's Law—that if anything can go wrong, it eventually will—with a kind of generalized third law of thermodynamics, that we can go on reducing the probability of irretrievable catastrophe in any particular system but we can never get the probability down to zero. If it is not zero, then the irreversible catastrophe will eventually happen, especially if time is infinite, as in the human imagination it almost has to be. As Garrett Hardin might say, "After the end of time, then what?"

It may be, therefore, that evolutionary sustainability is a different matter from the sustainability of any particular system within the process, for though all particular systems may become extinct, the evolutionary process may go on. We must have a sixth model, as suggested earlier, of isolated, or almost isolated systems. One suspects that on the earth this option is no longer feasible, short of a very massive collapse in human knowledge. It is hard to imagine a catastrophe that would destroy all the globes and atlases in the world and not destroy the whole human race. But even a catastrophe in which all atlases and globes were destroyed except one, together with enough social organization to produce a geographer who could read it and teach it, then the whole world would eventually be recolonized with globes and atlases.

A key problem here, which is quite hard to answer but of crucial importance to the long-run future of complex systems, is the potential isolability of particular subsystems within the larger framework, say, the earth. Suppose at the moment that the whole human race were destroyed except in New Zealand, in a catastrophe that left the rest of the environment pretty much unchanged. The universities, libraries, the knowledge structure of New Zealanders would almost certainly sustain itself and would be transmitted to new and larger generations. The knowledge of what the rest of the world was like would not be lost. New settlements would be made. In 1,000 or 2,000 years the whole earth would be repopulated with people descended from the original New Zealanders, with technology, perhaps, not very different from what we have now. Under these circumstances, the oil and natural resources would certainly last much longer than they are now likely to. If all human beings were destroyed except a primitive tribe in the forest of the Amazon, however, the world might also ultimately be repopulated with their descendants, but the developed knowledge structure would be lost, and it would have to be reestablished by the long and painful process that created it over the last 50,000 years. Whether the process was actually repeated would depend on the extent to which it has been the result of random factors that might not happen again. One has the uneasy suspicion that all evolution depends a great deal on luck.

The ethical and political implications of managing the commons are very large. It implies a view of the dynamics of the world that I think is essentially true but which is very destructive to what might be called "naive radicalism." Naive radicalism thinks only in terms of static redistribution. It is based more on hatred of the rich than on love for the poor, on envy rather than on pity. It thinks in dialectical rather than in evolutionary terms, in terms of struggle and conflict rather than in terms of ecological interaction and development. The ideological message of the commons is pretty clear: Naive radicalism, in which I would include Marxism with all its insights, is a dead end that is quite incapable of interpreting the enormous complexities of the real world; it can indeed march us over a cliff into irretrievable disaster.

The ideology of the commons, however, gives even less comfort to the naive conservatives, who believe that private property and the market can do everything, or those who think that a system of national defense can preserve a little island of permanent prosperity in a world of misery and decay. National defense is as much an illusion in the modern world as is Marxism, and faith in it can march us over a cliff even more rapidly and dramatically. The biggest tragedy is above all the commons between the national states, which gives us a positive probability of almost total nuclear disaster.

What one hopes will emerge is a new radicalism, more realistic than the old, with a better appreciation of the complexities of dynamic systems and evolution systems but without loss of the fundamental sense of compassion that inspires radicalism at its best. There is an ultimate necessity of regarding the whole human race and beyond as a potential community if the extraordinary evolutionary potential of the human organism is finally to be realized.

Notes

1. The hymn begins "I sing the almighty power of God" and is found in many hymnals.
2. Alfred Lord Tennyson, "In Memoriam," stanzas 55–56.
3. "There are many parts of Europe even now in which custom exercising the force of law prevents more than one son in each family from marrying; he is

generally the eldest, but in some places the youngest: if any other son marries he must leave the village. When great material prosperity and the absence of all extreme poverty are found in old-fashioned corners of the Old World, the explanation generally lies in some such custom as this with all its evils and hardships. (Note: Thus a visit to the valley Jachenau in the Bavarian Alps about 1880 found this custom still in full force. Aided by a great recent rise in the value of their woods, with regard to which they had pursued a far-seeing policy, the inhabitants lived prosperously in large houses, the younger brothers and sisters acting as servants in their old homes or elsewhere. They were a different race from the work-people in the neighboring valleys, who lived poor and hard lives, but seemed to think that the Jachenau purchased its material prosperity at too great a cost.)" Alfred Marshall, *Principles of Economics, Vol. 1,* 9th ed. (New York: Macmillan, 1961), p. 182.

4. Gerard O'Neill, "Testimony," *CoEvolution Quarterly,* No. 7 (Fall 1975), 10–19.
5. Adam Smith, *The Wealth of Nations,* Book I, Chapter II.
6. K. E. Boulding, *The Economy of Love and Fear: A Preface to Grants Economics* (Belmont, Calif.: Wadsworth, 1973).